8/23/2013

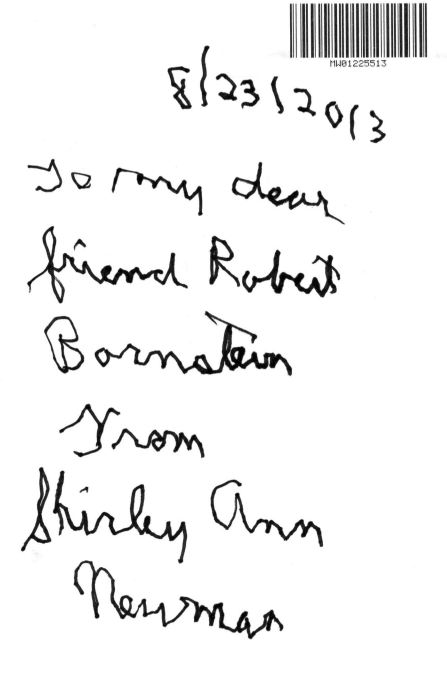

To my dear
friend Robert
Bornstein
from
Shirley Ann
Newman

Long Journey with Heavy Luggage

Mt. Sinai to San Joaquin Valley

Shirley Ann Newman

Moses Sees the Burning Bush

ISBN-13: 9781481034203

ISBN-10: 1481034200

I owe great appreciation to Gilbert Gia, board member and past president of the Kern County Historic Society. Thanks are not only on my own behalf, but on those of potential readers of *From Sinai to San Joaquin, The Jews of Central Valley*. Gil has given me so much support, encouragement, and the contribution of articles *he* has written and published, and also interesting photos, material directly related to this book.

Heartfelt thanks to Pam Allison for contributing her formatting skills, including the page numbers, Table of Contents and Index.

My profound gratitude to Angela Gia for donating her artistic talent to design the cover of this book.

Shirley Ann Newman

Also by *Shirley Ann Newman*

Deflecting My Death! Memoirs of a Jewish
  Resistance Fighter in Nazi-occupied France

We Brought Sinai to San Joaquin, The Story
  of the Jews of Kern County

Miss Day's Dismay! A Novel

Maniacal Midrashes, In Fun I Poke At Bible Folk

It's Curtains For You! Original play scripts

The Jews, A People of Plight and Flight

It's Curtains For You!–Original Play Scripts

Did The Ladder Fall So I Could Be Born? A Novel

Short Stories For the long-in-the-tooth

My Faulty Father's Foul Play! A Novel

TABLE OF CONTENTS

Foreword

Long Journey With Heavy Luggage--Mt. Sinai to San Joaquin Valley has substantial content, and follows the same theme as the book's first edition: *We Brought Sinai to San Joaquin, Story of the Jews of Kern County.* It is in part a historical account of the ancestral past of local residents who practice or trace their family background to Judaism. But it is also a cultural and sociological study of current or recent local residents whose Jewish family members immigrated to this country, mostly from Central or Eastern Europe. They had come here not only in the eager and hopeful quest for economic, social and educational opportunities, but for freedom, equality and justice.

The first edition was written in 1998, fourteen years ago. This book updates material, adds significant events that occurred in the interim, and depicts institutional changes in the Jewish community. These factors make this book current and relevant.

I'm sure that you will find it interesting to know that besides the data I researched and compiled for the book, quite a few other members of the community, Jewish and non-Jewish, contributed material. The book is a collaborative project that includes media, historical notes, documents, and memorabilia, as well as religious, political, philosophical and social perspectives, and strong personal convictions!

Shirley Ann Newman

Introduction

Why there had been such a strong impetus on the part of Jewish people to move to a new and very different cultural and political environment is an interesting subject. Was it really worth the risk of failure, the trouble and the *struggle* of having to adapt to a new language and any number of other social differences? Could the newcomer really expect to be rewarded with better opportunities than in his home country? Was the promise of freedom, of equality, real or mythical? Had these migrants truly experienced an uncomfortable or untenable political situation in their nation of origin, or were they simply malcontents? In some cases could it have been discordant family relations, a member who had been regarded, or had regarded himself an "ugly duckling," a misfit, who always felt and acted differently, incompatibly with their way of life and mode of Jewish observance?

After all, it demanded courage and initiative to fly out of the nest to the unknown, to put behind the familiarity of a homeland, and to be only *somewhat* sure of freedom, fraternity and financial fulfillment in a distant land. However, most migrants had grown completely discouraged in their present situation, weary of awaiting a change-for-the-better. They were people who no longer anticipated that anything worthwhile would happen to their Jewish compatriots.

That's why from countries like Tsarist Russia, large numbers of Jews sought a new way of life even in the wilderness of western America. This was a chance of fulfilling their dream, by making a fresh start in a new land even though it was far off across the sea with cultural and linguistic differences.

True, in all times and places, there are adventurous, restless personalities to whom the distant horizon whistles a beckoning call. It lures them to strange and very different places, to lifestyles that are vastly unlike their current ones. People like that go on the move simply because they choose to explore. They have a need to seek change, to gratify their curiosity.

But for most émigrés the resolve to separate from tradition and a long ancestral background had to do with the unbearable conditions for Jewish people in their homelands, where the "Sword of Damocles" hung over their heads, often threatening their very survival.

This book about Kern County's Jewish residents, past and present, includes where they had been born and, if not in the United States, or not in California's Central Valley, where they had come from and what had brought them here. To Jews from Central and Eastern Europe, America was known as the *Goldena Medina,* the Golden Land. Though not to be confused with the biblical Promised Land, it was regarded as a country of promise, a place of freedom and plurality, an unlocked door to individuality, to the acceptance of difference and to glowing opportunities.

In America and in the rest of the world, with the exception of the modern State of Israel, Judaism has always been, and still is, a minority religion. Nevertheless the legal right to practice the faith, to live "Jewishly," (however one defines it,) is firmly rooted in the United States Constitution. This makes our country a comfortable place for Diaspora Jews.

Life in Tsarist Russia was harsh, bitter, and fraught with deprivation. It was a myriad of social, political and economic injustices, the usual components of anti-Semitism. At times, Poland and Hungary were linked to the Russian regime. Consequently, the same discriminatory regulations applied to Jews there as well. The abject poverty of most Jews kept them huddled in broken down shacks, often further victimized by sudden pogroms. Bands of drunken soldiers would burst into Jewish villages to burn and pillage.

It was not unusual for young Jewish boys nearing the age of mandatory conscription into the Tsar's military to flee their home countries, to seek resettlement and then citizenship in a country of religious freedom, one with no official national religion. That, of course, was America! The youngsters would scrape together the money for a steerage class ticket on a ship crossing the Atlantic Ocean and docking in that blessed land!

News was screened and censored in Tsarist Russia, so learning of America's glowing prospects would come through whispered rumors. Not only was religious freedom and tolerance a major feature of America, so was the lack of required military service.

The *Goldena Medina,* the golden land gave these oppressed, downtrodden, deprived, luckless Jews of Europe the eager expectation of having a safer, more secure life than in the country they sought to leave.

Sailing across the Atlantic Ocean to America did indeed result in many a Jewish Horatio Alger, that rags-to-riches fictional character. He became an inspiration, a role model to youths on the first rung of the ladder, impelling them to look up to the top rung and chant in fervent hope: *I can make it, and I shall!*

To ignore or deny the existence of anti-Jewish prejudice, bias, and flagrant discrimination, even in America, is a flight into fantasy. Xenophobia appears to be incorporated in the human psyche. It seems to take great effort and dedication for people to accept those who differ from them in how or if they worship God. It is not always effortless for people of different faiths or different cultures to live together in peace, let alone in harmonious integration. If eventually they do reach that level of maturity, society will reap the benefit of *everyone's* potential, *everyone's* skills and talents that we frequently bypass and ignore.

How did Jews institutionalize religious life where they settled? There were three priorities: They established a synagogue, a place to worship, a place to study our Jewish faith system, our history and culture, a place where a Torah scroll can respectfully abide. Then the Jews consecrated a burial ground for their deceased. The third institution was a Jewish benevolent loan society. It was central to providing financial assistance, including interest-free loans to fellow-Jews.

In large cities there were usually Jewish Community Centers where Jewish residents met one another through social and cultural activities. Often it was where young men and women met their future spouse. These centers conducted lessons in Hebrew, and in Torah study. They had dances and club meetings. Usually they had a library whose inventory of books was a source of Jewish history and other important and enlightening subjects related to our faith system. No matter how old or young you are, try to learn, to expand your knowledge, to deepen your understanding of your own people. I promise it will help you know who *you* are. Maybe even why!

Jewish philanthropic societies support a variety of Jewish causes, including help for the State of Israel. Many of their members don't belong to a synagogue or attend religious services. They define themselves "secular Jews." They regard themselves as culturally Jewish, a term that is rather nebulous and hard to define, as culture often relates more to one's birth country than to one's religion. This is especially so if it applies to a person whose life is fully or almost totally devoid of Jewish ritual observance.

There are many whose Jewish practice is limited to a few specifics: having a rabbi conduct marriage ceremonies, circumcising their baby boys, "Jewish" burials, attending "High Holiday" services, or perhaps making or attending a Passover Seder.

In short, there is no clear-cut, unambiguous answer to the question: "Who is a Jew?" Currently in Israel and elsewhere, debates on the issue have flared into a hostile tug-of-war. This is partly because of a major political issue, the right to Israeli citizenship. Opinions are so divergent, ranging from "Anyone who defines himself Jewish" to "Only those who practice Judaism in strict accord with *Halacha*."

Ten years ago, in 2002, the Jewish community of Bakersfield became nicely rounded out with the acquisition of an Orthodox congregation. A branch of Chabad came into the picture. Now we have the three major divisions of Jewish practice: Orthodox, Conservative, and Reform. The first to "set up shop" here in Kern County was Congregation B'nai Jacob, a Conservative synagogue.

Regarding the expense of maintaining a synagogue - a special building is not a religious requirement. A congregation can exist merely by the presence of ten Jews who are at least thirteen years old. They assemble to reverently and earnestly pray, and to study the Torah, and its offshoots. The Torah contains the laws and rituals God gave Moses at the top of Mount Sinai. This was right after He liberated the Israelites from Egypt, where their living conditions had become highly oppressive.

The Covenant God made with the Israelites includes His promise of guidance and protection. It initiated the practice of circumcision.

Our sages viewed circumcision a major feature of Jewish identity, a testimony that we are unique in body as in soul. The mystical explanation is that as a little of the foreskin is rolled back, revealing the tip of the organ, a veil is simultaneously lifted from our soul, and that confirms our intrinsic bond with God. This ritual unites the Jews into "one people, one God," all having a stake in this intrinsic bond.

Circumcision does not forge this bond; it merely reveals it. In this sense circumcision differs from all the other laws, rituals and requirements. They forged new connections with God, whereas circumcision reveals our initial connection with Him.

In the mid-19th century when Orthodox Jewish practice was relaxed among many groups, and the movement known as Reform Judaism started, virtually all stops were pulled out. Early on, *Reform* had eased observance to such an extreme that after a time, many Jews viewed it with disfavor. Their desire was more moderate practice. "Middle-of-the road," Conservative Jews perceived Reform Judaism as having dire consequences, total assimilation, a return to the Hellenic period centuries ago, during the Roman Empire.

In attempting to clarify and describe the differences separating these three categories of Jewish practice and observance, it is necessary to point out that in each one there is considerable latitude. In some instances, the divisions almost overlap one another. A congregation may call itself "Orthodox" and yet be strikingly close to a congregation that titles itself "Conservative." Lately, Progressive and Reform Jews are abandoning their Anglicized services, and are now reciting prayers in Hebrew, and even chanting them in the faith's traditional language. They are changing services that for many years were recited only in a country's lay language.

We've resurrected a variety of holiday customs that for more than a century had been neglected, considered archaic and obsolete, regarded as quaintly historical, but no longer relevant. This revival was initiated soon after the rebirth of a Jewish State. The Jewish people were motivated to sing and play our hymns and holiday songs in Middle Eastern style music.

Besides the blurred lines separating Orthodox, Conservative, and Reform Judaism so is the definition of who is and who is not

Jewish. When a member of a Jewish family drifts completely away from practicing the faith, abandons it totally, or even converts to the Christianity, does their genetic composition mean they still *are* Jewish?

With more Jews marrying non-Jews the issue has been raised about categorizing the children of "mixed" couples. Judaism had been using the matrilineal designation, the mother's religion. Now it is accepted, at least by Reform Jews, that a child whose father is a Jew but whose mother is not, is nevertheless Jewish. However, this is only *if* the child is taught the history of his Jewish ancestry, and the faith system's laws and rituals.

An ongoing difference of opinion and of dispute relates to the "Jew by choice," a term for someone who converts to Judaism. Orthodox Jews adamantly refuse to honor a conversion sanctified by a Reform rabbi. Instruction hadn't been sufficiently stringent and detailed, they insist. Nor has there been a deep enough inquiry into *why* the person chose to be a Jew. The sincerity of a candidate is at issue. Indeed, the Orthodox deems the whole process too mild, too casual. Moreover, a conversion conducted by a Reform rabbi is invalid because in the opinion of Orthodox Jews Reform ordination is unacceptable. "Now they even think a woman can be a rabbi!"

Because of all these unresolved, conflicted issues and many differences in practicing the Jewish faith, this book is not just a historical account of this region's Jewish residents; it is also a sociological study of the Jews, and of their integrated communal life in Kern County, California.

With respect to the book's title: *Long Journey With Heavy Luggage—Mt. Sinai to San Joaquin Valley,* wherever a Jew lives, or when he moves and resettles, he is obligated to figuratively transport as his most sacred possession, the Torah. It contains the Covenant, a contractual agreement in which the Israelite people pledged their obedience to God's laws and God appointed them His vanguards of moral and ethical behavior.

PART ONE

Strangers in A Strange Land

Strangers in A Strange Land

Freedom, Fraternity, Financial Fitness

The early arrivals to Kern County were mostly sojourners making a trek through Tejon Canyon, proceeding alongside the foothills of Bear Mountain, then moving northward to the place that became Bakersfield. These people were en route to older areas of the state, already settled, and offering predictable opportunities. There is evidence that they came westward from Tennessee, Kentucky, Arkansas and Texas. Many of these people were basically adventurers, restless for a change. Their stopover was often to water their stock, and perhaps to give their children a chance to romp and tumble a bit. At times, however, they idled away a whole season in our area, fishing, hunting, growing a crop of corn to replenish the supply they had started out with.

Around the mid-1840s the region had a trickle of settlers, despite the risk of Indian hostility and from predatory bears. A little later, during the Civil War, there were outlaws, roving marauders and renegades from both the Union and Confederate armies. Production of hay, vegetables and beef were the industries of the first farmers. But the cattle business and mining were successful and these were attracting mercantilism and the banking industry. It was in this era that many immigrant Jews and those living in eastern states came westward and made the Central Valley their home and source of finances.

Lesser Hirshfeld, a retail storeowner, was called "Cristobel" because of the jovial relationship he had with his store's Hispanic patrons. He and his family of pioneer merchants became well entrenched in Bakersfield and Tehachapi retailing. Four Hirshfeld brothers had emigrated from Germany to make America their homeland. Herman Hirshfeld, the oldest, started his business in Havilah, the county seat during "boom" years of gold mining, 1866 to 1868. Herman Hirshfeld first started working for Morris Jacoby, also an early pioneer of merchandising, and among the Jewish settlers. Morris Jacoby's Company dealt in wool, hides and grain. He too had emigrated from Germany. After Herman worked in the business enough to acquire sufficient know-how he became Morris Jacoby's partner.

Marcus Hirshfeld came to Tehachapi in 1874 and bought a general mercantile business from Ed Green. Seven years later, in 1881 he sold his interests to Isador Asher and joined his brother Dave who was running the Pioneer Store in Bakersfield. Dave Hirshfeld had previously worked in Santa Ana. After a year he put his luck to the test with placer mining in Mexico. Two years after that venture, in 1874, Dave returned to the United States and linked up with the Hirshfeld Brothers, owners of Pioneer Store.

A historical account of Central California: *Pen Pictures of the Garden of the World* is a highly complementary depiction of Dave:

"Dave Hirshfeld occupies an enviable position as a sterling trait of character—that he never misrepresents anything in business, and that he never resorts to the 'Cheap John' way of doing business, holding out five-cent inducements in order to gain a $5 advantage over the unwary. Mr. Hirshfeld takes a lively interest in home affairs. This tends to advance the material interests and development of his town and vicinity. As a citizen and social companion, he is highly esteemed."

General stores sold clothing and all sorts of dry goods. In fact, every commodity miners, ranchers, builders and householders needed. Several of these small enterprises mushroomed into leading department stores, even chains of these stores. Partnerships were formed and dissolved; mergers and buy-outs occurred, sometimes between relatives, friends, or just former countrymen.

In September 1900 one of the enterprises of Dave Hirshfeld and Otto Belau, owners of Pioneer Store, was sold to the Hochheimer Brothers. It later became Brock's, a noted Bakersfield Department Store. The Hochheimer brothers, Amiel and Moses were German immigrants whose careers began and concluded as mercantilists. They entered the industry in the early 1870s after their jobs with Eppinger & Company in Dixon.

The younger of the two brothers, Moses, struck out on his own in 1876. He was joined in a partnership with William Johnson. Johnson and Hochheimer owned a store in Willows. Three years later Amiel came to Willows and bought out Johnson's interest. The firm's name was changed to Hochheimer and Company.

One of their four sisters married Sam Blum of San Francisco; another sister, Mattie, wed Julian Brock. Julian was a partner in Cohn and Brock, a clothing store in San Francisco. In 1878 Mattie and Julian had a son they named Malcolm. When he grew up his first full-time job was working for his uncles Moses and Amiel in their Willows store. He joined the family business in 1894.

In 1898, Ira Hochheimer, oldest son of Amiel and Bertha, graduated from the University of California. He came home to Willows and started working in the family's business. Ten years later, in 1908 Monroe Hochheimer, Amiel and Bertha's second son was added to the staff of next-generation family members.

By chance in 1900, during a visit to Bakersfield, Moses Hochheimer met Otto Belau. More or less as a joke Mr. Belau said his business was available for purchase. Within minutes a deal was struck: for \$20, 000 the store's lease, all its fixtures and stock were turned over to the new owner.

After the 1906 earthquake and fire in San Francisco, Malcolm Brock predicted its devastation offered huge opportunities for the construction business. He decided to seek his fortune by helping to rebuild San Francisco; the disaster had leveled it. He spent two years there, and after that he traveled to Alaska. His Aunt Bertha's father, Sam Blum had induced Malcolm to manage the new Blum mercantile business and bank in Cordova. This occurred in 1909.

Ten years later a devastating fire in Bakersfield fairly demolished the Hochheimer store. The loss amounted to \$750,000. Other businesses that also suffered losses were the American Jewelry Company, Weill's Department Store, and The Grand Hotel. Six weeks later Hochheimer set up a temporary business, stocked it, and readied it to resume selling. The site was 18th St. between "Eye" and "H" Streets.

Further misfortune befell the Hochheimers the following year. On July 11, 1920 their store in Willows was totally destroyed by fire, a loss of half a million dollars. Twenty-seven other decimated firms led to ten lost buildings, adding another half million to the total cost of the fire. Once again the Hochheimers managed to get along with a makeshift retail business, until their new store on 20th and Chester was ready to open.

Many Hochheimer's customers were rice and grain merchants. When the 1921-rice crop failed, and customers couldn't pay their bills, it badly hurt the Hochheimer Co. Thousands of dollars of permanent indebtedness forced the firm to consolidate. In January 1922 its store in Willows was closed.

Malcolm Brock still in Alaska began to have second thoughts about the territory's potential population growth. Between 1909 and 1922 he had acquired partnership and presidency of the Blum-O'Neill General Merchandise Co. and of the First Bank of Cordova. Nevertheless, he decided to rejoin and manage his family's business in California, experience adding his useful input regarding its reorganization. However, problems continued to plague the company.

Bankruptcy came under consideration to relieve the company of its vast debt burden. Malcolm Brock made a bid to buy the store, and the creditors approved and accepted his offer. Although the store made no major change in its merchandising policies it assumed the new owner's name: Malcolm Brock and Co. Later it became Brock's Department Store.

Pioneers can be defined as persons of vision, willing to take daring risks but foreseeing the potential of a great future! Among the early settlers in Kern County were Jews of varying backgrounds and work experience. Clearly, they were people who hadn't achieved success in their European home country or America's east coast, but whose hopes were aimed at this undeveloped region. Jews were attracted to the West for the same reasons as other Americans and immigrants.

But many Jews who had started their lives in Europe had an additional very special incentive: Centuries of discriminatory laws and attitudes had kept them from land ownership, from professions and from other desirable means of support and fulfillment. In their homeland many had struggled to eke out the barest existence, permitted to engage in occupations that non-Jews viewed with contempt, regarding them too lowly and demeaning for *their* acceptance.

Jews were tradesmen of cheaply designed, ill-crafted goods; they were moneylenders and brokers with sharp limitation on their upward mobility. In regard to craft occupations, Jewish artisans were denied membership in a guild, an umbrella of wage and price protection through the strength of unity. But overriding those countless economic and social limitations was another, more profound motivation that precipitated Jewish immigration to America. It was religious and political freedom.

The zeal Jews had for their new land rendered them colonists who bore arms against the British in the American Revolutionary War. They stood side by side with others fighting for the values our country treasures and consider a birthright: liberty, equality, the democratic establishment and administration of our laws. In every war this nation needs men to defend our values and philosophic convictions. Right from the beginning Jews risked their lives to obtain and *sustain* the United States of America.

In the 1800s, soon after America had freed itself from the British monarchy's control, Jewish immigrant shopkeepers with their mercantile ability, and some with experience, responded to the potential of a western frontier.

Though most Jewish people here had come from a country in Europe that barred them from university education, or their impoverishment meant they couldn't afford to attend school very long, most were literate, industrious, and not afflicted with impediments like drunkenness. They were hardworking and resourceful.

Many of the young and healthy had left Europe to connect with an uncle or brother or cousin already established here. Business owners frequently sent a note to their relatives in the old country promising a job to the newcomer.

Of course, sometimes the project, a job or partnership, didn't materialize, or not for long, leaving the recent arrival to fend for himself. If it didn't pan out and proved to be an unhappy arrangement it dissolved, and everyone went his own way. There were almost limitless solutions.

Marriages of Jewish immigrant men in the old west frequently were to Native American or Mexican women. In the 1840s, when ranching made its embryonic beginning in the Tehachapi Mountains, that territory was still part of Mexico. But then, as the Jewish population grew, around the dawn of the twentieth century, more and more young Jewish men sought young women of their own religious faith.

While California's most basic industry was cattle ranching, land grants were freely given. Perfunctory authorization was simply to set geographic limits on an owner's range. A petitioner submitted his request to the governor who passed it along to an official of that particular locale for his approval; this was followed by the registration of ownership.

In 1846 when war broke out between Mexico and the United States, Mexican ranchers left their land to fight the war. America won the conflict, and as soon as the Mexicans validated this they sold their land to American ranchers and to many immigrants from Europe.

The newly developing West had just discovered gold. Mining and sheep herding industries flourished simultaneously in the Sierra Nevada.

In the early 1860s, Solomon Jewett, a Vermont shepherd, was employed to take charge of Colonel James Vineyard's cattle flocks. A ranching business was established between Solomon, his brother Philo, and a San Francisco banker named Thomas Bull. It was located ten miles east of the not-yet-incorporated city of Bakersfield, and given the name Rio Bravo, (Wild River) because it bordered the Kern River.

The Civil War (1861-1865) not only raised political conflict, it resulted in lawlessness and violence. Among the crime gangs were Monroe and Hawkins, two sly guys who tricked Solomon and Philo Jewett, the unsuspecting owners of Rio Bravo Ranch. They convinced them they were sojourners merely passing through the area. The Jewetts invited the pair as their overnight guests. While Philo was showing them where to install their horses one of the bandits grabbed him and they threatened his life.

Fortunately, he jumped through a window and freed himself. Later he returned home and discovered the murdered body of one of his herdsman. Regarding property theft, luckily the only things the two outlaws stole were two rifles.

Later on, in the mid '70s Jacob Weill and Morris Jacoby who owned establishments in Bakersfield bought a store in Kernville that Allen D. Green owned. It was a time of rapid growth for the town and in ten months a dozen houses were constructed. A newspaper article referred to Kernville as "Little Chicago."

Other than developing quickly, it was like other towns in the county, saddled with crime and political dissent, a devastating consequence of The War Between the States.

Most of this area's pioneers had come from the south and were experienced in mining, farming, and the cattle industries. Although by now many of these gold miners and herdsmen had drifted away, those who did remain, built a stable mining community. Cattlemen became settled ranchers.

E.J. Boust had acquired a real property settlement and named it after himself: "Boust City." It had wide cement walkways of flimsy construction but that frequent fires did not destroy even when the city was brought to its knees. Their length stretched all the way to the sagebrush.

The rise of Boust City included saloons and other enterprises of diversion. In 1920, five years after Mr. Boust died, all his property was purchased by Sam Orloff. He built a modern residential area, naming it "Taft Heights," and left in place some of the original cement sidewalks. Many pieces of real property that oil companies owned were sold on the real estate market, and this promoted a housing boom in Taft.

Sam Orloff had truly pioneered Taft, constructing buildings in the downtown area of 5th and North Streets, and initiating Taft National Bank. Its opening November 28th, 1922, was temporarily in the Parrish-O'Brien building, 121 Fourth St.

Note: Details about Sam Orloff are from "Kernland Tales" by Edith Dane (May 1950), transcribed and edited by Larry Peahl (2006) and submitted to this book by Gilbert Gia, member and former president of KC Historical Society.

"Men of different temperaments, personalities, viewpoints and objectives contributed to the tapestry that describes the history of Taft. No one's story is more colorful; none has left a deeper imprint on the community than Sam Orloff's. If, while trying to shape Taft into a fine community and thus improve the lives of its people, a few times he made a fortune for himself, but viewing the financial gain inadvertent and unimportant. He had no qualms about putting his money at risk when another project came along.

Sam had been born March 10, 1880 in the Russian Ukraine. He was the seventh of Gregory and Nichomo Orloff's fourteen children. Ancestral Orloffs had been part of Russian aristocracy, and the family had owned a large portion of land in the Dnieper River Valley. They also had thousands of heads of cattle, and three gristmills. But when Sam was a child his family fell into hardship and tragic conditions.

Throughout its history Russia has been a land of darkness and brooding, a menacing one for its Jewish populace. They were periodically the victim of hate and injustice. Yet Sam was never embittered by his own negative experiences. He perceived life as an adventure, each blow of adversity a challenge. He judged the worth of his life by his capacity to give to others, not by what he had acquired from *them.*

Sam was still a young child when the family was obliged to leave Russia, departing without possessions, leaving them behind, literally walking away empty-handed. Their refuge was the city of Krolevetz, Little Russia, where they resided in conditions of oppression, poverty and squalor.

When Sam was only eight years old he worked for the owner of large fisheries on the Black Sea. Almost without help the boy taught himself to read and write in Russian, his native language, and to understand arithmetic. His employer began using him as an errand boy, taking him on trips to England.

Seeking to move ahead, to improve his situation, Sam took a new job, on a cattle transport boat that traveled the huge distance between Liverpool and Capetown, South Africa. He hoped that this was moving him nearer wish fulfillment, to immigrate to America.

After several cattle boat journeys the chance arose to be a sailor on a vessel bound for New York. It was in 1892 that he came there, a lonely twelve-year-old without money or acquaintances. But with courage and self-reliance Sam resolved to become a worthy citizen of the United States. His first job in New York was in a grocery store, his hours 3 a.m. to 7 p.m., his pay $3 a week.

He had learned to handle a paintbrush while he was a sailor, so he soon worked for a painting contractor. The man had him painting flagpoles, such dangerous work it yielded Sam $1 a day.

The Pacific Coast was Sam Orloff's Mecca. He secured the chance to work as a sailor on a ship bound for Havana, Cuba, then to Colon. From there he crossed the Isthmus on the Panama

Railroad, and worked his way to San Francisco on an American freighter.

He arrived in San Francisco in the latter part of 1896, at the age of sixteen. Sam's first California job was to paint bridges for the Southern Pacific Railway. His next was ship painting for the Union Iron Works. After that he became a house painter.

In 1901, when Sam was 21 years old he married Dina Kalfin, a daughter of Rabbi Harold David Kalfin. The girl was also a Russian born immigrant. In 1904, together with their two children, the couple moved to Eureka. Sam went into the men's furnishings business there and acquired his first chance to make a substantial amount of money.

A large schooner had been grounded on the sandbars while a storm had been in progress, and was battering the schooner to destruction. Mr. Orloff went to the bank and persuaded them to give him a loan, money to finance a salvage operation. He profited by about $80,000! His son Maurie related that a fine racehorse from South America had been part of the rescued cargo.

The family then moved to Spokane, Washington where loaded with cash Sam tried his luck at ranching. The endeavor proved to be unsuccessful. But undaunted by failure he cleared up his affairs in the state of Washington, and with his family moved back to California, this time to San Francisco.

In the fall of 1909 the new and booming town of Taft caught his attention and interest. Leaving his wife and children in San Francisco he came to Taft where he became a roustabout in the fields. However, he soon brought his family from San Francisco to Taft and established them on the north side of Center Street, between Fourth and Fifth Streets.

Here he set up a little notions store that Mrs. Orloff tended. It had living quarters in the rear. The store had a bell on the upper frame of the door that jangled while a customer was entering, alerting the proprietress and signaling her to halt any household duties she was engaged in, even feeding her young children.

Paralleling this, Mr. Orloff became a junk dealer. At the start he used a pushcart to collect waste materials from the fields. He worked long hours and built a good business. Thereafter he was very proud of his pushcart, often displaying it in a Taft parade.

In 1918 he started a furniture and hardware store, but soon sold it and entered in partnership with Whiting and Meade of Los Angeles. They sold lumber and other building materials. In 1921 Sam bought out his partners and created Taft Supply Company. The inventory was supplies for oil wells.

Permeating Taft in those early years was a sense of continual change, an attitude of impermanence. To some degree it remained many decades, making it seem risky to build or invest in a sturdy, high priced building, even for one's business or home.

However, Mr. Orloff keenly disagreed with this viewpoint. To prove his own confidence in the town's permanence he began to erect buildings equal in quality to those of *any* town its size. He started in 1920 with the two-story Orloff Building on Fifth Street (later called the Professional Building.) After that, in 1922 he built the State Bank Building. He also constructed storefront buildings, and a post office.

He had erected the bank building because of his concern that not a single bank in town was open on Saturday, an inconvenience for many people. Sam was inexperienced in the field of banking, but, with the help and under the guidance of Hellman of Los Angeles, he opened the State Bank of Taft, and arranged for Saturday banking hours.

Another of Sam Orloff's concerns was that the area still had few modern style well-built homes. So in 1920, against the advice and wisdom of others, and in the face of high odds, he purchased the ninety-acre Boust estate, south of Taft. It was the site of those wide cement sidewalks extending to the sagebrush, a source of astonishment to chance hikers unfamiliar with Taft.

Clearing the land, grading it, and platting it was a challenging project. It included a frustrating struggle to obtain utilities in this remote subdivision Mr. Orloff titled "Taft Heights." But with grim determination he persisted, and before long people *were* purchasing his attractive offers.

It took little time for local residents to start expressing pride in these well-constructed, commodious homes; including the really fine one Mr. Orloff had built for himself and his family.

Lovely green lawns, trees, flowers and shrubs made the subdivision a garden spot in the desert. Sam soon saw that creating "Taft Heights Addition" had been a wise decision.

While busily absorbed in all these business ventures, much to his credit he did not neglect his duties as head of a large family. He taught his children to respect the law, and he made sure they received the good education circumstances had denied *him*. Nor did he neglect civic responsibility; he earnestly supported programs focused on improving the community. He made generous donations to religious and social charities, and to other programs.

Although Sam Orloff regretted his own meager education, the rapidity of his thought process and wide scope of intellectual interests positioned him a peer of the well-educated. He would mentally initiate a project, plan the details, and in no time bring it to reality. The conception of an endeavor often occurred during the night, at three, four o'clock in the morning!

Many of Taft's physical features had been Orloff creations. Not all of these were financial successes, though. He dribbled away more than one fortune.

Sam Orloff died at age 69, while he was in Los Angeles. Survivors were Dina his wife, their four sons, three daughters, and fourteen grandchildren.

Jacob Asher, his name Anglicized from Auscher, was said to have been Kern County's first permanent Jewish resident. He entered in partnership with Mr. Sanderson, the men becoming co-owners of a "Two-Table Billiard Saloon" in Havilah. The timeframe of this was two years after gold had been discovered. Havilah was an important mining locale, its population growth soon reaching five hundred. When elections were started in Kern County, Sanderson and Asher's establishment became the first polling place. (1867) Jacob and Rose Asher's son Albert, born in 1871, was thought to be the first Jewish person born in Kern County.

At its height Havilah consisted of four hotels, twelve general merchandise stores, a paint store, two pharmacies, two billiard parlors, two barber shops, three produce stores, two bathhouses, three blacksmith-and-wagon shops and numerous bars and drinking saloons. *The Havilah Courier* once wrote that until banks started to open in the region, financial transactions were through the exchange of gold bullion, the only reliable and trusted medium.

Charles Asher was one of three brothers who came here as experienced mercantilists. Charles, Isador, and Arthur were born in Poland but had lived in Prussia before immigrating to the United States. After his arrival on American shores, and while still in New York Charles met and married Anna Marx.

In 1896 he brought her to Tehachapi, his destination because one of his uncles had established a business in the town. Anna was an immigrant from Germany, and also had family members in Kern County.

There evolved through business interests and marriages an intricate inter-connection of quite a few Jewish families. Many people in the area were blood-related: cousins, nephews, nieces, aunts and uncles. They became business partners and married into each other's family, Jews becoming a tightly enmeshed segment of the local population.

The Asher brothers opened stores in the communities of Tehachapi, Mojave, Taft, Randsburg and Lancaster. The Hirshfeld, Crystal, Marx, Brodek and Harris families were mercantilists too, and had all come with plenty of commercial experience. It included a familiarity with the intricacies of banking, so they began to operate local banks. As the population and industries of the county grew it became obvious that financial institutions were needed to serve the business community. Even today there are streets in Kern County bearing the names of these first settlers.

Note: Source of the following, a biographical sketch of Henry Alexander Jastro is a lengthy article by Gilbert Gia, member and former president of Kern County Historical Society.

Henry Jastro was respectfully called The Commodore of Kern County. He, in turn, was one of President Theodore Roosevelt's many admirers. Mr. Jastro characterized the nation's political leader as follows: "He's a big man, strong and fearless, and I'm convinced he's absolutely honest in his convictions. He means what he says, and I look forward to seeing some radical changes for the betterment of the country's conditions."

Bakersfield might have said that about Jastro. He too was thoroughly honest in his convictions. He did his best for Kern County, but although he was often lauded for his contributions to the community, at times he was maligned. For two decades his stewardship charted the course of Kern County, the reason for his title, "The Commodore."

In November 1892, at the age of forty-four Henry Jastro ran for a seat on the Board of Supervisors, defeating Henry Condict by a single vote. Condict charged his opponent with fraud, and Jastro counter-charged Condict with receiving illegal votes. The typed records revealed that illegal votes had been cast for *both* candidates!

Sorting through the newly corrected records the judge of this court case granted Jastro 399 votes and Condict 398. Henry Jastro won a total of twenty-three consecutive elections.

His birth is said to have been Hamburg, or perhaps it was Berlin, Germany. *Or* it might've been in Prussia, or in Poznan, Poland. And before he emigrated, his surname had been Jastrowitz! The only *certainty* about Mr. Jastro is that he had crossed the Atlantic from Europe, arrived in the United States and became a citizen in December 1889. He probably came to California in 1863 with his family when he was thirteen. The fact that Jastro was born in 1897 became known through the 1900 United States Census. However, Europe's 19th Century history complicates statistical data.

Virtually limitless opportunities in California's Central Valley were through land ownership and raising cattle, coupled with a man's business acumen. It enabled newcomers like Henry Jastro to amass huge fortunes. But before his own acquisitions, he had steered the vast Haggin Empire to higher and higher profits. His talent and abilities earned him recognition throughout the West.

When he became an elected official his public life was constantly in the news. Nevertheless, details of his private life were learned almost entirely from an interview he once gave to Sunset Magazine. Another source was Wallace Morgan's 1914 authorized biography of Henry Jastro. Family relations became known only through official wills and other estate data.

Henry seemed to be everywhere at the same time. He served on the boards of Western Cattlemen's Association and the California State Fair Association, and he testified before Congress on matters of the agriculture and international trade. He was an ex-officio Regent of the University of California.

The apex of his career was the Democratic Party's candidate for Governor of California. Campaigning obligations absented him from Bakersfield. When he didn't attend a Board of Supervisors meeting, voting was deferred. Few county projects were conducted without him.

In December 1904 and January 1905 while Jastro was in Washington D.C. giving speeches to the Forestry Congress about conservation and reforesting, he received accolades for his understanding of parliamentary procedure. He favored reciprocal trade relations with Europe, requiring their markets to accept U.S. beef products. He admitted America's meat trade was in deplorable conditions.

Jastro's endorsement to run for the office of governor had been at a meeting of the Kern County Democratic Central Committee. At the time he was in Europe, so it was viewed merely a courteous gesture by his friends and neighbors.

At the start of his life in Bakersfield, the young boy, 5 feet, 7 inches tall, with brown hair and brown eyes had worked for Phineas Banning as a livestock drover and freighter. In 1865 Jastro became a trail boss on the long cattle drives between San Joaquin Valley, Arizona and Nevada. Upon the death of a relative, and through the man's divided estate Henry Jastro's share was in livestock.

Sometime in the late 1860s his acquaintance with Alphonse Weill in Tehachapi led Henry to meet his future wife, Mary Whalen. She was Thomas Baker's seventeen year-old stepdaughter. By then Jastro was well into sheep ranching and sale of their wool.

Jastro's family members only became known after his death, and through his will. His sister Minnik was married to Leopold H. Harris, a man from Prussia who had come to the United States in 1854, and in 1855 settled in Los Angeles. In 1869 Harris made a trip to Europe for his marriage to Minnik Jastrowitz.

Incidentally, Minnik's maiden name did not appear in Jastro's will, or in the Harris will. It was found in a book printed in 1916, ten years before her death. Her Jastrowitz identity confirmed the origin of Henry's name.

The Harris couple had three children: Alfred, Rosa, and Sarah. Rosa and Sarah married their father's partners and Alfred joined his father's firm. He and his brothers-in-law were active in Los Angeles business, civic and fraternal affairs.

Herman W. Frank moved to Los Angeles in 1887, and the following year became connected to the I. Harrison Company, later called Harris & Frank, and after that Harris & Frank Retail Clothing. He had married Sarah Harris the year he joined her father's business. In 1896 Frank became vice president of Los Angeles B'nai Brith. They had a daughter, Martha, and she married Alfred Stern.

Henry Jastro's connection to wealthy California families kept expanding. His niece Rosa Harris married Melville Adler, making one family of the Jastros and the Adlers.

The estates of Henry Jastro, and of Leopold Harris identified a second Jastro sister, named Bertha. Her husband, H.M. Cohn, owned a kosher butcher business but later became a Los Angeles pawnbroker.

One day Henry's mother retired to her room to have a rest. Five minutes later her husband went to see if she was all right; he found her lifeless body faced down in her bed. The *Bakersfield Californian* published an article honoring her memory:

Possessed of rare unselfishness, abounding in tender solicitude for the welfare of others, blessed with a sunny, even temperament, she has walked through life a constant giver of blessings, a treasure to her friends, and a queen in her home.

By 1912 Henry Jastro's influence on the government of Kern County was in decline. J.A. Waltman, an aspiring Democrat for a seat on the Board of Supervisors assailed Kern County Land Company for controlling county politics. Another public challenge arose when H.A. Ingalls accused Jastro of wielding the power of his wealth and official position, to slow the county's development. The two men had a nasty conflict.

"Nearly a year ago I went to the Board of Supervisors. Their representative, Mr. Jastro, was not present, and the rest of the board advised me to see him first. I approached his 'majesty' as he entered the courthouse, told him that the desire of suffering settlers was for a road, reminding him that several former petitions had failed, that a road was necessary, and so on.

"He turned on me in that wise, patronizing manner of his, stating that he *knows* all about the matter, and that the settlers will get a road when he's ready to let them have it, or when it *suits the interests* of the Land Company!"

In 1915 the Board of Supervisors moved to reelect Henry Jastro Chairman of the Board. Before they voted he asserted: "I want to say that my health now is not the best. As you know, I've been prevented from attending a number of meetings in the past, and my ill health may interfere in the future. However, if you think I can serve you under these conditions, I shall interpose no objections."

He *was* reelected, responding: "I want to thank you sincerely. Not many men have been honored with an office as many terms as I have held Chairmanship of this Board. This, I believe, is my 21st year as Chairman of the Board of Supervisors of this county. I have tried to be absolutely fair. Many unjust assaults have been made against the Board, but the pendulum is swinging back, people seeing that these attacks were not made in good faith.

"As to the future, I promise to do the best in my power for the interests of the county. Any mistakes I make will be of the head, not the heart."

April and May 1915 Jastro was in ill health and not even in the county. But by June he *was*, and in July he attended a Board meeting to do an analysis of charges against J.W. Jamison, a man accused of extorting money.

On an evening in March 1916 Bakersfield Chamber of Commerce, in conjunction with the Kern County Board of Trade honored the Board of Supervisors, particularly Henry Jastro. The high point of the evening was when Col. E. M. Roberts toasted him.

As the honoree stood, the attendees rose en masse, cheering and applauding until the Colonel attempted to speak. Later Jastro said, "They may criticize us, but no man can point to anything for which he received a 100 % value."

The applause broke out again, and when the Chairman of twenty years finished and sat down, the attendees all stood to display approval. They accompanied it with lengthy applause.

Despite this fanfare, the Old Guard under Jastro's influence was minimized by a Republican Reform faction. The Old Guard was done in by the *new*.

Nevertheless, Henry Jastro remained active not only in local business but in the community's social structure: In 1920 Roland Dye, an executive of Boy Scouts of America thanked him for enabling young boys to spend a camping week-end at the base of China Grade bluffs. The following year he was elected president of the California State Agriculture Board.

Alas, soon after that honor he was in the grip of a serious ailment. Most likely it was a heart affliction that kept him in San Francisco for several months. In mid-April 1923 he came back to his hometown to dedicate the cornerstone of a new Masonic Hall. The strain was too great, and days later Henry Jastro suffered a heart attack. He was treated for it in Mercy Hospital.

But then, four months later the 71 year-old codger rose to another stressful challenge! He joined Governor Richardson at the Sacramento Street Fair, the two men engaging in a horseshoe-pitching contest. In January he was a judge in a debate conducted at Union High School, between Bakersfield College students and those of USC.

In February a shameful deed in Jastro's life was resurrected into view and publicly confessed. While addressing the Kern County Realty Board he revealed that a contract he made in 1887 with Haggin & Carr that entailed supplying Oakland mills with 5,900 bales of cotton had led him to commit an unethical deed. To raise and harvest a sufficient amount, and to conform to the terms of the contract, Jastro had illegally hired black laborers from the South. He was fined but didn't pay $5,000. He was given but didn't serve a six-month jail term.

Jastro admitted, "I still owe my country those six months. Although we found out that good cotton can be raised with cheap labor, it was the working conditions that made the plan both a legal and ethical failure." At the time of a stable economy, and when the unemployment rate was low in Kern County, workers' wages were adequate, but in 1884 when the economy slowed, Haggin & Carr had planted a thousand acres of cotton in a cost-saving move using black workers Henry Jastro had sent Mr. Owenby to South Carolina to recruit.

A heart attack he sustained in January 1925 resulted in his demise in April. Henry Alexander Jastro's funeral service was held April 18th in Masonic Temple auditorium. Bakersfield streets were empty and silent while Dr. Willis G. White of the Presbyterian Church recited his passionate eulogy.

Arthur S. Crites also spoke at the service, praising Jastro's philanthropy, his manifold deeds of kindness, many of which were not even known by the public. They were *well known* by most of Bakersfield's lawyers whose specialty was wills and estates!

Herman A. Spindt, principal of Kern County Union High School expressed gratitude for Jastro's interest in his school's activities; a special one was agricultural and vocational subjects.

Jastro made substantial donations to St. Paul's Church to meet the parish's 1925 obligations, and to Bakersfield's Mercy Hospital. He also contributed to each of the following: the San Francisco Orphans' Asylum, Catholic Orphans' Asylum, Russian Orphans' Asylum, and the Hebrew Orphans' Asylum.

Only when the end was drawing near, in the last few days of Henry Jastro's life did his family and close friends realize he *couldn't* recover. He had been transported to San Francisco so specialists there could offer their medical skills, but to no avail.

Regarding Henry's family life, while one of his daughters, Carolyn Louise, was a student of Marlborough School in Los Angeles she had lived in her cousin Rosa Adler's home. It was there she met her future husband, a Christian named Merriam Chadbourne. In 1900 Jastro's daughter May was wedded to William Greer, and in 1914 her second marriage was to Max Koshland, both Jewish men.

Guy Hughes, a contemporary of Henry Jastro iterated: "On my rare visits to Bakersfield during the later years of Henry's power, I'd sometimes meet him. I was of no political significance, just a young cowman with a few cows, striving to get ahead. Henry Jastro would greet me by name, seemed to know my neighbors, because he would ask about their well-being, and how their cattle were doing. To the very last he was a cowman heart and soul."

May Jastro Koshland's will included a $7.6 million endowment the University of California, its title: "Henry A. Jastro School of Agriculture." Decisions about where to leave her money would have pleased her father.

In the course of his lifetime he kept growing in both affluence and influence. As manager of the Kern County Land Company in 1903, he gained control of one million three hundred ninety-five

40

thousand acres of land. Although the company name implied that its holdings were limited to Kern County, in actuality it owned property in other parts of California, and in Arizona, New Mexico, and the nation of Mexico.

A subsidiary of the K C Land Company was the local utility company Henry had initiated. Later on, the company merged: San Joaquin Light and Power Company, and Pacific Gas and Electric Company.

Jastro had exerted strong power in the country's livestock industry during his five-term presidency of the National Livestock Association. Another of his enterprises was the Southern Hotel, which at the time was a leading hostelry. He was a board member of the Bakersfield Sandstone Brick Company.

When he ran on the Democratic ticket for a seat on the Board of Supervisors, he won with a high majority of votes and served from 1892 to 1916. Although his allegiance was always to the Democratic Party, he had a lot of support from Republicans too. He was well liked because of his service to the public, meanwhile keeping taxes tightly reined in. During his administration, county roads were paved, an elegant courthouse was constructed, and the county acquired a library system. For over twenty years Henry Jastro was the dominant political figure in Kern County.

He had been in the San Francisco Palace Hotel when he died. Henry was in the company of his two daughters, who had his body transported back to Bakersfield for the funeral. Since he was a member of the Elks, and the Masons both lodges participated in the service. Henry Jastro and his wife are buried next to each other in Union Cemetery.

Complying with their father's expressed wishes, in 1927 his daughters had a bandstand erected in a city park located between Truxtun and 18th Streets. On its facade it simply says, "From Henry A. Jastro." Sadly, as years drifted by the public's awareness of him and of his beneficence have dimmed.

Both in life and in death Henry Jastro's religious perspective, and the practice of his faith were kept under wraps. As a matter of fact, his private life has been pretty much that: *Private!*

Morris Jacoby, a civic-minded, prominent Jewish businessman of the mid-19th century offered to build a brick-constructed county jail for Bakersfield, *if* the city became the county seat. Acceptance or rejection of Jacoby's magnanimous offer that included a free five-year lease on the jailhouse was to be determined in the next election.

The flourishing mining industry had thinned, but agriculture was on the rise. This evolution led to greater pressure for the county seat to be moved from Havilah to Bakersfield. It was desired because Bakersfield was growing in importance not only in the farming industry but in mercantilism. It would be inconvenient to travel to Havilah on county business. In 1873 the Board of Supervisors received a petition with enough signatures to conduct a referendum on the issue of changing the county seat.

The vote was a close one but by disqualifying the ballots from three precincts, the Board tipped the balance in favor of retaining Havilah. Solomon Jewett, a member of the Board of Supervisors filed a claim against disqualifying ballots he insisted *were* valid. He requested a court hearing of this crucial issue.

In the interim, while the case was traveling through the court system, composition of the Board underwent changes leaving Solomon Jewett the only member involved in this dispute.

Ultimately, in 1874 Judge Alexander Deering of the 13th district court in Visalia ruled in favor of the questionable votes, thus making Bakersfield the new county seat. Its residents celebrated with flag waving, by lighting bonfires, exploding black powder, and clanging anvils. Morris Jacoby was made a Board member.

Around 1890 Charles Asher's roots were unearthed from his homeland and transplanted in this country. His and those of his two brothers, Isador and Arthur, became deeply and firmly burrowed in the soil of Kern County. Generation after generation resided in Tehachapi.

In 1896 the Hochheimer/Brock legacy made *its* start in Kern County, members of these two families becoming well-respected mercantilists and giving conscientious service to the community. A compatible partnership had connected the two German-Jewish immigrant families, both with hopes of a great future in America, the *Goldena Medina!*

Simon Hochheimer, born 1820 in Bavaria, Germany had settled in Pittsburgh, Pennsylvania when he came to the United States, starting his personal family there. He and his wife Hannah née Mayerheim, (also German-born,) had six children. Their two sons were named Amiel and Moses; their four daughters were: Mattie, Bessie, Julia, and Ettie.

The couple and brood of youngsters embarked on a difficult journey to California. It was a time (1859/1860) when travel was exhausting even for adults. Those with children needed not only good health and strength, but determination! The Hochheimers traveled by boat from the east coast to Panama. They boarded a railroad train that took them to the west coast, and then they journeyed northward by boat to San Francisco.

Moses, the younger boy, even at an early age displayed an independent, individualistic personality. After he and his brother Amiel, who was five years his senior, had worked awhile for Eppinger Company in Dixon, Moses was ready to strike out on his own. He formed a partnership with William Johnson and they opened a general merchandise store in Willows. Amiel came to Willows in 1879 to be part of the enterprise. He bought out Mr. Johnson's interest and the brothers changed the store's name to Hochheimer and Company.

Their father Simon died in San Francisco in 1891; their widowed mother lived until 1910. (Her family name is uncertain; it *may* have been Mayerheim.) Whether Simon and Hannah had ever even visited Kern County, an area enriched by their descendants is dubious.

Myer and Fannie Brock gave birth to Julien in Germany on February 26, 1839. Julien immigrated to the U.S. in 1870 and settled in California. When old enough *he* became a retail merchant. With a partner he opened a clothing store called Cohn and Brock.

Julian fell in love with Mattie, sister of Amiel and Moses. They married March 28, 1878 and had a son they named Malcolm. At age sixteen Malcolm started working for his two uncles, Amiel and Moses, owners of Hochheimer and Company in Willows.

Right after San Francisco's 1906 earthquake Malcolm left the employ of his uncles and involved himself in reconstructing the desecrated city. He spent two years doing that before his move to Alaska where until 1922 he worked in banking and mercantilism.

Twenty-two years earlier, in 1900, Moses Hochheimer found *his* place in the Bakersfield business arena. For the sum of twenty-thousand dollars he bought Chester Avenue's Pioneer Store from Otto Belau. He re-named it Hochheimer and Company. Moses, to whom much of the county's Hochheimer/Brock influence should be attributed, died in San Francisco November 11, 1911.

By then Amiel's sons: Ira and Monroe were in the family business, watching it thrive and grow! The former owner, Otto Belau had employed twelve people; the Hochheimers gradually increased their staff to a hundred-fifty.

Their father was involved in California politics, and a delegate to the Republican National Conventions of 1896, 1908, and 1916. In 1928 he died in San Francisco where he had resided for a while.

After Malcolm Brock sold his Alaska business interests in 1922 he came to Bakersfield to manage the Hochheimer store. When the financial crisis erupted he bought out the creditors and now was the firm's single owner, re-naming it Malcolm Brock and Company. Son of Julien Brock, grandson of Simon Hochheimer, Malcolm firmly attached himself to a legacy his forebears created. Industrious and highly motivated Jewish families had a strong hand in the growth of this region of Central California.

Early in the twentieth century, to these shores, a young fellow from Tsarist Russia by the name of Oscar Rudnick came to these shores. Born in 1890, it didn't take long for him to set his sights on migrating to the United States, as hordes of others were doing. Oscar was fourteen years old when he left his home and family in Vilnius and arrived on Ellis Island, New York.

An older sister and her husband, Alta and Louis Levine had come to America at an earlier time and were living in New York City. Louis went to meet the ship on which young Oscar was expected, distressed to be told there was no Oscar Rudnick on the passenger list! His reasonable conclusion was that his wife's brother had failed to board the vessel.

For some obscure reason Oscar's official papers were not in his true name. It was why the confusion occurred and nearly caused Oscar to be denied entry to America. He was terrified at the prospect of being shipped back to Europe. After a short detention on Ellis Island in the care of HIAS, Hebrew Immigrant Aid Society, and while the desperate youngster vowed to jump in the East River and drown himself, the situation was clarified and resolved. Oscar was united with his sister and brother-in-law, ready for life in the United States.

His first job was in Springfield, Massachusetts where he worked in Springfield Arms Company's factory. After about three years he joined Alta and Louis on their move to Los Angeles.

Oscar supported himself by working in a dairy, then a grocery store, and after that as an itinerant salesman. He peddled merchandise for Watkins Products, a company that sold household and industrial maintenance products in outlying areas. Oscar's "territory" included sparsely populated Bakersfield and its rural surroundings.

To reach his potential customers Oscar, who by then was perhaps twenty years old, drove a buckboard wagon hitched to a pair of horses or mules. The wagon was filled with Watkins' cleansers, brushes, buttons, and other items ranchers and their wives found useful.

Soon he was traveling all the way from Los Angeles across the Mojave Desert to Carson City, Nevada. Overnight stays were in people's barns, but often he had a hospitable invitation to sleep in a customer's home. Oscar's Orthodox, traditional Jewish background stood him in good stead. He quickly earned the reputation of being an honorable young man. He always credited this to the dicta of his early Torah studies.

Payment for many Watkins Products was done with livestock. Oscar would slaughter the animal himself and sell the meat, frequently generating more profit than through a cash payment. This was the seedling that ultimately bloomed into the Rudnick Empire in ranching and meatpacking,

Oscar gradually saved enough money for his first land purchase, a plot in the Fruitvale section of Bakersfield. It coincided with the discovery of oil, and led to an influx of men and their families seeking jobs in the incipient industry. They needed meat, which prompted Oscar to create his slaughter business. In the beginning the functions were done in the open air, under a tree!

There already was a thriving slaughterhouse, owned by Oscar Coleman. Before long the two Oscars became partners, until Rudnick bought out the Coleman enterprise.

He named his business Kern Valley Packing Company. At its peak the Rudnick enterprise owned vast pasturelands on which huge flocks of sheep and other livestock grazed before slaughter. Livestock of other ranchers were also brought to Oscar Rudnick to be slaughtered, and for the curing and smoking of butchered meat, marketed under the Smokehouse brand.

At first all his land was only on lease, but as Oscar pyramided his assets, he gradually made purchases, until his holdings were not only in California but Nevada, Arizona, and Oregon.

Oscar and his series of partners became landowners of over a million acres, besides extensive land leases. The following were these enterprising ranchers: Art Alexander, Gregorio Mendiburu, Leonard Bidart, Filbert & Michel Etcheverry, Juan Arrache, Frank, Tony and Jim Delfino, Leonard Stevens, Waldo Bozarth, Phil Klipstien, Simone Zorillo, Tony Leggio and Tex Chanley. Mr. Rudnick had a connection to virtually every sheep ranch, including the notable Tejon Ranch.

In 1912, at the age of twenty-two he had met a young Russian immigrant woman in Los Angeles; her name was Libbie. He and Libbie were married in Carson City, Nevada. His sterling character made him a good husband and a good father to their eleven children. Their son Philip holds treasured memories of his dad's character.

He recalls in his youth of watching Oscar buy livestock from rural youngsters at the yearly Kern County Fair. These boys were eager to earn money for their education, impelling Oscar to invariably pay them more than the prevailing market price.

To quote Philip: "My dad's behavior was based on his childhood study of *Pirke Avot,* "Teachings of the Fathers," as well as Torah's outline of ethical principles. He attributed his compassionate treatment of the less fortunate to his background in Judaism. Once when a customer suddenly fell into straitened circumstances, and his wife required hospitalization, the man desperately needed a hundred dollars to pay the hospital bill. He saw no option but to have animals slaughtered that were far too young and meager in size and weight. It would've been totally out of character for my father to exploit the situation. Generously, he gave the man the hundred dollars, telling him to return to his ranch with the immature pigs, and to bring them back when they were sufficiently fattened and could command the right price."

At the 1998 Centennial Heroes Awards Banquet, the deceased Oscar Rudnick was one of fifty honored residents. On behalf of his father, Philip accepted the honorary award for ethical business practices.

Ranchers would ship their cattle to Kern Valley Packing without knowing the price per pound, or witnessing the weighing process. Philip was the assigned "weigh master," who had to be diligent in balancing the scale, arriving with certitude at the correct weight. Oscar then instructed him to add twenty pounds to the total, thus ensuring that the absent seller received an advantageous tally. There was never the slightest chance of violating an absent customer's trust.

With his own children Oscar had been a demanding parent, a hard taskmaster, Philip declared in retrospect. But at the same time he imparted to his children the imperative of honesty in business dealings. Softness and gentleness emanated from Libbie, the hard-working mother of their brood of eleven children.

In the early lives of these youngsters, the Rudnick residence was next door to the packing plant. Not only did their mother take wonderful care of her children she prepared meals for the plant workers. Later on when Oscar and Libbie bought a house in Bakersfield although they lived comfortably, their lifestyle remained very simple, almost austere. Despite their massive wealth, Oscar and Libbie never displayed flamboyance, never practiced conspicuous consumption and never took a costly vacation. None of these factors generally ascribed to rich people were in accord with the personalities of Oscar and Libbie Rudnick.

The time-consuming industrious tasks of the Rudnick couple did not exclude their practice of basic Jewish rituals, such as making a Passover Seder, observing *Rosh Hashanah, Yom Kippur,* and other days sacred to the Jewish people. They supported both Bakersfield synagogues: Congregation B'nai Jacob and Temple Beth El. It was customary to make a donation when called to the Torah. On behalf of impoverished members, when *they* were called to the Torah,

Oscar would submit a contribution. He seemed constantly mindful of the blessings God had bestowed on him, and he sought to be worthy, to demonstrate his gratitude by helping others, Jews and Gentiles.

In the Rudnick early struggles, Libbie too showed her mettle. A delightful anecdote was depicted by the *Los Angeles Examiner: Woman seizes swindler in vise-like grip, drags the 'Flim-Flam' artist back in the store, and her husband gets his money back! Policemen pry her loose. Prisoner identified as a man who attempted the same game two weeks ago.*

In 1952, at the age of sixty, Libbie died of cancer. Oscar's second marriage was to cardiologist Dr. Sophie Goldman, widow of Herbert Goldman. The couple parented a daughter they named Rebecca. Oscar Rudnick died in 1959, always remembered and honored by his descendants, and also by the community. He exemplified Jewish ethical precepts.

Even Teddy Kollek, who became mayor of Jerusalem and was raising money from U.S. private sources for Israel's defense needs, knew that Oscar Rudnick strongly supported the Jewish homeland. Their acquaintance led to Bakersfield as the site of an early stage training ground for Israel's air force. Elynor Rudnick, interesting, colorful daughter of Oscar and Libbie gave herself a major role in the program. She and her brother Marcus persuaded their dad to allocate a portion of his land for an Airpark. It was near Highway 99 and Watts Drive.

Elynor became the Airpark manager. After meeting Teddy Kollek she offered to train young Israeli pilots. The curriculum was an accelerated, comprehensive one, its design based on United States Air Force training in World War II. Everyone in the Rudnick family, and joined by Bakersfield's Jewish community, contributed to the funding. The Israeli student pilots were not only men, but young women too.

At mealtime the students dined in a nearby restaurant owned by (ready for a few chuckles?) *Mr. Fox and Mr. Lion!* It was called The Saddle and Sirloin.

The Jewish owner of an army and navy surplus store provided the trainees with necessary equipment. For a little pocket money Elynor gave each student a small allowance from her personal resources.

Not all these flight students made the grade, and were able to achieve eligibility for advanced flight training. Only three out of the thirteen were proficient enough to become combat pilots.

A strict embargo imposed by several nations, the United States included, required the training to be covert. The ongoing danger of being ascertained by the F.B.I. put a restraint on the program. After three or four months the first group of trainees returned to Israel and joined the air force in varying capacities.

In 1986 Elynor was invited to Israel. Her contribution to their War of Independence was recognized with the Israel Air force Medal of

Honor. Ten years later in Palm Springs, California her noble life came to an end. The body of Elynor Rudnick was interred in the city of her birth, Bakersfield, California.

In 1924 the United States instituted highly restrictive immigration legislation. Many people viewed it xenophobic, anti-Semitic, monstrously immoral, and vilely discriminatory! Presidents Taft and Wilson had been urged to oppose the law, but since anti-Jewish feelings were not uncommon at this time, resentment of Jewish people's successes, and the country's general dislike of newcomers, it was easy to get the law signed by these Presidents.

The National Liberal Immigration League, and Citizens Committee for Displaced Persons, both funded by Jewish organizations recruited non-Jews from Europe's eastern and southern countries to protest the new law, to assert that claiming Anglo-Saxons and other Nordic people were superior, more worthy of United States citizenship was biased.

"True, Czechs are sturdy laborers, Jews good businessmen, Italians spiritually exalted, and artistically creative, a quality Nordic people rarely attain. However North Europeans, Anglo-Saxons made *this* country! Yes, the others helped but they came to this Anglo-Saxon commonwealth adding, even enriching it, they didn't make it. We're not going to surrender it to somebody else, or allow other people, no matter what their merits make it into something different. If there is changing to be done we will do it ourselves." (Cong. Rec. 5922, April 8, 1924)

Sam Young chose the quiet town of Keene as his retirement community. In the manner of a delicately bred Victorian lady discreetly raising the hem of her skirt to shield it from a muddy walkway, Keene held itself slightly aloof from the helter-skelter of Bakersfield. It gazed reticently on burgeoning traffic, patchwork of new housing developments and sprouting mini-malls.

Driving easterly on Highway 58, after a mere half hour from the center of town I was in a totally transformed landscape, exquisitely pastoral. In this setting was the home of Sam and Betty Young. May 1998, the time of my visit, in the company of Ross Abarbanel was to interview the couple for this book's first edition.

Most of Mr. and Mrs. Young's eight thousand acres was leased to ranchers, except for their home on a wide expanse of twenty-two acres. The interior décor of their house was a charming blend of elegance and country simplicity. In the relaxed and commodious aura of a spacious great room the Youngs had created an inviting atmosphere.

I had met Sam eighteen months earlier in a public assembly at Temple Beth El. He, Stefan Zellner and I had been speakers for a commemorative program marking an anniversary of *The Night of Broken Glass,"* Kristalnacht, a rampage of destruction by the Nazis. These people had burned, looted, and totally demolished synagogues and their sacred contents of books, scrolls, objects of Jewish ritual. This infamous night should never be forgotten!

Mr. Young described his own life in those times, and how he managed to avoid becoming one of six million Jewish fatalities in the Holocaust.

Even after listening to Sam Young address the congregation that evening I had not become acquainted with this remarkable man in the way I came to know him at the informal visit to his home. His early background had been in rural Czechoslovakia, where the family of Sam's mother, she included, had all been farmers. This made it abundantly clear why Sam's retirement was in Keene. It was compatible with his life-long appreciation of nature. Right here were grasslands and rolling, tree-studded hills. The whole setting was in pristinely clean air, an increasingly rare factor in Central Valley. On sleek, graceful horses Sam and Betty enjoyed riding, and they proudly showed these creatures at equine events.

Sam Young came full-circle, from the start of his life at the foot of the Carpathian Mountains to his retirement on rich fertile soil and the hills of Kern County. Leaving Europe right after WWII, he had immigrated to the United States in 1946, thus benefiting from the phenomenal growth in California's real property values. Astute in business, he became a highly successful building contractor and land developer. Sam had amassed substantial wealth.

Highly intelligent, deeply introspective, firm in his convictions, he spoke to me in unrestrained candor, projecting his perceptions and assessments of Judaism and its place within America's Christian and secular societies.

In regard to Sam's own approach to Judaism, he believed that the moral and ethical code of Jewish doctrine is the very foundation, the imperatives of all good societies. However, Judaism's ceremonial symbols in and of themselves have little importance, this university educated, scholarly member of a family of physicians emphasized.

Mr. Young also said he strongly disapproved of the political impact Israel's ultra-Orthodox wing was having on the Knesset, the government's legislature. Their stubborn belief in the Messiah was absurdly unrealistic, even detrimental. "Who has done more for world Jewry, David ben Gurion or leading rabbis who try to impose this narrow, archaic belief on us?" This was one of the subjects we discussed.

But clearly, Sam Young recognized how vital it was for the Jewish people to have their own land, a safety net that can prevent another disaster like the Holocaust. Or even one of the capricious expulsions that place us in a state of uncertainty, without a reliable refuge, a rightful living space on this planet. This has been our situation ever since inception of the Diaspora!

Despite Sam's secularist philosophy, paradoxically he credits Jewish laws of *kashruth*. They preclude the use of sick animals, and thus prevent the spread of illnesses like those that became epidemic in Europe. He recalled that in Czechoslovakia anthrax felled Christians with the disease, but not Jews and not those non-Jews who purchased meat from the kosher butchers avoided the disease.

He was convinced that placing high value on study, on education, should be credited with the survival of the Jews, despite a history of oppression, discrimination and predatory destruction.

Sam and his second wife Betty, had almost unlimited choices for a retirement residence, so it is indeed a compliment to Kern county that this jewel, Keene, was where they decided to settle in 1978. The Youngs were not only significant philanthropists but the fulfillment of one of God's most fervent desires: that man's dominion over the earth shall include respect for all His creations of the natural world: plant and animal life, air and water. Of infinite value are local residents who preserve rather than dissipate and destroy our precious heritage.

After Stefan Zellner, a Holocaust survivor, retired from a long career: as an engineer for a few major oil companies, followed by five years as a consultant, he began giving lectures about the Holocaust to schoolchildren. He related not only its history but his personal experiences.

Stefan had come to live and work in Bakersfield in 1973. Born in Breslau in 1929, a few years later his family moved to a small mountain town called Landeshut. Its principal industries were vineyards and the production of linen. The population at the time was 14,000, including about seventy Jewish families.

With crystal clarity Stefan recalled and related to me a troubling restriction the1933 Nuremberg laws had imposed on him: As a Jewish child he could no longer use the public swimming pool! What a serious loss to a four year-old who simply could not understand *why!*

Most adults didn't anticipate the depth and significance of the changes unfolding for Europe's Jews. Stefan's mother had played tennis on public courts, but now she couldn't.

The Zellners had been religiously observant. They kept a kosher home, attended an Orthodox synagogue, observed Shabbat and the holidays, including Passover's diet restrictions. Stefan studied to become a worthy bar mitzvah even though most of his Jewish education had been uncomfortable due to the difficulties the Jews of Europe were facing.

After the war it was at a Jewish Community Center in Long Beach, California that Stefan met Louise Seide. She became Mrs. Stefan Zellner. Louise had come to California from Connecticut and obtained her first position as a schoolteacher in Long Beach.

Although they were very happy there, Stefan's career required the move to Coalinga, a town so small it did not have a synagogue. The few Jewish families clustered together for limited holiday ceremonies, and had to travel to Fresno to attend a synagogue. Carpooling was how their children were transported to Fresno for their religious instruction.

When Stefan had a chance to work for Getty Oil, later Texaco, he moved his wife and two children to Bakersfield. They were elated to be members of a much larger community.

In 1987 when Texaco was downsizing it offered Stefan a retirement pension he considered generous enough to accept. For the next five years he worked independently as a consultant, and then retired from that.

Stefan Zellner was an ardent volunteer for several very important causes: He gave American citizenship lessons to immigrants endeavoring to pass the required test. He assisted low-income people with their tax forms. He and Louise were members of Temple Beth El, and both served in various ways. For many years Stefan was the congregation's treasurer and acted as liaison between Greenlawn Cemetery and Temple Beth El members, most purchasing grave sites there, through the temple.

He not only gave lectures in schools about his experiences during the Holocaust but Stefan gave his own children, Judy and Michael a substantial understanding of the consequences of a Nazi regime.

"Live by the Jewish mandate: *You shall not stand idly by while your neighbor bleeds.* Stand up for the rights of others even when there is great risk to you. Support civil rights for everyone; demand justice for all!"

The Night of Broken Glass resulted in *the nightmare of broken spirits* for many Holocaust survivors, a consequence of their hideous experiences, the terrors they suffered. That certainly related to Max Newman who had lived in Kern County only the last eight years of his amazing life. A Holocaust survivor and one of France's war heroes, he had also been an Underground Resistance fighter. He came to this country in December 1957.

Max (Neuman) Newman was the second husband of Shirley Ann Newman, this book's author. She became his third wife. They met, married, and lived in Miami, Florida from 1958 to 1962. Then, until 1981 San Francisco was their residence, *except for* a two-year interval: Malta two-and-a half months, Portugal two-and-a half months, and Spain eighteen months. Between 1981 and '85 they lived in Australia, returning to the United States with the intent to live in Bakersfield, close to their daughter and son-in-law, Heidi and Robert Allison.

Two New Miamians
Are Now Mr. and Mrs.

Two new Miami residents were married Tuesday in Temple Israel. Mrs. Shirley Ann Socher became the bride of Maxwell H. Newman who emigrated from Paris, France, eight months ago.

The bride is the daughter of Mr. and Mrs. Arthur Sachs of New York. She is a college graduate with a master of arts degree from New York University.

Mr. Newman fought with the Free French under Gen. Charles de Gaulle, and served in the R.A.F. He hold the Distinguished Flying Cross, Croix de Guerre, the Medaille des Evades and is a member of Jewish War Veterans of America, post 330.

The wedding party included the couple's two daughters, Heidi Socher and Christine Newman.

The couple will honeymoon in Mexico and make their home at 895 NE 138th St., N. Miami.

Anti-Jewish propaganda and its manipulation of attitude and behavior that had lain dormant or existed covertly became overt in Europe during the 1930's. In Germany it was bolstered by two factors: a collapsed economy and the build-up of the nation's military power when Adolph Hitler became Chancellor.

His political strength rapidly ascended. Anti-Semitism grew to an extraordinarily high level. The ideology of National Socialism became a propaganda device for channeling the despair and frustrations of the German people. The economic conditions that resulted from losing the First World War, coupled with the impotent policies of the administration before Nazism came to power were swept under the rug. Instead, a relatively minor segment of the populace was blamed: "The German people in general are not at all responsible for our country's disastrous condition. The Jews are the culprits!" Other minority groups were also blamed.

The doctrine of anti-Semitism that became widely disseminated in Europe during that era was institutionalized in Germany with the Nuremberg laws, a series of regulatory practices that completely separated and disadvantaged the Jewish people. They were convincingly classified "genetically inferior," an insidious threat to the well-being of others.

No significant protest was forthcoming, despite the fact that so many great contributions to the arts and sciences had come from Jewish scholars. Or the fact that Jews were traditionally devoted to moral and ethical values, to family values and to education. They were known to be a peaceful, industrious people, and that the very foundation of Judaism is to engage in deeds of benevolence and justice. However, now everything good about them was ignored.

As Germany conquered nation after nation: Poland, Austria, Belgium, France, Hungary, and with Italy and Spain under fascist rule, all those countries instituted, in some cases forcibly, in others collaboratively, anti-Semitic discriminatory laws that gradually led to rounding up the Jews, transporting the strong, healthy ones to work camps, the others to death camps. Even capricious on-the-spot-executions occurred.

When France was invaded, surrender was almost immediate. Max Neuman, a naturalized French Jew joined the Resistance Movement, the *maquis*. He did *not* comply with the legal requirement to register under his Jewish heritage, to attach a yellow star with the word "juif," on the sleeve of his outer garments, and to have a large 'J' stamped on his national ID card.

Max's birth had been in an Austrian city, but became a Polish one after the First World War. His family was, and is to this day, observant Hasidic Jews. Their point of view and ritual practice didn't match with Max's personality. Young Max was a *doubter,* young Max was a *pouter and* young Max was a *shouter!* A few months after becoming a bar mitzvah he took flight.

His objective was to come to the United States. In Italy he stowed away on a ship, was discovered in the mid-Atlantic Ocean and turned over to HIAS when the ship landed on Ellis Island. The Hebrew Immigrant Aid Society notified his frantic parents of their runaway child's whereabouts, and they wired the money for his return voyage. That's when Max's Plan B was implemented. He obtained a student visa to France and until his mother's rich and famous Parisian cousin, Helena Rubinstein, lost patience with him she reared him in a very indulgent manner.

After eighteen months in the maquis during which he committed perilous acts of sabotage against the Germans, and against France's shamefully collaborative, guilt-riddled Vichy government, Max requested a release from the maquis. It was

 granted so that he could attempt an escape from the country, and if he made it, join the fighting Free French headed by General Charles de Gaulle. Based in England, *Les Forces Françaises Libres* was an adjunct to the British Royal Air Force.

Max did accomplish his escape, but was imprisoned in Spain for nine months as an illegal entrant. When *that* release was affected and after six-weeks in Madrid to sufficiently recover from the deprivations of prison life in a destitute country, Max was trained and served as a tail gunner in a heavy bomber, its missions to destroy the evil power of Germany. Max Neuman was one of the 20 % of tail gunners to survive.

Abraham Goldwater was made particularly joyful on his 75th birthday with a surprise party, and by being proclaimed "Honorary Mayor of Nineteenth Street!" One of the reasons Al treasured the proclamation certificate so highly was because Mayor Mary K. Shell who had been one of the three hundred guests at the party presented the award to him. This bit of memorabilia occurred November 6, 1982.

It was Al Goldwater's many involvements and efforts in promoting civic and commercial interests and activities for downtown Bakersfield that earned him an impressive series of laudatory recognitions, and vocal expressions of appreciation. Through his notable retail business called Emporium Western Store he championed the community's youth, tirelessly supporting organizations like the 4-H Club, and the Future Farmers America. He sponsored many livestock events at the annual Kern County Fair.

The Emporium Western Store, now a familiar local landmark at 1031 19th St. was founded in 1909 as a general store. In 1928 it was purchased by Isaac Rubin, grandfather of the current owners, and it has been a family business for three generations. In 1946, managing the enterprise was passed to the leadership of Isaac Rubin's daughter and son-in-law, Rose and Al Goldwater.

Rose and Al

It was in 1948 that Al Goldwater transformed the store's inventory to solely Western apparel, one of the first in California history. Al also changed the name from "The Emporium" to "Emporium Western Store." Currently, it is owned and operated by the Goldwater's' son Stephen Goldwater, and daughter Carol Durst.

Steve recalls the affectionate ribbing he and Carol would give their papa while looking at his picture in a cowboy get-up: "We would chuckle, giggle and call him a *Yiddisha Cowboy,* or a *Schlep-a-long Cassidy.* He seemed like an oddity to us as kids, that he was completely out of character: Why would a Jew born in Liverpool, England in 1907 dress like a cowboy, talk like one, and. stock his store with only Western style clothes?"

Al Goldwater died at the age of eighty-five. He had been the youngest of Joseph and Bessie Goldwater's twelve children. When Abraham was twelve, in the company of his widowed mother, three brothers and two sisters he left England and sailed to America on the *S.S. Carmania.* The group arrived in New York in January 1920, and continued westward to Los Angeles, residence of Al's oldest sister and her husband. Another sister lived in Phoenix, Arizona, and for fourteen years the young boy remained in an unstable situation, continually changing his home base, sometimes Los Angeles, sometimes Phoenix.

In 1934, a year of the Great Depression, Al had an unsteady job in a Los Angeles tire store. But when he heard of a permanent job opening in a Bakersfield store, one with a good recommendation he secured it. He boarded a train and came to Bakersfield.

Soon negative thoughts filled his mind, doubts about staying here. Who would want to live in a barren, behind-the-times, rough-and-tumble town of unpaved, dusty streets and gun-slingers! On the other hand, what was the use of doubling back to sophisticated Los Angeles when work opportunities were so scarce? Al decided to stay in tacky town, after all.

He embarked on his new career life at Central Tire Shop on 19th St. close to Union Avenue. Morris Laba owned the shop. Three years later, in 1937 Abraham Goldwater and Rose Rubin became husband and wife! Rose's dad, Isaac Rubin, born in Poland around 1879 had made Bakersfield his home in 1918, soon after immigrating to America, He and his brother-in-law, Ben Siegel became co-owners of Paris Shoe Store, located in midtown Bakersfield. After ten years Isaac Rubin bought a general merchandise store from the family of Morris Chain, a leading attorney of Bakersfield. Mr. Rubin gave his store an appropriate name: The Emporium.

Cowboy Al

Rose Rubin was the third child of Isaac and Eva Rubin. Isaac had been one of the founders of Congregation B'nai Jacob, and in 1934 Al and Rose Goldwater became members. Later Al became President of the synagogue, serving five terms.

At the start of the Second World War Al was drafted into the military. But two months later he was discharged for a hearing loss in one ear. Although it was an honorable discharge he received no veteran's benefits since eligibility required at least three months of service. Upon his return to civilian life Al began to work for Rose's father in The Emporium. In 1946 he and Rose bought the enterprise and made most of the inventory Western style boots, blue jeans, and cowboy hats.

The store is a veritable museum of pioneer days, but it stocks apparel for people in San Joaquin Valley's present day agriculture and livestock industries, and ranch life.

Benny Shapiro could almost be termed *a Bakersfield boy;* he was very young when he came to live here with his parents. They had both been born and raised in New York City, but were of European ancestry.

Benny was the last of their three children; he had two older sisters. Their father opened a small general mercantile store on the northeast corner of 19th and K Streets, below one of Bakersfield's several hotels. In 1925 when Benny was ready to earn his keep he started working in his father's store. One of his duties was to travel to Los Angeles as the store's merchandise buyer. It was on one of these trips, while Benny was in conversation with a dealer's salesperson that he mentioned he was ready to seek his companion-for-life, to find a bride! It wasn't so easy for a Jewish man to meet the right young woman; the population of Jews in Bakersfield was so limited.

Another salesperson overheard him relate his "predicament" and interjected, "I know a darling girl you'd like." Her reference was to Clara Hoffman, indeed *a darling girl*. Clara was a clerk in her sister Sarah's shop. Right after the introduction Benny quickly returned for a second encounter; he presented Clara with a bag of candy! Their marriage was in 1925, on St. Valentine's Day, a romantic day one for marriage proposals, engagement celebrations and weddings, even for young Jewish men and women!

Petite as a little doll, Benny had found Clara appealing enough to promptly start his courtship. Less than a year later she became Mrs. Benny Shapiro.

He left his father's employ and opened his own business, an army/navy store on 19th and L Streets. It was very small but tasteful and attractive. He and Clara were in a thriving business until 1936, when a fire destroyed the shop. The fire insurance settlement enabled them to live on in comfort, even to finance considerable travel.

Their retirement began to pall and they became restive; the couple wished to become productive again. This time they were attracted to a

60

very different kind of business. A pawnshop owner who had recently fallen on hard times through unwise outside investments said he was willing to teach the details of his business to Benny and Clara. The arrangement wasn't a generous gift; the seller was going to be paid for his tutelage. Until the end of World War II Benny and Clara were successful pawnbrokers.

Another purchase Benny and Clara Shapiro made when they again settled down in Bakersfield was a home in the center of town, on Cherry and Oleander Streets. They found that they were neighbors of the Rudnicks, and Clara and Libby became close friends. Unlike the increasingly large Rudnick family that finally consisted of eleven offspring, Benny and Clara were childless (much to their regret!)

Shortly before the Shapiros resumed an entrepreneurial life in Bakersfield, Clara's niece Hulda, her spouse Melvin Magnus and their two children, Steven and Margaret moved here after the war.

Mel had spent the war years working in a Marin County shipyard owned by Bechtel Corporation. Before the war he earned a law degree and was admitted to the bar, but he hadn't started to practice his profession. Nor was he expecting to at the moment. There seemed little chance of working for a local law firm. He kept afloat as a men's clothing salesman!

Hulda's younger sister Ann was a war widow and mother of a little boy. It was definitely time for the family to converge, for Benny and Clara to help her two nieces. A proposal was laid out. Benny owned a parcel of real estate on the corner of 19th and M Streets. He had purchased it from his father. He would build stores on it, he said, open a department store for him and his wife, and Mel could work there too. A second store would be Ann's, one that sold children's apparel.

The plan couldn't come to fruition because of a shortage of construction workers and building material. The community was in need of homes for war veterans and their families. That was a priority. No chance of obtaining a permit to build stores!

An opportunity opened for Mel to teach a class in real estate at the evening high school. The next steppingstone for him came through an inadvertent meeting. It was with one of Mel's law professors who recommended him to the D.A. He was hired as a deputy. Melvin Magnus was launched into his profession! Most of his work was confined to tracking down "dead beat dads," obliging them to support the children they had brought into the world. Another seven years passed before he opened a private practice.

David Laba explained, "My parents came to America from Romania, their home country. Naturally, it was for the same reason all Eastern European Jews emigrated. They had grown weary of long years of oppression and poverty, nothing to look forward to!"

David was born in Bakersfield's Mercy Hospital and resided in this community his entire life. His father had been a child of eleven years when *he* came to America, uniting with his parents who had first resided in San Francisco.

It was not unusual for family members to come separately to America. These deprived people couldn't pay the cost of ship's passage for parents and their children all at the same time. David's father had left his wife and children in Romania, earned and saved the money for her *schiffskarte*, and later for their two sons. Before their mother left Romania she had placed the boys in the care of one of her brothers. He agreed to keep them until he received their transport money. The boys arrived in San Francisco in 1904, two years before an earthquake leveled the city.

The birth of David's mother had been in Bucharest, capital of Romania. Her own mother, a nurse, died in the flu epidemic right after WW I. Her father, Sam Himovitz, was one of Congregation B'nai Jacob's founders, and its first vice-president.

Sam's business, the Bakersfield Pipe and Supply Company was destined to be a huge success. Oil production was flourishing and expanding in this locale. Another thriving Himovitz business was the Union Pipe and Supply Co.

Although most people were still using horse and wagon transportation Sam embarked on the incipient auto industry, buying and selling usable parts of vehicles that couldn't run anymore. His California Auto and Wrecking business was on 19th and V Streets.

At first, cars were not equipped with glass, but with a material that cracked and deteriorated in the sun and heat of cities like Bakersfield. Mexico was producing glass. It inspired in Morris Laba the idea of installing glass in cars. Morris, who became a son-in-law to Sam Himovitz, started importing Mexican glass. He would travel from San Francisco to Mexico by boat, then return in a horse-drawn wagon loaded with sheets of glass. Later on it was by truck. The auto parts store Sam Himovitz owned became a place to buy imported glass.

Morris was always well dressed, in accord with sophisticated San Francisco. He had something else that made him attractive to Sam Himovitz: Morris was Jewish and single, ideally suited to wed one of Sam's three unmarried daughters.

Time after time Sam kept inviting Morris to his home on Maple Street. Each time Morris declined. He knew perfectly well why he had been asked to come to dinner. He just didn't feel ready for married life. He was enjoying bachelorhood and wasn't ready to abandon it. However, once when Morris found himself in Bakersfield, away from home and family on a Jewish holiday, this time he *did* go to the Himovitz house for dinner.

Because of the mother's death, the oldest daughter Rose Marie had assumed the role of hostess. After her father was afflicted with widowhood he had remarried a few times but at the moment he didn't have a wife.

Sam made a jocular introduction of his daughters to the thirty-three year old guest: "Take your pick! They're all available." He hadn't really been accurate; Rose was engaged, her fiancé a jeweler in Taft. It was her father who had had arranged the match, ready to pass his beautiful young daughter to a man twenty years older than *he was!*

Extraordinarily beautiful, with flaming red hair, Rose Marie easily captured the love of Morris Laba. The two began to correspond, became engaged and were married in 1925. Rabbi Benjamin Cohen officiated at the ceremony in Eagles' Hall.

Morris Laba didn't continue to be a traveling salesman. He bought an auto wrecking and supply store on sale. Soon he bought out Sam Himovitz, his father-in-law! However, by then the older man was ready to retire and become a footloose adventurer.

He went to Paris, where one of his brothers had chosen to live when the family left Romania, came to America and lived in San Francisco. While visiting his brother in France Sam met a lovely young Jewish entertainer who sang and danced. Her French charm captivated him; he proposed to her, and she used the chance to fulfill her fervent wish: to live in the *Goldena Medina*.

Lovesick Sam had no idea he had been the victim of a ploy. He brought her to Bakersfield, and after a few years she was restless to resume her career. She drifted off to Los Angeles and performed in various nightclubs. Madame Himovitz then settled in Murietta Hot Springs and remained there.

Abe and Bertha Popel, parents of Sonia Simrin and Stanley Popel, made selling furniture a lifetime occupation. Abe's father had been a talented designer and craftsman of fine wood furniture, including the artistry and intricacy of inlay. He instilled in his children an appreciation of beautiful home décor.

Although the migrations of the family crisscrossed the continent, and included Abe and Bertha's two interludes in Los Angeles the ultimate place of settlement was Bakersfield. It was related to the health of Stanley Popel. From infancy he had been trouble with asthma. The recommendation from the doctor was to maximize the child's comfort by removing him to a dry climate. The two options suggested were Phoenix and Bakersfield. Bertha Popel vetoed Phoenix as a choice. Her negative reaction was based on the experience of having once lived there. She didn't like it!

The Popels moved to Bakersfield where Abe's initial way of supporting his family was to sell furniture for Valley Furniture Company. Its owners were the Rosen family.

Abe never accommodated himself well to working for others; highly independent, his goal was his own business. By the time their daughter Sonia was born Popel's Furniture Company was a reality. The first of Abe Popel's stores was in East Bakersfield on Sumner Street, soon followed by a second store on Baker Street.

Sonia's and her brother's Aunt Evelyn lived in Bakersfield too. She was married to a man whose early exotic life shaped both his personality and career. The birth of Uncle Leo Horn had born in Harbin, a Manchurian region of China.

If one were to pose the question: "What business is least likely to succeed in Bakersfield?" a natural reply would be *furs*. That may very well hold true for those devoid of Uncle Leo's charisma and resourcefulness! When he opened a fur shop in Bakersfield every woman of monetary consequence came to buy a fur coat or jacket from Leo Horn. She was either cajoled by the furrier into desiring one, or badgered by intimidation. Under Uncle Leo's influence fur became *the* status symbol among Bakersfield ladies.

Just as Abe Popel and others were inclined to assume the same occupation as their predecessor, Leo was following *his* father's interest. The elder Mr. Horn had been an importer of furs.

For a long time Leo's fur business was limited to custom-made garments, he himself a walking advertisement, a promoter of garments made of animal skins. He sported fur hats as part of his own attire, and out of fur pelts even made personal items his niece Sonia described as "intimate unmentionables."

The Popel furniture business didn't stay on a steady rise. For a while things went well and the family gravitated from a rental apartment to their own home, a house on Cherry Street. But when over expansion led to a disastrous downturn in Able's finances he scuttled his entrepreneurial condition and started to work for the Summer's Furniture Galleries. The house on Cherry Street had to be vacated, the family again in a rented apartment.

For an interim period the Popels moved back to Los Angeles, but returned to Bakersfield in 1949. Popel's Furniture Co. was on Nineteenth Street. After a while it was moved to Sage Shopping Center on Columbus Avenue in the College Heights district, and finally to Chester Avenue.

When Stanley Popel was old enough and ready for an occupation a second store was opened, also on Chester Avenue. Both of Abe Popel's children now worked in their dad's stores.

Stanley Popel married and had four children with his first wife, Joy. He then married Dorothy who had been divorced from *her* first husband, and had two children.

When Sonia finished college and married Stanley Simrin it connected her to a "pre-fabricated" family. Stan had been married before and was bringing his four children into his new marriage. They ranged in age from eleven to six. Sonia moved into their home on Blade Ave.

Stanley was a pharmacist for Rufener's Drugstore on Alta Vista Boulevard, but with aspirations for a different profession. He fulfilled his goal and became one of Bakersfield's high-profile criminal defense attorneys. In 1972 the Simrins bought a house on Alta Vista Street.

With the exception of ordained rabbis, Stan's avocation, Torah teacher of Temple Beth El was performed with the dedication and ability few people display. On Thursday evenings he and his well-attended class met in the synagogue's library. At times class attendance swelled to the point of requiring the group to assemble in the social hall.

Sonia Simrin became the very capable and successful owner of Rand Personnel Agency. Her zeal and energy extended beyond that. Sonia, Jackie Rudnick and Mary Speare managed the Temple Beth El gift shop.

"Even we, Max and Shirley Ann Newman, felt like *strangers in a strange land* when we moved to Bakersfield in late 1985. We found it difficult to adapt to a town that to us was pretty unsophisticated. Of course, I was comparing it to cosmopolitan New York, my hometown and where I had lived until age forty. For Max the comparison was with Paris, his beloved residence from age fourteen until he was in his forties.

My parents didn't practice any of Judaism's rituals or ever go to a synagogue. That reminds me of a comedian Buddy Hackett anecdote. In reply to someone's question: 'While growing up in Brooklyn, Buddy, did you go regularly to a synagogue?' 'Did I *go* to a synagogue? Hah, hah, Brooklyn *is* a synagogue!' Buddy fired back, arousing roars of laughter from his audience. Having also grown up in Brooklyn, believe me, I can attest to the character of that New York City borough.

Every year on the High Holidays, Rosh Hashanah and Yom Kippur, only maybe ten to fifteen kids would show up in the elementary school I attended, P.S. 186. It was the same when I went to Seth Low Junior High. These students and perhaps six or eight non-Jewish teachers had to busy themselves with who-knows-what? Of course I couldn't know because I was one of the absentees.

Though I was given no Jewish education, nevertheless, on the holidays I dressed up and walked around the neighborhood chatting with my friends, appreciating my good luck of getting days off from school. Yes, I knew I was Jewish but I had no idea what that meant!

Our home wasn't kosher, and yet my mother cooked Jewish meals, whatever *that* means. Maybe it was because they were European style: German, Russian or Polish, Austro-Hungarian or Romanian. We used to wisecrack, calling certain Jewish food K-rations: *Kishka, Kasha, Knishes, Knaidlach, Kugel...*For readers that were born after World War II and had never heard of K-rations, it's a military term referring to a war combatant's packet of emergency food.

Here in the southwest, Jewish people seem to mish-mash even Shabbes dinner, casually combining chicken noodle soup with burritos, or fajitas with potato *latkes.* New York Jewish home life was deeply entrenched in tradition. A typical Friday night dinner consisted of: chopped chicken liver on salted crackers or challah, chicken soup with rice or noodles, carrots, and a few globules of fat floating around. The next course was roast or boiled chicken with potato latkes, rice, or spaghetti. Dessert was likely to be strudel or pie or maybe honey cake or sponge cake, with tea and lemon, or black coffee. Even in non-kosher homes anything with milk was usually *taboo* in a meal that included meat. *No pork!*

In religious homes, on Friday at sundown the mama lights the Shabbes candles. Then, when everyone is seated at the table for dinner, the first thing they do is recite the blessings over bread and wine. In one hand they hold a chunk of challah, a cup of wine in the other hand. Of course, young children are only allowed to take a sip of wine, so Mama keeps her eye on them to make sure a mischievous imp doesn't do more than that with the alcoholic liquid in his glass.

Many Jews who keep a kosher home bypass the strict dietary laws *outside* their own house. I used to wonder if that means they have two stomachs, one they feed with kosher food, the other with *treif.* Another distinguishing feature in Jewish diets is to exclude not only pork products, but shellfish. Because of these childhood memories I can't imagine reaching into a bucket of Kentucky-fried Chicken planted in the middle of the dining room table on erev Shabbes!

New York is a city of almost limitless forms of entertainment. If not nowadays, while I lived there they even had Yiddish language theaters on Manhattan's lower east side. It appealed to the nostalgia of immigrant European Jews.

My neighborhood in Brooklyn was largely residential. We had Mom and Pop grocery stores, fresh produce stores, and butcher shops. Proprietors and hired help were mostly Jewish people. It went without saying, and without a sign notifying customers that the store will be closed on upcoming major Jewish holidays. Whether or not the owner observed the holidays was irrelevant; there wouldn't have been customers those days.

A store that was owned by an Orthodox Jew was always closed on *Shabbes*. So were stores on streets like Delancey, Rivington, Hester and a few others on Manhattan's lower east side, Jewish neighborhoods virtually replicating a Polish ghetto. Business was alive and bustling on Sunday, but totally dormant on Saturday.

In short, New York in the days of my childhood and young adulthood was in some respects like the modern State of Israel. Not entirely populated with religiously observant Jews, but deeply immersed in Jewish culture and tradition.

I'm used to Bakersfield after living here since November 1985 and I've learned to react casually to Merry Christmas and Happy Easter greetings from neighbors, acquaintances and sales clerks.

I recall that when I first moved to Bakersfield, except when with my daughter, son-in-law and my two grandchildren I felt lonely and isolated, that the gulf of distinction between the dominant populace and me possibly could not be bridged. I soon learned I was quite mistaken, but until my discomfort was fully abated, becoming an active member of Temple Beth El buoyed me up! I regularly attended services and Torah class. As my understanding of the Jewish faith system, and my eagerness to know my people's history expanded, so did my appreciation of the Jewish religion and culture.

Paradoxically, it was in Bakersfield with its small number of Jewish residents that I learned to embrace my Jewish heritage with such fervor. In considerable depth I discovered who I am. What a wonderful feeling!

Among the Jewish community's heroes of the Second World War, men who experienced the perils of combat were Hyman Seiden, Abraham Goldberg, and Stanley Schwartz.

At the funeral of Abraham Goldberg, Mike Miller recited one of the eulogies. The deceased proudly served our nation in the Marine Corps, Mike informed the attendees.

"Remember those golden, olden days before the Internet, cell phones and HD TVs? It was in 1953 that Abe linked up with our local Jewish Community. Yes, it was when Dwight Eisenhower was our President, when Edmond Hillary conquered Mt. Everest, and when the 1st issue of TV Guide was published.

After the war, and when Abe returned he always wore his Marine Corps pin to Shabbat or holiday services. After all, his Marine service had been a sacred duty. Abe viewed fighting and destroying evil a requisite, one as obligatory as the very principle. The Marines, whose many battle sites were islands such as Saipan, Iwo Jima, Tinian and Okinawa, fought the enemy with the bravery and dedication of truly patriotic Americans. Abe was a fine example of this. I frequently prevailed upon him to disclose some of his wartime experiences. There is one I'd like to share with you.

"Abe's company was engaged in battle on one of the 'forgotten' islands, and he received word that Yom Kippur services would be conducted near Marine Headquarters, which was not far from the fighting on this very small island. Nevertheless, Yom Kippur services had been placed on the Jewish chaplain's agenda. At sundown on *erev Yom Kippur* the man stacked a pile of ammunition boxes, set his portable Torah scroll on it, and now was ready to go, to lead these warriors into asking God's forgiveness for the deaths and other destructive practices they had committed. It was in defense of their sacred nation, on land He had blessed them with in the late 18th Century.

The weapons of these Jewish warriors remained on the ready during the service, the men hearing tracer rounds streaking past them, artillery rounds exploding alarmingly close! The Chaplain recited the entire service nonstop; while all around him marines and sailors came and went, military duties their first order of business!"

Abe's patriotic commitment, his struggles to stay alive notwithstanding, he attended religious services whenever he could. When the Japanese surrendered, the ravages of war were removed, and the islands' natural beauty and tranquility restored, but many of Abe's friends and fellow marines had lost their lives there.

Friend and TBE Member Since 1953

Abe had come home after the war to promptly resurrect his former life, and again become a worthy American citizen, an admirable neighbor, a gentleman and a good Jew! He left Bakersfield on April 2, 1997, a week after turning 96, but forevermore remembered for his soul of *a Marine!* Here's to you, Abe: 'Semper fidelis.'

A Flying Tiger named Stanley Schwartz, born August 1, 1922, was the oldest of three Jewish sons of Charles and Bertha (Korman) Schwartz. The lives of these boys started in New York City's lower east side. Their paternal grandparents had come to America from Austria, their mother's family from Poland. Stan, his parents and brothers lived in Brooklyn for a while and then moved to the Bronx, where Charles became owner of a kosher poultry store.

Stan joined the Army Air Corp in 1941 and after his training was sent into the China/Burma/India (CBI) theatre of combat. He was a top turret aerial gunner in a B-25 bomber, stationed in Kunming, Unanni, Shenztu and Queilin with *The Flying Tigers* of the 14th Air Force.

"Our job was to find Japanese subs and troop ships, as well as cargo ships, low level bombing and staffing of the enemy," Stan depicts. "Information was given to us by Intelligence Operations to successfully bomb various targets. We bombed Canton, Mcua, Shanghai, and Hong Kong among many other targets: wherever the

Japanese happened to be! One time, we were returning to our home base in Kunming, very badly shot up. We couldn't land at any other bases because of the heavy traffic, so we had no choice but to make our way to Kunming.

We were about a mile and a half out when the pilot told me (I was the radio operator) that we're 'dead stuck,' and to inform the tower of a 'May Day.' We had run out of gas and had to be ready for a crash landing. I reported to the tower that both our wing tips had been knocked off, half our tails gone, that we had only one landing gear, and a sputtering port engine. Both engines were shut down, so we skidded in. What a rough landing, but the pilot had done a great job getting us home in one piece! We were promptly interrogated, the usual debriefing procedure, and then allowed to go to our quarters.

Once, on Passover we were flown into Bombay, giving us the chance to go to a Seder at one of its synagogues. They had their own ovens out back, and there baked their own matzo."

In May 2012, tribute was paid to Stanley Schwartz and other heroes of the Second World War, by the Honor Flight organization. Twenty-one military service veterans were invited to go on Kern County's first Honor Flight, to Washington, D.C. It was a memorable trip, although quite a tiring one for these old men, ranging in age from 82 to 101. Stan was two months short of turning 90. However, the assistance of guardians brought them through it without mishap. Viewing the different memorials of World War 11, the Korean War, Vietnam, and Iwo Jima, those of Army, Navy, Marines and Air Corps was sensational, especially to witness the changing of the guard at Arlington, Ft. McHenry and Franklin Roosevelt memorial sites.

Stan's discharge was in January 1946. He went to work for his father in the poultry store, and this is how he met his beloved wife, Norma. After a whirlwind, seven-month courtship they were married on Nov. 16th 1946. With the war over and all these men returning, apartments were scarce. Stan and Norma lived with her parents for several years. It didn't keep the young couple from bringing their first son into the world; they named him Jeffrey. Living in New York continued until the boy was four-and-a-half. In December 1951, with Norma in the seventh month of a second pregnancy they traveled to California, seeking a fresh and more productive start.

Stanley Schwartz, Hero of WWII

Stan promptly found a job in Lockheed's aircraft factory. They lived with Norma's older brother in Covina until after the birth of their second child, Holly (of blessed memory). In May, they struck out on their own, moving to an apartment in Pasadena. After his job with Lockheed, Stan worked for the Edison Company, and then as a salesman for Fuller Brush Company. By this time, 2 more children had been added: Lisa and Jack.

Things were growing tough for the Stan and Norma Schwartz family, so Stan started to work as a salesman for Shell Furniture Store. His boss, Shell Cohen, decided to open a second store, this one in Bakersfield. He asked Stan to get it started. The first question Norma asked her husband was, "Is there a synagogue in Bakersfield?"

It was very important that they keep Judaism in their lives, as well as in the lives of their young children. By this time Helen, their number five, was in the picture. They looked for a house, and found one they liked in a northeast neighborhood of Bakersfield, on Redlands Drive, across the street from Siemons Park and Nichols elementary school. They moved there when Helen was a year old, in August 1963. Stan and Norma's children are now grownups, out of the house the Schwartz family had moved into forty-nine years ago. Nevertheless, it's still the home of Stan and Norma.

After working for Shell Cohen a number of years, in 1971 Stan left the furniture store and started his career in life insurance. It was with New York Life Insurance Co. After about 5 years, he embarked on his own business. He opened an office as an independent agent connected with a number of companies. His success as a life insurance agent included the wonderful opportunity of attending conventions, thus traveling extensively, accompanied by Norma. They had the great pleasure of visiting the Bahamas, Bermuda, Hawaii, England, Spain and other countries of Europe. They also visited Israel, Canada, Mexico, and many states of our own country. Many times, their children were with them on those trips.

Stan and Norma had been B'nai Jacob Congregation members for a number of years, but then changed their connection to Temple Beth El. They still are devoted members of the Reform synagogue. Their children all celebrated their bar and bat mitzvah services, and confirmations at Temple Beth El. Three of their grandchildren also had their bar or bat mitzvah services there.

One of their grandsons, Jeremy, lived and studied in Israel for several years, and is now a rabbi. Receiving the offer of a position in the University of Illinois, meant he, his wife and daughter moved back to the United States August 1st 2012. Stan and Norma have good reason for great pride in their children, grandchildren and *fourteen* great, grandchildren!

Unfortunately, we lost Stan in March, 2013, at the age of 90. He will be missed.

Hy Seiden, who started his military life as a corporal in the U.S. Army Royal Hawaiian Coast Artillery Corps had been stationed in Pearl Harbor on that fateful day, December 7th 1941. The Japanese attack was a shocking incident that led us into World War II. Hy had enlisted five months earlier and was stationed on the Island of Oahu, site of the attack.

A factor that made him proud of America, and to be an American was that our country shields and protects the right of Jews to worship God, to conduct our lives in accordance with the teachings of the Torah. The Pearl Harbor memorial services at Union Cemetery were very important to him. So much so that he made sure they occurred every December 7th for 20 years after the Pearl Harbor Survivors Association chapter was disbanded. Its importance led Stuart and Richard, Hy's sons, to attend the service every year since 2007.

In February 1915 Hy was born in Yonkers, New York, finishing his life in Bakersfield at the age of 96. He was the sixth child of Harry and Celia Seiden's eleven. Harry had been a painting contractor, and Celia a dressmaker. Typical of Jewish parents who were low on finance resources, they committed themselves to bank loans for sending their children to college.

Hy's turn came in the midst of the Great Depression, in 1935 when the doors of banks had been shut and no money was available for his *college* education until the G.I. Bill was initiated after the Second World War. However, Hy initially worked to pay for his advanced education, his first college year in Yonkers, the second in Stillwater, Oklahoma. After the war, with the help of the G.I. Bill he enrolled in UCLA where he earned his bachelor's and master's degrees, becoming a highly qualified geologist.

Apart from Hy Seiden's professional and family life with his wife Ruth and their 2 sons, he was firmly entrenched in both the secular and religious institutions of Kern County. The Seidens were members of Congregation B'nai Jacob, where Hy served as treasurer and Board member, actively participating in Sabbath and holiday services, and in the practice of Jewish rituals, laws, and ethical principles. Judaism was the very essence of Hyman Seiden. Not only was he proud to be an American, but especially so to be a *Jewish* American. And the community was enormously proud of Hy grateful to have someone so kind and good-hearted, always ready to extend his friendship and service.

Hy's professional training in geology, and his achievement of honors in the subject, soon guided him to the successful strategy of striking oil in this area of petroleum resources. He is credited with discovery of the Asphalto Oil Field, and thus our county's ability to reawaken its slumbering oil industry in the 1960s.

A leading interest and involvement of his, a deeply personal concern was Down's syndrome, the birth defect of Richard, one of their two sons. Ruth, Hy and Richard had worked as a team, enabling lovable, friendly afflicted Richard to have a remarkably active life, a lively, eager-for-more-experiences, happy one.

"Nobody thought he would reach 50," said Rabbi Paul Gordon at Richard's birthday celebration in 2008. That was because heart disease is common in people with Down syndrome.

Upon Hy's death in March 2011, Richard expected to be moved close to his brother and sister-in-law who are not residents of Bakersfield. He declined to leave this community: his work in a BARC thrift store in the downtown area, services at B'nai Jacob synagogue, dancing class and bowling. These activities had been helpful in relieving some of the overpowering grief he sustained at the death of his mother. Incidentally, the Kern Regional Center of BARC offers a valuable service to our community's developmentally disabled. It helps them live as independently as possible.

The transition of losing a second parent and moving in with another family was a hard enough adjustment for Richard. Had he been moved to another city, imposing on him was the trial of reshaping his life would not have been a wise decision. Even from a distance his brother and sister-in-law, Stuart and Mary-Alice provide loving guidance. Their anxious eyes are always focused on him, always apprised of how he feels and how he's doing.

PART TWO

The Torah is a Light

"THE TORAH IS A LIGHT"

History of the Jewish Justice System: The Sanhedrin

The Sanhedrin, the Jewish legal system, is said to have consisted of 70 men, and was based on the dictates of Moses. It was the restart of the Israelite nation after their release from Egyptian domination. It was the return of self-government.

As the first men in the Sanhedrin died or became unfit for service, new members were ordained. The Sanhedrin continued until the Second Temple was destroyed and a few hundred years passed. Then a new legislature called The Knesset was initiated.

The Sanhedrin undertook many functions to strengthen the spiritual life of the people. These formed the sacred spiritual legacy of the Judaic faith system. From then until now, the Jewish people have been living in general accord with their heritage, and this is to continue until the coming of The Messiah, when God will bestow on them *fulfillment* of the prophecy.

For this section of the book several Jewish residents of Bakersfield have written about how their Jewish faith and its principles influence and impact their everyday lives, particularly their careers. "Do you think your attitudes, your behavior, your treatment of other people have a connection to your Jewish upbringing and from what you learned in religious school and synagogue services?" I asked. "Have the moral and ethical dicta of the religion affected your daily decisions and overall lifestyle? Will you share with the readers of my book your earnest thoughts and feelings on the subject?" In these next pages are the responses to my inquiry, the personal perspectives of a cross-section of Jewish people in our community: people of different ages and occupations. *Us!*

A memorable event for me was a bat mitzvah celebration five years ago. Here's my reaction to it:

Amelia Goes to "bat" For Us

At a bar-or-bat mitzvah service I find the symbolic act of passing the Torah from generation to generation particularly meaningful. The process is demonstrated with an actual scroll, ending with it in the arms of the youngster expected to perpetuate our Jewish heritage. I'm deeply impressed by the demonstrative gesture, and infused with a comforting reassurance. Its message is "Yes, with all my strength I hereby accept this heavy responsibility."

Recently I had the honor to be present at the bat mitzvah of Amelia Egland. As the service moved along it became abundantly apparent that this girl had a deeply sensitive, compassionate nature. Amelia will dedicate herself to promoting the ethical principles of Judaism. The emotion she displayed convinced me she will experience life to its fullest. She'll feel impelled to work for changing the world's evils to those of goodness.

Empathy will motivate her to share with others not just their joy and pleasure but their pain and sadness. Despite the personal discomfort she will feel through the ugly and tragic circumstances of other people's lives, it will provoke her anger and frustration, and she will work to make good things, happy things evolve. Amelia Egland is someone I know we can count on, a fellow Jew committed to making the world a better place, whose religious studies enabled her to see that indeed, the Torah *is* a light!

Through the years Temple Beth El has had many youngsters who instilled confidence and comfort in us. Many more are waiting in the wings to relay their messages of commitment to our wonderful heritage, and to tell us they accept the responsibility of achieving *tikkun olam*.

Sarah Neal: *"Wrestling With Religious Conviction"*

When I was a high school freshman, fourteen years old, I was skeptical about God. The existence of a Supreme Being just didn't seem feasible. Everything was a debatable subject to me. In fact it still is!

But I've gone through changes: Three years of high school, being an officer of my temple youth group, taking part in my confirmation service, and having leadership roles in various secular organizations of which I am a member.

During this last year, my sense of who I am has greatly strengthened. I brought about many new developments in an organization known as the International Order of Job's Daughters, which is now making an accommodation to our Jewish members. I take pride in having sparked understanding and tolerance in my order. In 1999 ritual revisions made a non-denominational order *truly* non-denominational.

Judaism is not a belief system that applies only to one's personal self, home and family life. It relates to the community, the nation, to the whole world. I defended who I am, and my conviction that the organization must open up to girls of all races and creeds. I know that for me, some of the most important aspects of my life include not only my belief in God, but also my Judaism.

There must be something out there that provides the blooming of a rose, the laughter of a baby, or an orange and purple sunset, or even the radiance of a rainbow glistening in the sunlight after a rainstorm. That something is God. Though there are still questions that linger in the back of my mind, the need for God in my life is everywhere. It may be before a test, before a report card comes out, or even just to say "Hello" to a listener. Sometimes the most open ear to what I have to say is in the One who doesn't talk back. That ear is the ear of God.

When things are not going very well, a test is too hard and the teacher's grade is too low, perhaps even written in red ink, does that mean no one has been looking out for me? I don't think so.

I think that what has helped me come to a higher understanding of what God means has been through my parents. We may sit and argue and debate for hours and hours on both the tangible and the abstract—my favorite subject of debate—or on the feminine and masculine aspects of God, but because of the knowledge they already have and now the knowledge that I have, I am able to realize that through all the discussions I have always somehow felt there is something out there. My task was to find out what that something is.

In conclusion I would like to say that my security blanket—God—has had a new fiber woven in. This is the golden thread of understanding. I have come to realize that without exploration and questioning everything is meaningless routine. Most of all I now deeply comprehend that there is something very profound and abstract. Who knows, we may actually be the "shadows of God." After all, aren't we created in God's image?

Rebecca Andrews: *"Growing Up Jewish in Bakersfield"*

Crowded streets are constantly packed with all types of people. At a glance, certain people stand out and others blend in. A tall, thin lady walks down the street holding her two-year-old boy's hand. She is wearing a long blue dress, heels and a strand of pearls. Her classy ways show in her strides. Her little boy is dressed in slacks, a button-down shirt and suspenders. In the opposite direction walks a middle-aged man with an old T-shirt, running shorts and a baseball cap. He quickly jogs past a group of school children around the age of nine. They carry their backpacks and books with them as they drag their feet and chatter. It is amazing how different people are, and how much a religion or lack thereof can affect each and every one of us.

Anyone can stand in a public place and admire the difference in humans. However, as the key turns in the ignition, everybody's car turns down a different street and they walk into a completely different household. As many people walk through their doorway, they are greeted by Christmas trees or various reminders that Jesus is Lord and Savior. However, for me it was always the *menorah:* the candelabrum or the *mezuzah* attached to the doorpost of our house. Touching and kissing my hand to the word of God has always given me a chill down my spine. But being greeted by different objects that serve as reminders of God has always given me a sense of pride as well. I love having a religion that is different from that of most of my classmates and friends. And they have always been fascinated by my Judaism, starting in Kindergarten when I passed out *gelt:* chocolate candies in the form of coins wrapped in gold foil. Also I'd give the children *dreidels:* tops. I lit the eight-branched *menorah* and explained the holiday of *Hanukkah.* Perhaps the best part for me was explaining that I receive eight times the joy since my holiday consists of eight nights!

Many Jews feel indifferent to our holidays, or they suffer from a sense of exclusion. Some people have a strong need to be the same as others. It just feels better to join in with the carolers, decorate and place an angel atop a Christmas tree, and enter into an Easter egg hunt with their friends. As for me, as a child I used to enjoy finding the *afikomen* at the Passover *Seder,* and acting the role of Queen Esther on the holiday of *Purim,* and lighting the candles on the *Hanukkah* menorah.

Security plays a large role in the ability to live comfortably as a member of a minority group. People with insecurities find it too hard to stand alone and to retain the beliefs of their heritage. I have never treated people differently who pray to Jesus from those of us who pray to *Adonai,* just as I never felt that the lady wearing a strand of expensive pearls is better than the man jogging in faded denims. We're all human beings, all with a heart and all with a need for faith. If it makes a person happier to pray to grass, then why not let him do so without criticism or reproach?

Whether my best friend is Jewish or Presbyterian, let her demonstrate her faith in whatever way she believes is correct. Growing up Jewish has always been considered a treat to me. I never resented it, and never will. The fact that Bakersfield has such a small Jewish population has made my experiences even more special. I continually have many Jewish friends and, admittedly, do feel a special connection to them because of our similarities in beliefs. Even though I've grown up and gone to school in a predominantly Christian community I consider myself just as prepared to go out into the world practicing Judaism as anyone raised in a largely Jewish-populated city, such as New York.

Who knows whether the people on crowded streets are Jews, Christians, Islamic, Catholics, Atheists, or Mormons? What is unusual about Bakersfield is that many cultures and religions are represented here and most people respect that. If anti-Semitic acts were encountered more often—they do occur on rare occasions—I'm sure my experiences in growing up here in Bakersfield would have made me feel different. Fortunately my knowledge of those acts that occur here has been limited to occasional and minor incidents. Thus, I've never felt under threat, unsafe in practicing my religion. I'm thankful for a divergence from the majority, and for growing up Jewish in Bakersfield where I never worry about expressing who I am.

Joshua Andrews: *"Why Is This Day Different...?"*

The day started out like any other. Although wintertime, there was no fog delay or anything else that seemed would make this day in any way unusual. Up until today I never really felt there was any difference between me and anyone else at school. Sure, at the holidays it was obvious that I was different from most, but others too, had differences in their religious beliefs. I looked forward to the opportunities of sharing and exchanging stories of each other's heritage and traditions. So, off to school I went on this day, ready to cope with all the normal issues that might come my way during history, English, math and all the other subjects. There were no signs; there was no way to know in advance that this was going to be a day very different from every other.

I had been proud to share the upcoming *Hanukkah* celebration in class recently when my teacher asked me to do so. I didn't know that lurking in my midst, disguised as a regular guy was lying in wait, the biggest hurdle I was yet to deal with in my life. It was one of those unbelievable things I'd heard about but never expected to personally experience. I had just recently turned thirteen and was knee-deep in studies for my *bar mitzvah* which was only a month from then.

I couldn't understand the hatred and disgust one of the students suddenly began to be expressed toward me. I wondered how he could dislike me so much when we hadn't had any personal involvement with each other. There never were any physical or verbal confrontations that would explain this. Why would my religious beliefs be of concern to him, I wondered.

When the lunch period ended that day my friends and I all went to where the pile of our backpacks lay. Each of the students took his before returning to class. "Hold on, you guys," I shouted. "Someone has mine; it's not here." Several of my friends had the same kind as mine—a green Jansport.

All of them checked to see that they had taken the right one, and they had. Mine was just not there. I was left standing in disbelief. I stared down at where all the backpacks had lain a few minutes before and where I, too, had put mine with the others twenty-five minutes earlier. I realized it had in fact disappeared and I went to the office to report it missing. I knew what I would have to confront when I went back to class without my books and my schoolwork. At the moment I was merely puzzled. Had someone accidentally gone off with my backpack, or had it been deliberately taken? Was I justified in feeling angry over this? It never occurred to me that it would be four months before I again saw my backpack. It was when I was sworn in on the witness stand that a deputy district attorney showed it to me.

I looked at the backpack then, at the disgusting sayings: "Kill the Jews." "Kill the Kikes." There was a mass of swastikas and other profanities scribbled all over it. I was asked what I thought of it. All I could express was, "Boy, that sucks!" Disbelief gave way to reality. I had to face the fact that one of my schoolmates, who goes to church and attends religious school regularly—and has done so all his life—had intentionally committed this evil act.

The court ruled him "guilty as charged." The judge in the case had presided over many felony charges; this one, he remarked, was a particularly difficult and trying case. The deputy district attorney said everyone involved was emotionally drained because of the stressful nature of the charges. But in the end justice was served.

When it was over I went back to the normal "kid stuff" no longer having to deal with the fear I was experiencing before the matter was resolved. What helped me get over it was the support of many friends who told me how wrong the offending student had been, and that they would no longer have anything to do with him.

DeeDee Chavez: *"Growing Up Jewish in Bakersfield"*

I have lived in Bakersfield all my life. I don't know what it's like to be Jewish elsewhere, but I can share my experience as a Jew in Bakersfield. My name is DeeDee Dianne Chavez, I am 13 years old. I have attended only two schools in my life and I am ready to begin high school in the fall. Since I have not moved around, I have had the same friends for a long time. I have known some of my school friends since the age of two when we started dance lessons together. Then we ended up in the same school in kindergarten and that's why I have known them so long. Now we are entering high school together.

I attended Noble Elementary and just graduated from Washington Jr. High School. In the fall I will attend East Bakersfield High School. I am probably one of very few Jewish students in the schools of Bakersfield. This has never bothered me and it has never bothered my friends that I am Jewish. I have heard stories about Jews who are made to feel uncomfortable by others, but I never felt "different" or uncomfortable. After all, there are many different religions and as long as we respect each other's beliefs we can live together in peace.

My parents were not born Jewish, but by the time I was born they had been practicing in the Jewish faith for years. So I was raised Jewish. When I started regular school at five years old I already understood I was Jewish and that we tried to keep *kosher*. I didn't eat the school cafeteria lunch on days they served pork. On those days I brought a sack lunch from home. My friends understand that as closely as I can I still keep *kosher*. In fact they are very happy on "Pepperoni Pizza Day" because they know I will be giving them my slice of pizza!

At Washington Jr. High everyone, including most teachers knew I was Jewish. When we returned to school after the winter break some of the teachers asked their students if they had enjoyed Christmas. But they would turn to me to ask if I had a nice *Hanukkah*. One teacher even gave me a *Hanukkah* card. I really appreciated that my teachers took the time to acknowledge my holidays. In fourth grade I joined the choir. During the winter concert we always sang Christmas songs. Although I don't celebrate Christmas I sang the songs with the choir because I enjoy singing. However, the choir teacher always included a couple of *Hanukkah* songs, too. I always felt proud and more comfortable that songs of *Hanukkah* were included.

Once, when I was in third grade a little girl started to argue with me. She told me that because I am of Hispanic nationality I was Mexican and couldn't therefore be Jewish. I replied that Judaism is a religion, not a race. A lot of people believe as she did, but they are wrong. This experience was the only negative one I can remember.

My very best friend is Christina Garcia. I've known her since third grade. We often discuss our religious differences. She asks me questions about my religion, and I ask her questions about hers. Although many of our religious beliefs are the complete opposite we agree that each of us worships the same God. And we agree that everyone's religious beliefs should be respected. At Christmas time I give her a Christmas gift and for *Hanukkah* Christina gives me a *Hanukkah* gift. We each celebrate our own holidays and acknowledge each other's.

My grandparents, aunts, uncles, and cousins are either Christian or Catholic. At first our Jewish faith was new to them. But they learned that our faith, although different is just as important to us as theirs is to them. I like the idea that my extended family has all these differences and that we all feel comfortable with our own choices. We can gather together as a family by respecting each other's beliefs. My aunts and uncles know not to serve pork to us, but instead make sure to also have food we are permitted to eat. I think that is very considerate of them and makes us want even more to share their holidays with them.

My family and I are members of Temple Beth El where I have very special friends. They are sort of brothers and sisters to me and it is with them that I feel most comfortable. We are all Jewish and our parents are Jewish. We gather for *Shabbat* services, we laugh and tell jokes, we have serious conversations, we all attend the religious school where together we struggle to learn to read and write in the Hebrew language. We help each other when one or another takes a turn to be pulpit assistant and also when the time comes to prepare to become a *bar* or *bat mitzvah*. At times we argue, but we have a bond: we are Jewish. When we gather at the temple the end of the week it is as Jews. We pray together as Jews; we sing together as Jews. We understand each other; there is no need for explanations. Now that I am entering senior high school I shall be eligible to join B.O.T.Y. (Kern Organization of Temple Youth.) I will go on field trips with the group and meet Jewish kids from other places. Activities will include fund raising events, camping and other sorts of "fun stuff".

I have been fortunate enough to attend a Jewish camp during the last few summers. I have been able to earn one of the camperships that are funded by donations by temple members. At camp I find myself in the company of hundreds of Jewish kids. We celebrate the *Shabbat* under the stars. I learn songs and dances that are new to me. When I return after my few weeks in camp I spend the rest of the summer teaching them to my baby sister, Rachel.

I have a good life in Bakersfield. I have my friends and teachers at public school, my grandparents, aunts, uncles, cousins, my parents, brothers and sister, as well as my Temple Beth El family—all here in Bakersfield. I have been able to share my religious life, including my own beliefs, with everyone involved in my life. I have received nothing but love and respect from those who have watched me grow up. I have been respected for my individuality and my personal beliefs. I think it has been very good for me to grow up surrounded by different people with different beliefs. It has taught me to respect other people's faiths. I have also learned that someone else's religious beliefs are as important and special to them as mine are to me.

June 1, 2008 DeeDee becomes Mrs. Chris Chambers

Stanley Simrin: *"Learning Judaism Prepares Us for Law School"*

Every Jewish child, the quip goes, is a law student. To study Judaism is *not* to read, listen, and commit to memory, repeat. Every word, every phrase, every concept is open to question, discussion, debate, dialectic, and commentary. There is no dogma in learning *Torah,* the Bible of the Jews. Its study is always in the company of authoritative commentary, often encompassing a broad spectrum of difference and disagreement.

Attraction to the law profession demands a passion for analyzing words, ideas, feelings, deeds, and placing them in a context that promotes an acceptable judicial decision for the client one is representing. Perhaps this phenomenon accounts for the preponderance of Jews in the legal profession. The proclivity is nurtured in childhood when one's Jewish education commences. Within the one hundred-sixty family membership of Temple Beth El are several of Bakersfield's well-known attorneys: Milton Younger, Stanley Simrin, David Stanton, Philip Rudnick, and David Neumeister. For those who become judges, Judaism is a formidable foundation through its unyielding emphasis on unequivocal justice. No favor may be bestowed upon the wealthy, the poor, the powerful, the impotent, or due to skillful eloquence, neither out of sympathy for the inept of speech, and surely not for one's kin.

Let us examine the thoughts of one of our Jewish lawyers, the influence and impact he believes his Jewish background has had on his work as an attorney. The final Court of Appeals: Judaism is a way of life, more than simply a religion or an ethnicity. It derives from the Hebrew Bible, our memory and experience, and what our Sages deduced from those things over the centuries. It tells us how we must live. We do not dwell on an after-life, and are uncertain there is one.

We know that if there is one, places are reserved there for those who merit them based on our behavior in this life. The *Talmud* teaches us, so the legend goes that we will be interviewed by a heavenly court when we apply for admission into the world to come, whatever that may mean. We will be asked questions and the first questions will be: "Were you ethical in business?" not "Did you love God or people?" not "Did you have faith?" not "Did you follow the prescribed rituals?" Those things are less important than how we behaved in business because it is in business that we have the most potential to touch the lives of others, for both good and evil. That ethical imperative is my guide to professional behavior in my capacity as a lawyer. The first place it impacts is in the area of fees.

Tradition teaches that everyone who does productive work should make a fair wage or return on investment, not a measly one, and not an exorbitant one. Nobody should be able to become overly rich and nobody should be kept in poverty. My fees, therefore, are not "what the traffic will bear" or the prevailing rate in my community. They are generally lower—enough to meet expenses and make a fair living. I also expect to do some free work for the community as part of the dues I pay for being a member of that community.

The Bible tells us that the wages of a laborer must not remain with us overnight. That means that I must pay my bills as soon as I receive them, and I do—except on the rare occasions that the money is just not there.

Tradition teaches I must provide good and sufficient service for what I charge my client. As a consequence I decline to take cases when I feel I cannot give adequate service, cases I know are outside my limited field of expertise, the criminal law. Cases I accept are only when my workload will permit me to do a proper job. I routinely turn down more cases than I accept. The tradition wisely teaches me that I can wear only one pair of shoes at a time, so I really do not need more than two.

The Sages tell us that we Jews are to be "a light unto the nations" and so I feel compelled to speak out on issues I feel competent on, to act as an example for others to follow, and let those who deal with me regularly know that I am a Jew guided by my Jewish values. We are also taught that everyone, regardless of the charge, is entitled to representation.

Given the time to do it right, I accept cases without first determining guilt or innocence and without regard for the nature of the crime charged. Even the guilty have a right to a sentence within the law, not beyond it, and even the guilty have the right to challenge the government's case and to have at least one person entirely on their side, within the law. That person is me.

Finally, although a lawyer's conduct is largely dictated by the canons of ethics set forth by the State and the profession, there are many ethical decisions those authorities do not cover. When that happens—and it happens often—I look to the tradition to determine my path. My business and professional life, therefore, is significantly directed by Judaic principles.

Michael K. Miller: *"My Approach to the Manufacturing Industry"*

Owners of commercial enterprises whose relations with employees and clients are respectful and based on high ethical standards elevates the community. Their virtues radiate and nourish the business environment as beneficially as sunshine and gentle rain enhance the quality and nutritional value of our agricultural products and livestock.

Kern Tech, a manufacturing company that had been co-owned by Michael Miller and Cliff David represented these admirable qualities. Bakersfield was fortunate and proud! Although Michael Miller no longer owns a business he is still involved in civic projects, and plays an active role on Temple Beth El's Board of Trustees. The Jewish community couldn't have a more worthy example than Michael Miller. His leadership is founded on integrity. His profound commitment is to the universality implicit in the Mosaic Code of Law. Michael Miller truly internalizes its message: the brotherhood of mankind.

All trades, including those in the manufacturing arena, provide a wellspring of situations that are best addressed in Leviticus 19. It is at the heart of what Jewish scholars term the "Holiness Code."

An employer has a responsibility to those who devote a substantial segment of their waking hours performing tasks that benefit the enterprise. People's wages should be paid in a timely manner so that they can meet *their* commitments. Employers should keep this in mind when considering how much to withhold on payday. Beyond the obligation to dole out their salaries on time, another obligation is implied. If an employee asks for an advance in wages the employer should extend a loan of what would be considered a reasonable amount.

After all, where else can the employee seek the money he says he needs? As a matter of policy, the loan should not exceed the amount of the worker's next paycheck. Company policy should include deducting no more than a day's wages per week for paying back the loan. If the employee had been in great need of it, requesting faster repayment would likely be a hardship for the worker.

The second precept relates to customers, and is derived from verses 35 and 36: "Ye shall do no unrighteousness in judgment, in weight, or in measure. Be just and fair in weighing and measuring." When a customer orders a replacement part made of #6061 aluminum, and your present inventory only includes #2024 it would be immoral to substitute the material without revealing it to the customer and requesting permission, *even if the available part is regarded superior!*

Also, if the part is found to have the slightest irregularity, it is your obligation to inform the customer, and await his response, about accepting or rejecting the item. The customer's payment is based on the original understanding. The manufacturer's smallest deviation is a breach of contract. Mike Miller urges the study of Leviticus 19 in its *entirety*. Some of the finest thoughts about our ethical and moral duties are to be found there. According to Jewish tradition, the first question confronting us on Judgment Day will be, *"Were you honest in business?"*

Rachel Brill Neal: *"California Has Become a Mini-Cosmos!"*

The California Department of Education recognizes that for education to be truly effective teachers need to have at least a minimal understanding of the varying cultural backgrounds of students. The teacher training curricula of California's university systems now include cross-culture education. Many school districts in the State, including the Bakersfield City School District are requiring already-credentialed teachers to supplement their existent training and experience with this add-on to their education.

At the time of writing the first edition of this book Sue Krause had been a librarian in Bakersfield's Washington Middle School. She had been in the Kern County school system three decades!

Sue Krause enrolled in the cross-culture curriculum at C.S.U.B. and found it a truly enlightening experience. Not only to acquaint herself with a variety of European and Asian cultures, but to even discover how many of these cultures had representation right here in our own Kern County community.

Mrs. Krause was a long-time friend of Heidi Allison, a member of Temple Beth El, and a teacher in Washington School. It was through Mrs. Allison that she also met Shirley Ann Newman, this book's author, and mother of Heidi Allison.

No doubt it was because of these connections that Mrs. Krause selected Judaism as the subject of her course project; focusing on one specific culture was the course requirement.

Mrs. Krause and two classmates who had also chosen Judaism as their area of special study prepared a presentation. They enlisted Shirley Ann Newman, Bruce and Rachel Neal as resource persons. Mrs. Newman related to this group of college students that a consequence of the Holocaust had been the deaths of over six million European Jews. She disclosed that the impact these horrendous events were having was not only on the survivors, but on the world's Jews. Regarding the effects their traumas were having, particularly interpersonal relations: spouses, siblings, parent-and-child, and many others.

Bruce Neal, a Bakersfield schoolteacher who had been a student in a Yeshiva, told the class about Jewish holidays and their historical foundations, their meanings and the traditions associated with them. His wife Rachel, a teacher in a Lamont middle school sang Jewish ethnic songs, played the guitar, and taught the class an Israeli folk dance. The project's committee of three brought a few typically European Jewish style foods for the class to nibble and taste.

"Out of the depths of darkness and mystery are emerging new understandings and clarity," I declared. Mrs. Krause smiled in agreement. "These studies will not only result in more qualified educators, but will enhance them as members of humanity! I hope that ultimately teachers, students, and the populace as a whole will unite through a familiar understanding and appreciation of each other's cultural differences. Only then will we have an *authentic* public school system. Only then will we obliterate the insidious, destructive societal disease of xenophobia. An important early lesson to be taught a child is: I'm OK, you're OK; everyone in the world is OK. That, I say, should be the foundation of education, the foundation on which the building blocks of learning are added."

"Before a child puts a foot across the threshold of the schoolroom he should have learned that the world does not exist merely for providing him with what *he* needs, and wants. It operates on a system of reciprocity. You may have been born with a high I.Q. but the sooner you develop a high S.I.Q., *social intelligence quotient* the sooner you will find yourself in step, in rhythm with the rest of us in the parade."

"Leaping in among the marchers without falling into step puts you off balance, bumping into those in front of you and blocking the progress of those behind you. Marching in step is easier, smoother and earns you the camaraderie and good will of the others."

"This does not mean you cannot eventually come up with an innovation, something appreciated and ready to be adopted by enough participants. Then it becomes you who is moved to the head of the procession. Taking the lead is best done by popular approval. Devise something new but within the range of acceptable societal values. That is a good description of democracy—far and away the most desirable system of communal living."

"What has this philosophical metaphor to do with teaching? It is intended to illustrate that the *subject* of instruction is really secondary: Whether it is language arts, mathematics, biology or history, a teacher can and should be able to include within the curriculum's framework a means of teaching positive, constructive societal values. And does anyone who has had the education courses to become a teacher really have the ability to inculcate values? Only one who has internalized those values, who truly *lives* those values. The issue is not only how much of the subject matter the teacher acquired, or the teaching methodology, but primarily who is this person? The teacher, to be effective as a purveyor of values must personify them."

"The accepted societal values of our civilization derive from Judaism, Christianity and Islam, the three major world religions. The United States Constitution was contrived by men who believed in God, who relied on biblical doctrine to establish the guidelines, the framework of secular civil law."

"No matter how secular is the conduct of public school curricula, no matter how devoid of the manifold differences that set one religion apart from another, or one denomination from another within the same religion, there are values common to all people. Even the social contract of secularists evolved from conceding that civilization functions best if we sublimate enough of our infantile self-need gratification in favor of a system of justice and fairness. We all fare better and are rewarded with a measure of security and tranquility when some of the fears and anxieties of a jungle environment are mitigated."

"Your next thought may be: All we have to do is give everyone a set of these rules and say, 'Here, go and learn them.' It doesn't work that way unless the youngster, the student is convinced that those who establish the rules are *also* living by those rules. Otherwise they will be considered fraudulent and meaningless. The youngster is right to expect his teacher to be one who instructs him to do what he, too, knows how to do—and who *does* it. I give no credence to the phrase: *"Those who can't do teach."*

"Education is a Jewish Value: As did many of my ancestors, I too value and respect education. To be educated and to be a part of the education system is to celebrate the wonder of life. Life *is* for *learning.* We are merely 'putting in time' if we live without learning. There are so many things to learn, so many wonders to share and participate in throughout this adventure we call living."

"My hope is that my students love learning. Whatever the subject matter, the teacher ought to demonstrate that learning is exciting and makes you feel alive. Watch children as they begin to walk or talk. They experiment. Each child's learning process has a unique quality, and yet is similar to everyone else's. In observing the stages they all have certain aspects in common. The child is amazed at each new stage of development he finds himself in, and proud of his own accomplishments. "Look, Mommy, look at me! Watch me!"

"A mother's job is to encourage her child, to share the wonder. The job of a parent or teacher is to admire the youngster's accomplishment. Some people say a good teacher is a coach who encourages and cheers his team on to victory!

"When I began my brief time of teaching, I thought I knew how to make each lesson exciting and filled with variety. I regret to say I did not live up to this high ideal. I had neither the energy nor the creativity."

"When I was a college student I remember being interested in every one of my subjects. I enthusiastically nourished my great hunger to learn; I longed to explore what life had to offer me. My high school English teachers contributed to that valuable input. My instructors in college built on that early foundation and continued to make the acquisition of knowledge exciting."

"The whole process was a cooperative one, however. I was a responsive partner to their commitment to teach because I came as a student-at-the-ready. It related to something I had already learned at home, from my parents and their Jewish values."

"We Jews are called 'A people of the book.' At Sinai, after redemption from Egyptian slavery we were given the *Torah* as a blueprint for good living. We're required to study it, analyze its

96

subtleties, and compare our conclusions with those of others engaged in the eternal quest for understanding and meaning. It is a veritable whetstone on which one sharpens and refines the mind and emotions. Because learning leads to a broader, wider, deeper life, as individuals and as a community we begin to treasure the value of study. We become sensitized to the meaningful messages we receive, and to appreciate the process. After awhile we love to learn! Only then can the cooperative relationship of teacher and student become a successful and fulfilling enterprise."

"*Torah* has also given me my political values. As both an American and a Jew I was taught to value people—all people."

"When I began working as a teacher in the farming community of Lamont the student body was comprised mostly of Mexican-Americans, many whose parents were migrant workers. Their culture was totally alien to me, but my own parents had struggled mightily through the Great Depression and had experienced the deprivations of the Second World War. To that extent I could identify and empathize with these youngsters and their families.

"But my own young adulthood was during the 60s, an era of idealism. I was conditioned by the philosophy of the time that undiluted tolerance of everyone's idiosyncrasies would result in peace, harmony and love. The whole world would come to resemble the biblical Garden of Eden."

"When my students failed to respond to my optimism, that they'll eagerly embrace and appreciate the day's lesson, my patience sometimes thinned; I grew frustrated and disenchanted, often a bit intolerant. I reproached myself afterward and endeavored to pray: 'Set these words that I command you this day upon your heart. Let them be a symbol before your eyes...' I'd promise myself I will increase my dedication to my noble profession. As a teacher my job should include helping the next generation of the world's population become better than the present one, so that ultimately we can bring about the repair of the world: *Tikun Olam.*"

Marlene Benson: *"A New Teacher In A New Community"*

At the time of writing this (for the 1998 edition) I had lived in Bakersfield about eleven months. I drove here from my home in Pikesville, Maryland that had a substantial Jewish population. My parents did their best to instill in my two brothers, my younger sister and me, Jewish values and traditions. During the high holidays my father would attend synagogue services while my mother prepared the food. She had been raised in Canada in a family whose religious practice was close to Reform Judaism. My father, raised in Washington D.C, had been brought up to follow the stringencies of Orthodoxy. My brothers were first sent to a *Talmudic Academy.* They then went to public junior and senior high schools. My sister and I attended public schools but went to a late afternoon Hebrew school three times a week.

In Pikesville as in other Jewish communities, you were bound to be influenced by the Jewish culture and traditions. I remember during *Rosh Hashanah* and *Yom Kippur,* Pikesville High, our local public school would be virtually closed. Few if any students showed up and even the non-Jewish students looked forward to these days because there was practically no formal teaching. The school provided the Jewish students with forms for their parents to sign requesting permission to be absent from school during those days.

When I arrived in Bakersfield it gave me quite a shock. I felt like the proverbial "stranger in a strange land." My roommate was a kind-hearted Catholic Mexican who helped me a lot. Even in the office where I did telemarketing that summer, to tide me over. I remember co-workers discussing a friend's death and their concern over whether her soul had been saved. They were curious about Judaism and I answered their many questions as well as I could. Attending synagogue services was never especially important to me in my hometown. There were many places to choose from so before the High Holidays my friends and I decided which one we'll go to from among them. I ultimately elected to attend Reform services on the campus of John's Hopkins University.

When I first arrived in Bakersfield I did not give much thought to seeking out a synagogue. When September came, the season of our most sacred holidays I began to realize how much I do need a synagogue in my life.

The High Holidays in 1997 evoked a great deal of uncertainty in me. As far as I knew I was the only Jewish person working as a teacher in Taft. I had to ask my principal and co-workers how to be excused for these holidays. After being granted permission, I was faced with a much more limited choice of synagogues than I was accustomed to. By chance, one day as I was wandering through the downtown area I happened to pass the building of the B'nai Jacob Conservative congregation. It was there that I met Howard Silver. After awhile he realized that I was not feeling totally satisfied with the services there and suggested I meet one of the young women who was a very active participant at Temple Beth El. He gave me the telephone number of the temple and also of Lisa Schwartz.

I also had to face many of my discomforts about being Jewish while working in Taft. Something I never had to do before. Growing up in a metropolitan area with a large Jewish population, I never had to come to certain decisions about how to deal with Christian holidays. Now as a teacher of all Christian students is it expected of me to decorate my classroom with their traditional decorations for Christmas? Would it create a problem if I were to tell them about *Hanukkah,* my own religious holiday which occurs at the same season of the year? I was relieved of my predicament when two of the other teachers invited me to share with them an explanation of the history, the miracle, of *Hanukkah.*

Inasmuch as this was my first year of teaching I didn't even have any prior experience to guide me. This system of "team teaching" at least provided me with a measure of support. I explained to the children what the *Hanukkah* and the *dreidel* are; and I taught some of my Special Education students the Hebrew letters. We painted the letters and pictures and then I displayed them on a bulletin board outside the classroom, without giving any consideration to whether it was appropriate to use what might be construed as religious symbols. Later I was told by many people in and out of Taft that this was a very courageous thing to do. Some teachers found my display quite interesting, but others expressed a bit of uncertainty about a public school's bulletin board decorated with representations of the Jewish religion.

Ironically, since I came here less than a year ago I am now more active in a synagogue than I have ever been. I think that when I lived in a metropolitan area with a large Jewish population I always took my Judaism for granted. Although I provided childcare for the East Bank *Havura,* a fellowship chapter in Maryland, I was never fully active in temple events. In this new phase of my life in Bakersfield, I have recently begun to explore deeply my Jewish beliefs. I have since become a member of Temple Beth El. I feel that living in a small Jewish community pretty much obliges one to become an active participant in synagogue life. Each one of us must truly do his share in keeping the community constructively functioning. Realizing this has set me on the track to going all out in exploring my Jewish heritage. I find that others have set for themselves this same goal!

Timothy Fromm: *"I'm Hooked on Judaism!"*

I am of the Jewish faith, and for a quarter of a century I've been a teacher in the Bakersfield City school system. One of the first things I did when I started teaching in Bakersfield was to inquire of Temple Beth El whether they need religious school teachers. To my surprise, not only did they, but it was for the third-grade, the same grade I was teaching in secular school.

To be precise, my public school class was K-3, children with behavior disorders. Initially, I was convinced no student really has a behavior problem if his/her environment is right. I worked very hard that first year, implementing an innovative behavior management system I developed, adapting it every three or four months. I was patient, nurturing and caring. The class seemed to be progressing very well.

However, what surprised and disappointed me was the lack of parental support. Judaism places high value on education but I soon noticed this was not true of many of my students' families. For quite a number of children it was only in school that they were shown a patient, caring, nurturing attitude. It made my days a continuum of uphill struggles.

As a significant Jewish prayer commands: *teaching must be at all times and all places; when you rise up, when you lie down, on your way*—which alerted me that not only during class time, but also at recess, and during the children's lunch period as long as they were in school I was obligated to carry on with their education, with my function as a teacher. Even after school hours, ("on your way...") when I made a home visit.

Religion school was different. My students seemed to be highly motivated. Even I was! While preparing a lesson, I was learning from it. Class became a strong learning environment for us all. The students were eager to learn and I was eager to learn in order to teach! Bible stories were read, discussed, evaluated in terms of our daily lives. The children learned the meanings of different Jewish holidays and their connection our historic background. This made them important, interesting and exciting. They were celebrated more at home because they had become meaningful. Judaism at it's best!

I began to explain about the Jewish holidays to my students in public school. On *Rosh Hashana,* the Jewish New Year we discussed what year had just begun on the Hebrew calendar. We nibbled a slice or two of apple dipped in honey, a tradition related to the Jewish New Year. Later on I gave an equal amount of time to explaining the Chinese New Year, which comes in January.

By teaching the meanings of my own Jewish holidays the children understood why I would be absent from school when. *Yom Kippur,* the day of repentance, happens. Observant Jewish people spend the day fasting and praying.

One year I brought treats to school, distributed them and then explained we were going to fast (for two hours). The students complained they would feel too hungry to wait before eating them. When it was over, they understood; the example enlightened them on self-discipline. It applies to studying for a test even though your friends are urging you to come outside and play basketball with them.

I felt that it was very important to explain *Hanukkah* and to make it clear that though it falls around the same time of year as Christmas, the Jewish holiday is *not* a 'Jewish Christmas.' We made *latkes,* potato pancakes; I taught the students the *dreidel game,* spinning a tops. Temple Beth El gift shop donates *dreidels* to young students. I brought gifts for the children, one per child, on each of Hanukkah's eight days.

My school had a very interesting tradition of incorporating a nativity scene into the Christmas program. At my urging, and after several years in which I expressed my disapproval, the term was changed to "Winter Program." I decided to take a stand against the custom of teaching only Christian tradition by introducing my own, and those of other ethnic groups. I started an annual *Hanukkah* display. I spent weeks educating my special ed. students about the holiday and they wrote a play script that our class presented: A Jewish family celebrating *Hanukkah*. It presented a brief history that led to an annual celebration, about rededicating our sacred Temple in Jerusalem after it had been desecrated and then rendered functional.

Passover is another major holiday (my favorite!) I explain to my public school class. I have the students bring their lunch to the classroom, and when lunchtime comes around I take out mine, a bag containing *matzo, charoses,* apple, egg, *gefilte* fish and horseradish. As soon as some students notice my meal is so different from theirs, I take the opportunity to relate the story of Passover. I let them sample foods unfamiliar to them.

Later, in the classroom, we have a special education version of the Seder. I once demonstrated something I had read in a Jewish journal about an innovative Seder, students incorporating into it an explanation of the plagues. One of the plagues we acted out was the turning of water into blood, which we demonstrated with red food coloring. We also used plastic frogs, farm animals with spots, and wild beasts, all as "props" for my show-and-tell demonstration. I divided the kids into family groups, the oldest boy of each family pretending he died, representing the killing of the first-born son in each Egyptian Israelite family.

Sometimes I teach the meaning of another Jewish holiday: *Purim* or *Shavuot,* or Israel Independence Day, or *Yom HaShoa:* Holocaust Remembrance Day.

My Judaism is reflected in every subject I teach; it includes the importance of education. As Leo Trepp wrote in: *A History of the Jewish Experience,* "Study in Jewish tradition is more than gathering facts; it forges a chain that joins us and spells survival."

I once had a student who resisted learning to read. I brought out a Hebrew book and showed him the Hebrew letters. Provoking his interest and curiosity motivated him to put more effort into reading the English language!

In math I use the monetary system as a teaching device. I point out the importance of math in daily life. It helps my students learn to add, subtract, multiply and divide using their own allowance money. Clearly, I have a firm commitment to the ideals of the Jewish religion, including the *obligation* to educate, and in the process, to imbue in my students a genuine appreciation of learning.

Addendum, July 2012: My weekday teaching in public school has continued. And so has my instruction in Temple Beth El religious school. I have been teaching there for nearly fifteen years, on Sunday morning and Wednesday evenings *"With meaningful diligence I instruct children of my Jewish faith in the Torah."* And in those preparing to become a bar and bat mitzvah I teach the sacred language of Hebrew.

However, a Sunday school teacher now has to deal with the problems a secular teacher also confronts. My religious school students seem to have a greater need for adult support and guidance, in addition to the usual, teaching them to structure their lives ethically and morally, based on the precepts of the Torah.

One year, the class I taught was Special Ed children, all from only one family. I didn't mind it much even though the situation was a bit redundant for me. These youngsters had been traumatized by their parents' divorce. It resulted in their chancy, irregular attendance. They showed up about 50% of the time!

My success in teaching is also challenged by Jewish students who with their parents are so busy these days with "other things," that doing their homework or studying for a test has little or *no* priority. To cope with this dilemma I added two features I hope will motivate them to learn, and to *enjoy* learning!

I use "Bibliodrama," the acting out of bible stories. The students might forget a tale just by reading it, but they *remember* that time they acted the part of Moses at the Sea of Reeds, watching the waters part, and their fellow Israelites making their escape from a bitter life in Egypt.

Another thing students like is the game of "Jewpardy," answering questions about what they learned from the performance, and getting a prize for the right answer.

At a religion teachers' conference in Los Angeles, the inclusion of parents was suggested. I conducted a few "Jewpardy" games for Temple Beth El parents. The first year it was pretty successful; the next year no parents showed up!

So there it is, how changes in family life have impacted education and the role of teachers. We're substitute parents, police officers, defense attorneys, medical advisers, psychological counselors and nutritionists...

In a multicultural community such as ours has become, our children (and their parents!) have to learn to behave in a kindly manner, to be tolerant of our differences. Years ago it was Jewish children who needed the deference of others, even from some of their fellow students in Sunday School who were of a different ethnicity and culture. My job is to bring all these children together and teach them that the bottom line is: *we're all one.*

Dr. Robert D. Allison: *"Personal Reflections."*

As I reflect on the past seven decades, it is apparent that Judaism, in terms of religious practice had little impact on my early life. In 1935 my father, a Russian immigrant, married my mother, the daughter of a Russian immigrant. She was born in San Francisco. This was during The Great Depression, a time of economic and social struggles. Many immigrants left their Jewish Orthodoxy on the doorstep of their homeland *shtetl.* Nevertheless, they remained culturally Jewish. So did my family, continuing to celebrate and commemorate the major holidays, attending High Holiday services, and certainly retaining their Jewish identity. They had a sense of connection to a people different from others.

After my father died in 1943, and my mother's remarriage in 1948 was to a non-Jew, our separation even from the cultural aspects of Jewish life became total. Yet I never lost the sense of identity and ethical values we associate with Judaism. A major one is education; I *did* go to college, as far as I know the first member in my family to do so.

I don't recall many discussions about religion during my childhood. However, my mother was bent on infusing in her only child Judaism's behavioral precepts: integrity, reliability, diligence, the importance of an education, and many other religious and cultural principles associated with the world's leading faiths. Very likely it was because of my Jewish identity that many of my friends in high school and college were Jewish, and why I connected with Jewish groups in college. Hillel was one, although that likely was more for social than religious reasons. In San Jose I attended the Reform temple occasionally, mostly because my best friend's family was a prominent member. My marriage was to a Jewish girl named Heidi Newman, (daughter of this book's author).

Heidi and I met each other one evening at a dance in San Francisco's Jewish Community Center.

It was in Bakersfield that my wife and I linked up with a Jewish congregation, Temple Beth El, the Reform synagogue. I even became a board member and officer. Heidi quickly grew active in the Sisterhood, for a time holding office in the group of highly involved female temple members. Finally, I was motivated to acquire the Jewish education I had missed as a youngster. Even my bar mitzvah observance had been bypassed. I was forty years old when I finally had the experience of standing on the bema, facing the congregation, my family, and my guests, and displaying my ability to read from a Torah scroll. Twenty-seven years late, of course, but happily my performance preceded my son Mark's.

In college I had majored in chemistry and minored in engineering, and upon completing my masters degree in chemistry joined the faculty of Bakersfield College. At the time they were looking for a chemistry instructor, and since I had been recommended through UC Berkeley's community college program, that was enough to satisfy Ed Simonsen, the BC President, and for him to hire me. It turned out to be a good fit. I planned to stay for just one year, and here it is, a half-century later and I'm *still* working at Bakersfield College.

I taught chemistry and occasional math. When technology became available, I collaborated with colleagues in integrating the use of computers into instruction. I also taught computer science courses. I later earned a doctoral degree, became chairperson of my department, instructional dean, interim president, and Vice-President for Instruction (academic vice-president).

After retirement, I served as Kern Community College District's interim instructional Assistant Chancellor and strategic planning consultant. Later I founded the Levan Institute for Lifelong Learning at B.C., funded through an endowment from Dr. Norman Levan. I'm currently its Program Director (a part time job).

As I said almost at the start of this brief biographical account, while I was still a young child my mother began to instill in me the importance of an education. That may have had a strong influence on why I made teaching my lifelong career. As Jews, our ultimate goal is called *tikkun olam:* "Restore the world to its initial state of purity." It is a monumental endeavor, and we can only try. But believing we can make a difference in view of the world's innumerable flaws, leads to another Jewish characteristic: *chutzpah*, the audacity to think that we can actually make even a small dent in those flaws.

Heidi and I are still married after *forty-eight years!* We have two children, both with advanced university degrees, and we also have two grandchildren. My wife and I are well entrenched here in Bakersfield, cheerfully involved in community activity and organizational life. Most of our friends, our nearest and dearest, are also local residents.

This book describes the involvement of local Jews in initiating and strengthening our public and private institutions as well as their dedication and active participation in moving Bakersfield toward the thriving, multicultural cosmopolitan city it has become.

I would like to affirm that for *me* both the religious and secular components of my life in this community have been both interesting and rewarding.

Note: Indeed, it *is* surprising that this world-traveling couple, Dr. and Mrs. Allison, find Bakersfield interesting! They've toured Europe several times--all the way to Russia and Turkey. They visited India, headed north to Alaska, and south to Antarctica. They toured Pacific regions: Thailand, New Zealand, Australia, China (twice!), Japan and Vietnam. They've been to countries in Central and South America, dropping in on the Galapagos Islands!

Robert and Heidi Allison

Shirley Ann Newman: *"Learning Might Keep You From Burning!"*

Education has always been of major importance to Jews. For a long time in our history it was just for men--until "feminism" bubbled up, the liberation of women. Achieving an education and becoming a teacher is a double-edged instrument. No, I do *not* mean a double-edged sword. It's a double-edged magical wand! As you teach and impart knowledge to your students, you often learn from their questions, their oral answers, what they express in a report, a test paper, their homework (at times bringing you to laughter!) Students are often a challenge; they give their teachers the incentive, the stimulation and motivation to expand and widen and deepen their own understandings.

Well, why is improving yourself through the art of teaching unique, even special? Doesn't a doctor try to learn more and more about medicine? Doesn't a lawyer wrack his brain over what the Founding Fathers *really* meant in the U.S. Constitution? What will be the consequences of a recent judicial decision, what will new legislation and regulation: federal, state and local, result in, and how might it impact on the populace?

Virtually throughout history we Jews have been a people of plight and flight. Needing a speedy get-a-way means traveling light, choosing only our most valuable and *portable* possessions— if we still have any left after one of those sieges of confiscation and destruction, of pillaging at the hands of our enemy! Often it results from the capricious whim of some drunken soldiers, or through the evil legislation initiated by a Jew-hating administrator in authority.

Believe it or not, you won't even need an eighteen-inch suitcase for transporting your most valuable assets, the ones I consider the best and most dependable possessions for helping you survive, and if you do, that enable you to adapt to whatever your vague, ambiguous future, wherever you next reside.

Set off on the journey with a strong, healthy, vigorous body, and *a strong, healthy vigorous mind!* Food and education have kept our people in existence close to six thousand years. Despite the many times we suffered oppression, discrimination, and been

108

on the brink of annihilation, the numerous occasions of being reviled, spat upon as unworthy of living on this planet, we're determined at all costs to survive as a people.

Yes, of course your three story mansion-like home is magnificent; so are the furnishings, and your four shiny, nearly new cars, your satins and silks, your jewels and furs (Furs? Shame on you!)—Forget about these; smother your attachment to all those treasures the first moment you awaken to the bitter reality: that your only chance of seeing the Messiah is to hightail it out of the country of hate, taking with you as little as possible, *except* for the two I keep urging you to count on, a strong healthy, resilient body, and a highly educated, resourceful, inventive, calculating, sharp, canny mind. Study and learn as much as you can. *Learning might keep you from burning!*

PART THREE

Honorable "Menschen"

Honorable "Menschen"

June 17, 2012 We Lost A Woman Of Valor, Our Beloved **Wendy Wayne**

Data are from an article by Steve Mayer, *Bakersfield Californian* staff writer, and from what Shirley Ann Newman knew personally about her Temple Beth El fellow congregant.

It was truly devastating to learn of Wendy's death. She had been one of the community's best serving citizens of all times. Hard work and dedication had begun in the late nineteen seventies and part of the eighties when she was a nurse and childbirth educator for the Clinica Sierra Vista.

By exemplifying compassion, a major precept in her Jewish faith system it, led her to make a highly affirmative impact in shaping the community's social services and humanities. Armed with motivational force, training and skills, she turned her noble perspectives into overt action, acquiring the nickname "Mother Teresa of Bakersfield." It was quoted more-or-less confidentially so as not to trouble her modesty.

Wendy not only downplayed her countless contributions to society, her endearing manner of praising and complimenting others encouraged *their* desire to do more for others, and to develop their potential in the arts and sciences. I too had been endowed with motivating comments from Wendy.

Best friend and co-religionist, Susan Reep, once remarked, "Wendy had a way of making you feel like *the* most important person in the world! There was always another seat at her table. There was always another bed in her house. Wendy has always been my role model."

State Sen. Michael Rubio once said of her, "She is the type of person who wakes up and thinks, 'What can I do today to make this world a better place?' She has that mentality from the second she wakes up until the moment she goes to sleep!"

Wendy grew up in Southern California but came to Bakersfield in the mid-1970s to help her then boyfriend, Gene Tackett. It was with his grass roots and ultimately successful campaign to unseat a three-term incumbent on the K. C. Board of Supervisors. She never left Bakersfield as her home city. Gene and Wendy soon married, and raised two sons, Larkin and Benjamin.

In a commencement speech Wendy gave at Cal State Bakersfield last year, she spoke about learning to take risks at an early age. "When I was 20, I decided to leave my comfortable home in L.A. and my five siblings, and travel halfway across the world to Africa to be a Peace Corps volunteer. Now, mind you, I'd never even been camping." But it was Wendy's willingness to jump into uncharted territory, to risk failure that launched her into a life of achievement on her own terms.

At least it was with a good background in education. She had graduated from CSUB in 1978 with a degree in nursing. Wendy would go on to earn a master's degree in public health and a doctorate in educational leadership.

In the mid-1980s, even as poverty programs were seeing cuts on the national level, she was appointed director of Community Connection for Child Care. It was yet another chance to dive into uncharted waters, into a level of administrative complexity and responsibility she had not previously experienced. She helped develop child health programs, day care and health education, and an effort to combat Kern's high poverty level. Local impoverished areas sometimes weren't so unlike Africa's third-world conditions she had experienced. It had given her a keen sense of realism and had produced an ever-present can-do attitude in her local efforts.

After Wendy had been in east Africa, living in a mud hut with no running water or electricity, later she came to Bakersfield to work as a nurse practitioner, public health nurse, childbirth educator, credentialed community college teacher, Kern County planning commissioner and chief administrator at two local nonprofit organizations dedicated to the health and well being of children.

Although she retired in 2004 she was nowhere near ending her efforts to help others in need of it. The following year, impelled by the disastrous results of hurricane Katrina she volunteered her services, spending a month in New Orleans, Louisiana. Working in conjunction with the Federal Emergency Management Agency, she sent home dispatches detailing the devastation and human toll she had witnessed.

Some of her observations were published in *The Bakersfield Californian*. In her every word Wendy Wayne's compassion was clearly evident, not boastfully worn on her sleeve like a badge of honor, but simply embedded in her nature.

In the fall of 2006, Wayne returned to Kenya, where in 1969 and 1970 she had taught desperately poor students. Now she had the chance to visit former student Jedidah Muthoni and her family. In spring 2007, she traveled to Nigeria and India to administer vaccinations to children.

She regarded her experiences in Kenya, Nigeria, India and elsewhere a gift, one *she* had received, not that she had given to others. She said many times during her extraordinary life that she gained much more from her volunteer activities than she was able to give. Unselfishness was one of the guiding principles of her life.

Always on the ready to deal with a new challenge, Wendy served for about two and a half years on the Kern County Planning Commission, finally resigning her position in 2007. She started another new adventure, taking up the reins of troubled First 5 Kern, a commission that distributes the state's tobacco tax funds to local groups that help children.

The organization was in turmoil when she entered it, still reeling from the controversial tenure of its former director. Hope was high that Wendy Wayne, through her administrative skills and personal integrity, could restore the reputation of the commission. Many believe she did, but she didn't have as much time as she was hoping for.

In March 2008, Wendy left the post after she was diagnosed with non-Hodgkin's lymphoma, a form of cancer that attacks the body's white blood cells. She began an aggressive regimen of treatments to fight the disease, and for a time, the lymphoma went into remission. Eventually it returned, but not before she had more chance to travel, spend precious time with her family, and continue to share the philosophy she formulated from her first trip to Africa: "Through giving, we receive."

In the course of Wendy's lifetime, she was honored many times by those who recognized her achievements. She received the

John W. Doubenmeir Award from the American Society of Public Administration in 1994. And in 1996 she was named Kern County Democratic Woman of the Year. Her synagogue, Temple Beth El, honored her in 2005 for her lifelong commitment to helping others. And she was inducted into the Cal State Bakersfield Alumni Hall of Fame in 2008.

More than four thousand graduates listened, laughed and cheered in June 2011 when Wendy Wayne gave a commencement address at the CSUB Outdoor Amphitheatre. As she shared what she called her five WWWs (Wendy Wayne's Words of Wisdom,) she talked about the importance of setting goals: daily goals, life goals and in-between goals.

During her first swim in the Indian Ocean off the east coast of Kenya she realized she had swum in three of the world's five oceans. So, she depicted to her audience, she set a goal to swim in all five, including the Arctic and Antarctic oceans. "And then I thought," she related smilingly, "while I'm doing *that*, there's seven continents, and I want to make love on every continent!"

The crowd erupted in cheers and roars of laughter. "I'm happy to tell you today that three years ago, I traveled to Antarctica," she added, then pausing a moment, related, "and I swam in the Antarctic Ocean!"

Wendy Wayne went on to soberly advise these graduates to find the time to really listen, to take risks, find their passion, and commit to doing at least one random act of kindness a week. "Because the kindness you give is a kindness to *you*. You know, I feel I've had a very magical life," she confided to the gathering. "I can tell you that I am the luckiest person in the world."

By Rabbi Cheryl Rosenstein, Temple Beth El:

Dear Chevrei--

"Wendy was an inspiration to us all in so many different arenas of her life. Please continue to live her legacy of goodness by doing the kinds of mitzvot she can no longer perform in this world. In this way, we can all help carry the great load she bore as one who labored hard in the effort of *tikkun olam*, repairing this broken world."

Note: The following, a further tribute to Wendy is Rabbi's message to the congregation in the July 2012 *Shofar*. (None will ever be too many! *S.A. N*)

At this writing, the arrangements for the formal celebration of her life are set for the Temple sanctuary on Sunday, July 8th at 1:30 PM. (Please note: our Temple service is intended to be the second and more intimate service, for us and her family; a much larger, public tribute will be observed earlier that weekend at the Fox Theater downtown. In truth, we ought to celebrate Wendy's life every day, by doing the numerous mitzvot her passing leaves undone.

Now that Wendy is gone, it is even more important that we keep her generous, giving spirit alive. Long before she knew what the words *tikkun olam* meant, Wendy lived them every day. Wendy would not have described herself as a "religious" Jew, but her daily deeds and conduct were exemplary of what a Jew should strive to do and be.

May Wendy's life continue to inspire us to live up to her good example, and may our deeds prove ourselves worthy of having known her. In this way maybe help the Holy One bring consolation and solace to her beloved family.

Dr. Jerry Sudarsky

Note: Details about Jerry Sudarsky were gleaned from an article (2008) by Gilbert Gia, Kern County Historic Society; edited 2012 by Shirley Ann Newman

Jerry Sudarsky was one of nine children, over whom he held the role of leader. However, they were all quite competent and all became successful adults. In adulthood Jerry was a trained scientist and exemplary humanitarian:

His father, Selig Sudarsky, had been born in 1881 and raised in Lithuania near the border of Germany, which was probably East

Prussia and thus under the control of Tsarist Russia. He didn't emigrate from his homeland until about 1914 or 1915. The family had been in the brush business in Lithuania, but then in the early 1900s Selig's younger brother Leister came to the U.S. to establish a brush factory in Chicago. Selig didn't emigrate until about 1914 or 1915. This was before the development and use of nylon, so Uncle Leister kept making trips to Russia to buy hog bristles.

Jerry's parents, Selig and Sara (née Ars) were married in 1916. Right after their marriage Selig's brother needed hog bristles for the factory in Chicago and asked him to make the purchase in Russia. Unfortunately, due to the country's involvement in WWI, after arriving there Jerry's parents weren't permitted to leave. They stayed for two or three years, which explains why Jerry's birth on June 12, 1918, was in a Lithuanian hospital, Nizni Novgorod, Russia.

After the war his father resumed his business interests in Europe, and in 1920 the family settled in Berlin where Jerry learned the German language. By attending an American school he also learned English. The Sudarskys lived in Europe until Jerry was ten. During that time his two sisters were born.

As a youngster Jerry traveled a bit with his parents, and visited the extended families in various places. He spent one year in London, and for a time lived in Madrid, where his father had other business interests. In 1928 they came to the United States and took up residence in Brooklyn, close to other branches of the family.

Jerry Sudarsky's entrepreneurial father owned several movie theaters in New York City, and also import-export businesses. He and his younger brother Efraim Sudarsky had an office in the notable Woolworth Building.

Jerry's mother proudly attributed a success potential in Jerry, as well. At home and his parents addressed him by the name Mila, Russian for "Sonny." His actual given name was in memory of his deceased grandfather, who had been endowed with the biblical name Jerahmiel, one of many respected Jewish prophets.

His namesake, Jerry related a humorous tale about his fifth grade teacher in P.S. 92: One day Mrs. Sweeney told her class they had a new student. *"Won't you stand up and give us your name, please,"* she requested of Jerry. He rose to his feet and announced, "My name is Jerahmiel Sudarsky."

Mrs. Sweeny sat down in shock, proclaiming, "Well, from now on your name shall be Jerry!" That was the source of it for him.

A few years after the historical Wall Street crash, and in the depth of the Great Depression, Jerry's father suffered a substantial financial setback. This was 1934; the year Jerry, his parents and siblings became citizens of the United States. Jerry was sixteen, and in high school.

Mr. and Mrs. Selig Sudarsky made plans to return to Europe, but Jerry opted out. Daring to make it on his own in those bad economic times required the boy to have a strong self-image, and the capacity to strengthen it!

While still in high school he shared a room with a classmate in the other boy's home. The house was across the street from Jerry's Uncle Ephraim.

It was incredibly hard to afford college during the Depression, so how did Jerry Sudarsky manage it? He was on the baseball team in high school and since his coach knew the coach at the University of Iowa he discussed an athletic scholarship for Jerry, who would become a Hawkeye player.

He enrolled in the chemical engineering program, but as it happened the scholarship only paid Jerry's tuition, and since he had no other source of funds to pay his other expenses, he needed a job. Through the school's employment assistance he obtained them. One was in a hospital, washing lettuce an hour a day for 30 cents. Work of that nature moved him through three years of college.

In 1939, at the end of his third year, devoid of money Jerry quit the University, went back to New York and took a job testing yeast in the laboratory of the Atlantic Yeast Company. He also enrolled in Brooklyn Polytechnic University, took evening classes and in 1939 earned a bachelor-of-science degree in chemical engineering.

After that he attended Columbia University for a year. Jerry became plant superintendent of Atlantic Yeast Company, but he worked there only briefly, until 1943.

Just before World War II his parents and two sisters, who were living in Latvia wanted to return to the United States. They made it to Norway, and in 1940 boarded one of the last ships to America before our country entered WWII. When they returned they needed Jerry's help. Living was a struggle, but at least they were *living!*

In January 1943 Selig Sudarsky died at age sixty-two. Jerry's reminiscences included the impact his father had made on him. The older man had been a highly respected member of his family, however, regarding feelings of *closeness*, Jerry found the issue too nebulous to define, too amorphous to explore.

After acquiring his chemical engineering degree Jerry joined the Navy. He was sent to Treasure Island, California, in 1943 where he trained to be a radar specialist. After that the Navy shipped him to the Island of Guam.

He had formed a liking for the Bay Area, so in 1946 when he received his discharge, he decided to settle in San Francisco instead of returning to New York.

He started to manufacture autolyzed yeast, supposedly effective in curing ulcers. He had scraped together $30,000, not very much for the kind of equipment he needed. One piece, a double drum dryer, he couldn't afford to buy brand-new so he started to search the ads for a used one. Wasco was the location of most of the equipment Sudarsky needed, and the way he expected his business to be outfitted when he started the ball rolling.

Just before one of his frequent trips to Los Angeles, someone gave Jerry the phone number of a Wasco friend of his. As he walked into the person's living room, his eyes fell on a beautiful girl by the name of Milly. In the twinkling of an eye he knew he loved her, impetuously popped the marriage question, and Milly said yes to his proposal! Jerry was 22 years old.

The young woman took a job in Los Angeles and after three months they were married. They honeymooned in San Francisco and came to live in Bakersfield. It started out in the Padre Hotel, a place so overrun with cockroaches that they felt impelled to quickly leave.

The next move was to Hotel El Tejon, where they stayed until they found an apartment on Chester Lane. Apartments were scarce right after the war. They furnished the flat with the two thousand dollars Milly had saved.

When an article in a national medical journal reported that autolyzed yeast was *not* good for ulcers Jerry stopped producing it and he looked for another product to manufacture using his drum dryer. In Los Angeles were three beer brewers. He started buying their used and discarded brewers' yeast, reprocessed and sold it to animal feed producers as a nutritional additive for livestock.

Nevertheless, he couldn't make a substantial amount of money because of the expense of hauling material from Los Angeles in trucks, converting it to his product and hauling it back. In fact, things were so tight he would seek payment two hours after delivery.

Little by little he learned about the feed industry. Soon it was about antibiotics; pharmaceutical companies were making and selling to animal feed companies their residual molds and bacteria. It had in it what they claimed was an animal-growth factor. They didn't really know what was in it, but somebody found out it was more effective than brewer's yeast in helping animals grow. Jerry considered making it his business and started looking for microorganisms that might produce residue with a greater animal growth factor.

For a short time Milly Sudarsky worked in her husband's business, but then because of her lack of science training she sought a job elsewhere and found one in the advertising department of Weill's Department Store.

In the late 1950s George Gelman, a biochemist and attorney, who was an associate of one of the company's investors became president of the firm, and in charge of finances and sales. Mr. Sudarsky handled the technology in the still quite small and modestly equipped laboratory of his company called Bioferm.

Sudarsky's technical department discovered a microorganism that could create a good deal of Vitamin B12, but it turned out that Merck owned the patent rights of the chemical molecule, and filed a lawsuit against Jerry's company. An out-of-court settlement resolved *that* issue!

Did the company ever grow to the point of competing with Merck? No, it did not. However, it worked out a deal with Squib Company, and that built up the company, including equipping a substantial research lab.

Because Bioferm's chemical wasn't crystalline B12, manufacturing its products was less costly. Property was bought until five acres were owned. A nearby ice plant was also purchased. Wasco was glad of the company's presence.

Also of relevance to the lives of Jerry and Milly Sudarsky were their contributions to the social and intellectual development of Bakersfield. The scientists that Jerry brought in from New York and Chicago were highly educated and cultured. They promoted the community's increased interest in the classics: music, lectures, theater, museums and other educational and cultural features. Of advancing the business, but their sophisticated, cosmopolitan background enhanced the quality of local life.

Milly Sudarsky was one of the people actively involved in fundraising for the Henrietta Weill Child Guidance Clinic. At first it was through an annual theater party, but that resulted in far too little. In the early 1960s The Guild House was opened and *that* became a very good source of funds. It was first located on Chester Avenue, south of California.

The Sudarsky couple bought a place on 18th Street for The Guild House that could accommodate up to 100 people for lunch. It soon became a good source of money for the Weill Child Guidance Clinic. At the start Milly was one of the cooks in that charming restaurant.

With the help of a man named Charles Jones, chamber music was added. Other people involved were Jack Geiger, the orthopedist, and Dr. George Ablin, a neurosurgeon, who lived in a Frank Lloyd Wright house near the Bakersfield Country Club.

Bioferm Company eventually employed two hundred people. Robert Fisher, one of the 200 was a very good research director. Other skilled research scientists were found through word of mouth, people seeking to relocate.

Some of the scientists had advertised their potential and lived in the east and mid-west. From these sources a fine staff was assembled. Unfortunately, a Chinese scientist the company wanted to hire could neither rent nor buy a house. Kern County's discrimination was shamefully apparent in those days.

Milly was indignant and went to bat for the ill-treated man, with threats to several real estate companies. She accompanied the scientist to Boydston Company and looked at houses with him. When this Asian man found one he liked, it was in the same neighborhood as the Sudarsky home. The real estate agent called her to say, "You know, we can't rent to people like that."

"What do you mean, *people like that?*" Milly snapped back angrily.

"Well, they won't be accepted!" he retorted in a mumble.

Bioferm was doing research for a company in San Jose, and Jerry would fly there every week out of Wasco Airport. His company hired a pilot but didn't own the plane. It belonged to the San Jose company. Things sure were a lot easier for Jerry now that he had become so wealthy through Bioferm. However, he sold it in 1960.

That's when he and Milly had a home built in Bakersfield, on the west side of Oleander, a couple of blocks south of Brundage Lane. Architect Whitney Bigger designed the house. He was not only a fine architect, but a good friend of theirs.

Selig Sudarsky had always been interested in Jewish statehood, and for many years Jerry was a supporter of Hebrew University in Jerusalem. He donated a few million dollars to build some of its facilities.

The Israeli government petitioned him to come there and establish and organize their chemical industries. He and others planned a fundraising drive to raise seven million dollars for developing the university's Life Science compound. Jerry's contributions to Hebrew University were dedicated to the memory of his father. "Things are a real mess in Israel," was how Jerry Sudarsky described the situation he had encountered on a trip there.

Politics made life there difficult for the Sudarskys, and with the passage of a year Jerry had hardly accomplished anything. Things were hard on Milly, but she stuck it out with her dedicated husband. It took five years to get Israel Chemicals Co. off the ground. For those five years Jerry acted as chairman and director of the enterprise. Nevertheless, it ultimately became a huge success, Israel's largest company. In 1972 Jerry left, and joined the board of Daylin Corporation in California, as its Vice Chairman.

In 2002 Jerusalem's Hebrew University awarded him an Honorary Doctorate.

"Israeli life had been difficult for my family," Jerry recalled reflectively: "The job I was doing had been outside my field of expertise. It was more political than technical, and the hardest thing I've done. But in looking back, oh, I'm happy I did it! It was a major accomplishment. I enjoyed my business life, but I'm more proud of what I did for Israel than anything else I've done."

Dr. Norman Levan

(Edited from an article by Dianne Hardisty for *The Bakersfield Californian*)

The keynote of Dr. Norman Levan's philosophy is a precept attributed to Andrew Carnegie. It has had a powerful impact on the doctor's attitude toward his affluence, his now-or-later decision regarding the huge resources he amassed. In his mid-nineties he is not waiting for his demise to result in enormous donations to Bakersfield College, to several universities, and to a hospital in Jerusalem. *He's doing it now!*

His former assistant recalls pointing out that to the doctor that time is running out, and instead of leaving his money to worthy causes in his will, which is what he intended, while he's *alive* it would be nice to pass along the millions he acquired through lifelong investments.

"I wanted to see him smile again. I wanted him to see the buildings his money built, and the programs that would be started. And I wanted to nominate him for an award," she stated.

Carmen succeeded in getting Dr. Levan, a recently retired dermatologist, to start giving away his money. And to smile a lot! The contributions campaign came at the right time, shortly after the death of Dr. Levan's beloved wife Betty. Ages ago the two had met on a tennis court, and before long became the center of each other's life. But the marriage had been childless.

Dr. Levan profoundly missed his wife. Her death narrowed his world to a one-day-a-week medical practice and to reading books many hours a day.

Four huge donations, each nearly six million dollars, went to three colleges and a Jerusalem hospital. With each donation he received accolades, invitations to events, encouragement to watch the construction of buildings and the start of programs in his name.

Although coy about the size of his wealth, it appears the now 94-year-old plans to give more.

Each donation has been structured to reinforce his lifelong belief that no matter what your career, to be a truly educated person you are obliged to study the humanities. Dr. Levan is an outspoken critic of his medical profession; he considers it dominated by people focused solely on science, and the financial remuneration for healing their patients.

The first of his multi-million dollar donations was allocated to Bakersfield College, for developing the Norman Levan Center for the Humanities. Dr. Levan's $5.6 million donation is the largest the college ever received; part of it paying to renovate an existing building that will house the center and its programs. A portion of the money financed the Levan Institute of Life-long Learning, its curriculum comprised of interesting, pleasantly diverting classes for the area's residents 55 and older. Director of this program is Dr. Robert Allison, long-time Bakersfield College professor and administrator.

University of Southern California, where Dr. Norman Levan earned his medical degree, and later headed the Dermatology Department, received a huge donation to fund the Norman Levan Institute for Humanities and Ethics, designed to encourage students to explore innovative ways to the thought process.

Another nearly six million-dollar donation went to Jerusalem's Shaare Zedek Medical Center. It opened the Dr. Norman Levan Center for Humanistic Medicine to promote compassionate care in a hospital more than a century old.

St. John's College in Santa Fe, N.M., received a six million dollar gift to build the Norman and Betty Levan Hall in its Graduate Institute of Liberal Education. The college curriculum is based on studying Great Western books. Levan says the advanced degree he earned from the institute "Changed my life!"

But what started Dr. Levan's "wealth ball" rolling? What made his medical career income grow to untold *millions?* Norman Levan's profession and his passion for studying the humanities are as remarkable as the millions of dollars he accumulated, and now is doling out.

He was born in a Cleveland suburb, where his father, Joseph, worked as a toolmaker. His mother Rose stayed home to raise

Norman, her youngest child, and his three sisters. Their parents divorced, so his mother and teenage son moved to Detroit where his sister Goldie had found a teaching job. This was during the Depression when jobs were scarce. Norman and his mother later joined Goldie on the West Coast.

A good student whose education was jump-started at home by his teacher sister, Norman skipped grades and graduated from high school at age 16. He then entered USC and majored in English. Teased by a brother-in-law that he would end up teaching like his sisters, or selling newspaper ads, Norman took the USC medical school entrance exam, passing it with a top score.

This was remarkable, since Norman had shunned "boring" science classes, and regarded pre-med students "quite dull." But he acquiesced to the school's demand that he complete at least a course in organic chemistry, and went on to earn a medical degree from USC. He served as a medical officer during World War II, with assignments in the Pacific zone of combat.

As a teenager Dr. Levan had been plagued with acne, and it became a factor in choosing dermatology as his medical specialty. It was that, and his wartime experience in treating servicemen with skin impairments.

He established a private practice after the war, and also offered volunteer services, teaching in USC's fledgling Department of Dermatology. When the department expanded, he became a full-time faculty member, and chairman.

In 1961, a group of Bakersfield doctors asked Dr. Levan to travel to Bakersfield once a week to treat the city's difficult cases. When he retired from USC a few years later, he and Betty moved to Bakersfield.

Typical of Dr. Levan's modesty he credits his financial fortune to luck! He said he was motivated into investing 8% of his faculty salary in a university account that would be matched by USC. He kept adding another eight percent of his income to a private investment account. The funds in these accounts became the source of his fabulous wealth.

"That was when the Dow was 400," he reminisced. By the time he started to give out his vast fortune, predominantly to promote education, the Dow Jones Industrial Average had climbed to more than 14,000.

Dr. Levan appeared to have a rather humble attitude in depicting his decision to use his money for charitable donations. But then with his eyes in a twinkle, and a smile on his lips, he quoted 19th century American industrialist Andrew Carnegie: "The man who dies rich dies disgraced." *Dr. Norman Levan sure won't end his life in disgrace!*

Milton Younger

Note: Data about Milton Younger contributed
by Gilbert Gia, Kern County Historical Society (2008).

The father of one of Bakersfield's leading attorneys, Milton Younger, was Louis J. Younger, born in Hungary in 1893. As a teenager of fourteen, Louis had been saddened by the loss of both parents. He migrated to America, arrived in N.Y.C. and from there went to Sumter, S.C. to live with relatives. He drove a peddler's wagon from which he sold candy and cigarettes. Louis left Sumter and traveled back to New York where he worked in a clothing store. His next move was to Los Angeles, and there too his job was in a clothing store. In 1920 he gravitated to Bakersfield where his employment was in a second hand apparel store owned by Mr. and Mrs. Abe Riegler.

Milton's mother Celia was born in Austria. Her parents died before she reached her teens so she came to the United States to live with relatives in Pittsburgh, Pennsylvania, then in Bakersfield with her cousins Abe and Anne Riegler. That is how and where Milton parents met each other and were married.

The birth of his sister Betty preceded his own. Milton was born in Mercy Hospital July 8, 1931. His godfather was Abe Riegler, a man who reveled in gambling and made substantial money on this risky endeavor. His ostentatious appearance included a diamond stickpin he wore on his tie.

Retailing had been a typical industry for America's Jewish immigrants. The lucky ones plied their trade in a store. Those that didn't have the resources to buy or rent a store were either employed in one, or vended clothes from a horse-drawn wagon, or used their two legs to transport wares in a cloth bag they slung on their back! Milton's parents owned and managed Younger Workingman's Store, in the heart of downtown Bakersfield.

Louis Younger had the good fortune to be connected to Abe Riegler who very likely had financed the start of Louis's business. The store was open full-time Mondays through Saturdays, and half time on Sunday. When Milton was twelve he started to assist his dad in the store, approaching potential customers, and promoting a sale with the sophistication of an adult salesperson. Actually, this was not an unusual ability in teenagers, nor was it typical only in "olden days!"

Milton's father had the gift of languages; he spoke several. From the oral communication Milton engaged in with his mother he could tell her intelligence was high enough to have achieved professional status. The bigotry, the political restrictions imposed on Europe's Jews had led to the poverty of huge numbers. Their deprivations included receiving an education. Nevertheless, Milton Younger's "genius genes" were precious endowments from Louis and Celia Younger.

Milton's parent added to this by instilling in their 'prince,' their beloved one-and-only son, a strong sense of self-worth and self-confidence. They kept urging him to fulfill his potential. Milton had been blessed with the greatest treasure, loving parents whole-heartedly aiming for the best of everything for their children.

Milton's 4th grade teacher, Miss Fox also recognized his special qualities, including his creative writing ability. She too focused attention on his future, motivating him to acquire a profession.

Miss Carol, another of his teachers went a step further, recognizing his oral communication ability. She regarded his endless chatter a lawyer's essential characteristic!

The bottom line is that Milton's parents *and* his teachers kept pressing him to *learn, learn, learn.*

That happens to fit right into my firm convictions, my personal viewpoint: that education has been a vital tool for helping the Jewish people survive thousands of years of plight and flight. When peril confronts my people and impels a hasty departure devoid of their material property, to endure the difficulties and uncertainties they're likely to encounter they need two qualities: a sturdy, healthy body and a well-developed, resourceful brain. This is their light and right baggage, a Jew's survival kit!

In childhood Milton took violin lessons. They led not only to an enjoyable hobby but to joining his high school orchestra. He was also in Kern Philharmonic, and he played the violin while a Stanford University student. Appearing in public was a useful experience for his future law career.

His violin teacher supported the theory and practice of communism, so when each lesson ended the two would have a discourse in politics. This was another worthy experience.

Milton's strong interest in politics attracted him into student body activities. Elvin Hedgecock, his debate and speech teacher encouraged that in him and had an important influence. The boy's extroverted personality rendered him a winner when he competed for an office. In about 1948, a time of growing interracial conflicts even among students, Milton joined the interracial council.

While in high school he worked as a sales clerk in his father's store, but at the conclusion of his freshman year at Stanford, and for the next six summers Milton found employment in the oilfields, plugging away seven days a week, twelve hours a day, for the reward of $2 an hour. At the start he was a "production roughneck," for Blue Barnes Core Drilling. Amazingly, he came close to paying expenses of his undergraduate years at Stanford.

Milton's dad, Louis Younger had been strongly involved in the Jewish community. He was one of the founding members of B'nai Jacob Synagogue, and gave lengthy, dedicated service as its president. Milton's mother Celia had been president of B'nai Jacob Sisterhood, her functions also performed with wholehearted devotion to her heritage and religious faith. Louis had been overseer of Jewish benevolence. An Aid Society was always part of Jewish communal life.

In 1957 Milton was admitted to the Bar. He had graduated from Stanford University Law School, joined the Army Reserves and was stationed in the Presidio of San Francisco. When his stint in the military was over, he came back to Bakersfield and began his law career with Morris Chain. At first he dealt with criminal cases but then with the kind he liked, and made his life's work: personal injury claims.

"One of the proudest things I've done as a lawyer was to represent people injured in the oilfield, the result of defective equipment. It's a misunderstood point of law that you can't sue your employer for injuries. Workers' Compensation isn't much better than welfare, public assistance. I was one of the first in this area, to secure compensation from manufacturers for men who had lost an arm or leg because equipment did not have safety guards. Soon the industry's interest in protecting employee safety changed; a feature that no doubt saved the lives of many men who might've been killed or maimed." Milton Younger.

Marsha Parr

To make an occasional day more cheerful for the temple's shut-ins *(No, I don't mean 'shut-downs' or 'shut-ups!')* the Caring Committee sends a visitor for the needful member's enjoyment, perhaps a bit of live-wire conversation. I view *my* visitor as worthy of top rating; Marsha Parr who started her visits on her own, not through the Caring Committee, really adds to the pleasure, interest, and provocative thinking of my bed-bound life! We're both members of Temple Beth El book club, and now that my vision has become seriously impaired Marsha reads the monthly book selection to me.

She is a Temple Beth El Board member, its Recording Secretary of long-standing, a Sisterhood member, and she sings in the choir. Marsha belongs to "Chaverah," a group of Temple Beth El men and women that spends one Saturday a month together, alternating in each other's home. Having recently discontinued morning services, the group begins with lunch, followed by a bracing discussion. The theme relates to something connected to Judaism's culture and history, or to a political or sociological topic currently at issue. It draws to a close shortly before dinner is served. Following the meal is a short Havdalah ceremony marking the close of the Sabbath and its condition of purity, and a return to the profane: the other six days of the week.

In her secular life Marsha plays an active role in the Retired Teachers Association, the 3Rs, a retired ladies-only school admistrators group, and the U. C. Irvine alumni association. What pairs Marsha and me so well is the burning and yearning for learning we have in common. The desire to keep expanding our knowledge and understandings is a major factor in the beauty of her life and mine.

Beyond all *these* links in Marsha's varied and very active life is her love, and deep devotion to her family. Their needs and desires are always in the forefront of her attention. She is steadfast and faithful to one of the highest values and ideals of the Jewish faith: *family!*

I keep trying to figure it out, but I'm still a bit puzzled: Is Marsha symbolic of the Star of David, or is the Star of David a symbol of Marsha Parr? Oh well, it doesn't matter I guess; whenever I happen to see the 6 point star, Marsha comes to mind. When I'm with her, an image of the star often looms up in my thoughts!

A Chicago department store by the name of Goldblatts became a metaphoric Cupid for two of its young employees: Albert Abram Kaplan, born and raised in New York, and Bess Rosenthal, born and raised in Winnepeg, Manitoba, Canada. They met on the job, fell in love, married New Year's Day 1941, and became the source of our Marsha! For Albert this marriage was the 2nd time around. A son from his first marriage was 10 years old at the time.

In regard to the couple's formal education, Bess had finished high school but the Depression precluded college. Even high school was out of the question for Albert, first of his parents' five sons.

Marsha was born in Chicago and attended kindergarten there. But then the family moved to Los Angeles to be close to Bess's mother and sisters. Elementary, junior high and high school for Marsha were in Los Angeles. She graduated from high school in 1965 *third* in a class of 745 boys and girls! Marsha had been in a variety of her high school's clubs and organizations.

She entered UC Irvine the year it opened, graduated with a degree in Comparative Literature and a minor in Social Sciences.

She entered USC under the auspices of the Teacher Corps, and earned a Masters' degree in Education with a minor in Spanish, acquiring elementary and secondary school credentials.

Though her two Jewish parents both had a substantial background in the faith system, Marsha had been deprived of studying its history, laws and rituals in her own childhood. Her parents would've liked to become members of their neighborhood synagogue and to enroll Marsha and her sister in its religion school. However, there was a prohibitively high, non-negotiable fee for the *'privilege,'* one they simply couldn't afford! Marsha is pretty certain that as a consequence her dad never again set foot in a synagogue--except for his grandson's bar mitzvah service (Marsha's nephew.)

Bess, Marsha's mom, had grown up in a kosher home, but since it was a rather costly religious ritual it was abandoned during the Depression. Marsha remembers that they did observe the High Holy Days, and also Hanukkah and Pesach, but that was about it.

Although candles weren't kindled on the eve of the Sabbath, the family treasured Grandma's old brass candlesticks. Marsha's parents fulfilled a major obligation, instilling ethical behavior in their girls, including the imperative of service to others, bedrock of the Jewish faith.

Right after grad school Marsha married Rafael Valdez, a Mexican man born of a very Catholic mother. The couple moved to Bakersfield in 1973, where Marsha became a bilingual teacher. In 1975 she gave birth to a baby boy they named David, but Marsha divorced her son's father in 1979. She remained a single parent for ten years.

After eight years of teaching in the bilingual program, she became a reading lab teacher with the California Demonstration Programs at Sierra JHS. Three years later she became curriculum specialist in Emerson JHS. She then left BCSD, and became an assistant principal in a Delano school. After another three years she moved to Shelbyville, Illinois, hometown of her second husband Guy Parr, and was a middle school principal for ten years. The last four years before Marsha's retirement were spent teaching Spanish in a rural Illinois high school.

In 1989 Guy converted to the Jewish religion and practiced the Reform mode of worship. But adopting the faith had been done principally to please the wife he loved so intensely, and Marsha soon faced up to the fact that this was a breach of ethics, Judaism's foundation!

Marsha asserts: "Sometime after divorcing my first husband I joined Bakersfield's Reform congregation, Temple Beth El, and saw to it that David was brought up in a Jewish home. My first close contact with other synagogue members was while I was part of a group forming a cooperative pre-school. Then it was in a circle of divorced people. My next close contacts came when I joined the choir.

I enrolled David in the temple's religious school and Jewish camp in summer. David received two camperships that made this possible, thanks to generous congregants. His bar mitzvah and confirmation services were under the leadership of Rabbi Steven Peskind. I was elected to the Board of Trustees, and have been Recording Secretary for several terms, served on Religious Practices Committee, joined The Chaverah, attended rabbi's classes, and joined the Sisterhood. Now I read to my dear friend Shirley Ann Newman, a fellow member of the TBE Book Club. Shirley Ann's impaired eyesight renders this an impossible task for her to accomplish on her own.

While living in Illinois my husband and I had attended worship services at the Mattoon Jewish Community Center (the smallest reform congregation in the U.S., and for a while at Moses Montefiore synagogue of Bloomington, Illinois.

Guy's death from cancer occurred almost five years ago, and four months later, I moved back to Bakersfield. Temple Beth El was a *major* reason. I have known quite a few synagogues in California and Illinois, none growing as meaningful to me, none *ever* displaying the caring, generous character of Temple Beth El.

Having the free time of a retired person, I am engaged not only in religious life, but in secular community life. I play an active role in the Kern Division of California Retired Teachers, currently co-editor of its newsletter. The organization promotes scholarship funding for aspiring teachers, and grants for first year teachers. I have given three years of instruction to the Kern Adult Literacy program. I belonged to the Bakersfield Keynotes, a local singing group that raises scholarship money for music students.

Keeping very busy has its reasons: The pain of losing my husband made it necessary that I fill my time with meaningful activity and with people. And furthermore, in recognition of my life's treasured benefits and blessings, for example a fine education and admirable upbringing, I feel that as a retiree, it's time to give back. I am seeking to justify the use of this earth's resources, of taking up space on it! This philosophical perspective motivated me to work on behalf of my synagogue and of our overall community, the two constituting 'my home.'

"My son and his wife Brandi are raising their three young daughters with a commitment to the Jewish faith. The oldest girl, Alexandra, celebrated her bat mitzvah in January 2012. The younger two are enrolled in religion school in Reno, Nevada, close to where David is currently stationed. He has thus far given thirteen years of service to our country's Navy, and wherever he is transferred, he, his wife and daughters join a synagogue. David also joins the men's club if his temple has one. He has helped in the congregation's Judaica gift shop, and if needed he serves as the non-ordained rabbi when at sea. He is currently co-music leader of religious school. Fried latkes are one the many joys of Jewish life for my son; he consumes them with gusto and prepares them for temple functions. The close connection my son feels to his ancestral heritage is my legacy.

"Judaism grows increasingly important to me. On June 2, 2012 I had the honor of participating in a b'not mitzvah service with four other ladies. For all of us it was a deeply emotional experience. The flowing fullness of spirit that Temple Beth El members display has certainly brought a positive change to my life!"

Nancy McCombs, Janet Blumberg, Pamela Elisheva,
Marsha Parr, Jill Egland

"Farewell, Rebbe Stan Simrin,
Devoted Torah Teacher!"

Note: The following is an edited version of Michael Miller's
endearing tribute to the memory of Stanley Simrin.

One of Stan's passions was teaching his Torah Study Class, on
Thursday evenings. We had these weekly meetings in the library,
for over fifteen years. I can't imagine a more dedicated teacher!
Stan always had an agenda, a point he wanted to emphasize, a
particular lesson he wanted to convey.

This was not readily apparent just by reading the text. He used
the Socratic method of teaching, posing provocative questions
about what his students *thought* the text meant. And even though
we read the same verses over and over, it was very difficult to
come up with the answers Stan was actually *seeking*. However, if
you did get it right, if you got lucky, he would honor you with his
coveted "BINGO!" The class would then congratulate the

"Bingoee." Sometimes we even lobbied for a Bingo we thought someone had earned.

Stan never wavered or fell out of focus from the lesson he had carefully planned. One evening a student, convinced she knew the right answer to a question, raised her hand, and Stan gave her the "go ahead" nod. The woman (Guess who? Your author, Shirley Ann Newman!) embarked on a lengthy, detailed response, anxiously awaiting a precious *Bingo.* Imagine her embarrassment and how crushed she felt to hear a resounding "Wrong!"

"But Stan," she protested, "I really believe I'm right." And Stan said like the placating parent of a kindergartner, "Well of coarse you do, or you wouldn't have said it."

Stan made us *engage* the Torah, and wrestle with every word, deeply enriching our lives in the process. We would discuss the lessons on our way home and whenever or wherever we met a Torah classmate.

Frequently, as a means of confirming a Judaic precept Stan would iterate a charming anecdote he had derived from our fascinating ancient heritage. One of those tales became synonymous with our beloved teacher. The storyline was about a few Rabbis arguing over which stones a certain baker could use in his oven. Well, it turns out that those particular stones were not even available where the baker lived. In any event, the man had been dead some fifty years. But that didn't halt the heated conflict!

Rabbi Eliezar proclaimed: "If I'm right, may the Carob tree outside move forty feet. The men rushed to the door, threw it open, and peered outside. Sure enough, the Carob tree *had* moved forty feet!

The other sages shook their heads from side to side, and gave their negative response in a chorus. "We don't take our law from Carob trees!" Thus the arguing continued until finally Rabbi Eliezar uttered vehemently, "If I am right, may a heavenly voice proclaim so." Sure enough, a heavenly voice proclaimed, "Rabbi Eliezar is right."

Whereupon the other sages reacted with, "We no longer take our law from heavenly voices. God himself gave us the law at Mount Sinai."

Can't you just picture the puzzled look on those pale creviced faces of the long-bearded fellows seated on rickety wooden benches, across the table from each other, in a one-room hut? Oy!

When the Torah class met on Thursday evening to study under Stan's tutelage, it was as though we were being transported, carried back to that special far off land of long, long ago.

None of us, Stan, will ever forget sitting across from one another, debating, arguing over what this or that verse in the Torah was *really* trying to feed into our minds and spirits. Oh sure, we'll continue to attend weekly classes, much better prepared as a result of the insights you imbued in us.

As Barry Goldner once said "Stan is the lion at the gate, guarding our sacred traditions and eternal values." I can't even imagine a more thoughtful, a more learned sage, than our own Stan Simrin. He was a gift God himself blessed us with.

Sadly, there is nothing we can do for you now in recompense for that myriad of gilded hours at the library table. Nor for those life-improving lessons you lovingly instilled in us, that major precept: *Justice* in all forms.

Not only we the students but you too, Rebbe Stan, enjoyed the surprise element of your classes. By the time a Torah lesson ended Thursday evening, it had proven to be a great source of satisfaction to Stan, to realize something new, interesting, and profoundly *different* had been acquired by his students.

"Yes, We Should Tell Them, But When?"

Is teaching about the Holocaust too traumatic for school children prior to college age? Lately we have been doing more to familiarize Middle and High School students with different cultures, even minority ones that are inclined to experience painful discrimination. After all, not everyone is a *WASP,* White Anglo-Saxon Protestant!

We tell about the disadvantaged in our own country and the social programs we've instituted in recent decades that tries and make a more level playing field for the not-well educated, the poor, the disabled, and the aged. But we also try not to tread too heavily on the feelings of young schoolchildren. We have certainly soft-pedaled teaching about slavery, and the wiping out of our country's natives.

For decades there's been a difference of opinion, level-headed debates and politely expressed conflicts among teachers, school administrators and the parents of school children, over the wisdom of pouring into children's tender-hearts the evils, the horrific deeds the Nazis imposed on the Jewish people of Europe in the nineteen thirties and first half of the nineteen forties, until their defeat in the Second World War. Adolf Hitler's objective was a total annihilation of the world's Jewish people.

A social studies teacher in Washington Middle School of Bakersfield presented her early teen-age students with a pretty open and frank understanding of the painful subject. And then, to assess their attitudinal reaction to such an appalling situation she followed it up with a project: She made posters filled with nasty, ugly, bigoted words that played into their senses and emotions, prompting angry, indignant responses from the boys and girls around the age of thirteen. She also asked them to compose poems that expressed their feelings about the treatment Jewish people were receiving. The children's sentiments showed deep compassion for the afflicted, and anger against the ones imposing it on them. After requesting and receiving parental permission, here are a few poems our *"mini menschen"* composed:

By Nick Hernandez:

I Know Torture!

I know torture
I hear cries of the Jews
I hear the evil laugh of the Nazis
I hear the Jews being beaten to the ground
I hear the sizzle of the Jews' branded skin
I know torture
I see Jews being shot to the ground
I see the numerals being burnt in the Jews' skin
I see blood dripping on the ground

I know torture
I smell the rotten blood on the ground
I smell the death of Jews
I know torture
I feel the sizzling numeral in my skin
I wonder how it would feel to die?
I know torture

By Eneida Nunez:

I Know Torture!

I know torture
I hear Nazis insulting Jews
I hear screaming for mercy
Then, the "S-S-S-S" of the gas chamber

I hear Hitler laughing and laughing
I Know Torture
I see numerals in the skin of people
I see branded skin
I see hatred
I Know Torture I smell gas
I smell death
I Know Torture
I wonder: Why not fight back?
I feel sorrow; I know torture

By Darlene Cervantes:

I Know Torture!

I know torture
I hear crying of sorrow
I hear the sizzle of burning skin
I hear shouting and cursing

I know torture
I see people dead on the ground
I see maggots feasting upon the bodies
I see people getting beaten

I know torture
I smell the gas of gas chambers
I smell decaying bodies
I know torture; I feel unwanted
I feel alone…I know torture!

By Patrick Trihey:

I Know Pain!

I Know Pain
I hear screams
I hear the whip
I hear the taunting of the S.S. soldiers
I hear the general moan of the entire camp;
I know pain

I see the blood on the S.s. boots
I see the bodies in the mud
I see the walking dead
I see the grinning and bloody S.S. man
I know pain
I taste the dust and decay
I smell the stench of unwashed bodies
I smell the smoke from Nazi cigarettes;
I know pain

I sense death is near
I feel the pain of the camps
I wonder how long I'll live.
I know pain!

I mustn't think I'm fighting that final fray,
Though gloom and dark are defeating a sunny day!
My dreams of the future have been clouded in fear,
My trudging steps drowning out light ones of good cheer.
How I'll miss our lands green with grass and leafy trees,
Even our northern lands of freezing cold, snow and icy rain.
If I *do* gain admittance into heaven it will be in great pain
From deep sorrows, strong anger, uncontrollable disdain.
God, why *did* You permit the Nazis to spray

My blood on Your land?
Ah well, despite the evils You overlook,
My Jewish faith will still stand!

S.A. N. (Adapted from *The Partisan's Song)*

PART FOUR

Spiritual Philosophy and Leadership

Philosophic Essays and Spiritual Leadership

"It's Your Call!"

There's a quip about one fellow saying to another: "I started having the most intensely spiritual experiences lately. And now, at last, I found God!"

"Really?" replies his friend, "Gosh, that surprises me. I didn't even know He was lost!"

No, He wasn't lost; God is *never* lost. Sadly, people often lose their *awareness* of Him. Or they just never acquire it. Before we're born, immediately upon conception God is right there to cheer us on, and guide us to the start of life. He's there during gestation and He's there to welcome the newcomer into this world. It is at the very moment the fetus pokes his head out that God greets him with His kiss. The gesture is of huge significance; God is implanting the soul He chose for this child.

I was surprised to hear this from my old friend. We usually discuss some current political issue, or talk casually about what each of us watched on TV the evening before, or about the bargain one of us was lucky to find last week in the shopping mall. Until that day we had *never* discussed religion, never even mentioned *God!* However, I don't think I'll ever forget this particular day when, like a bolt out of the blue, my friend started to confide in me that she had been feeling "empty," lonely and useless, but then, suddenly her emotions brightened.

"It was like when a day starts out cloudy and gloomy and all of a sudden the sun starts to glow, making everything bright and cheerful," was Mildred's metaphor that moved our conversation to the spiritual.

I refuted her initial comment, challenging it with, "Oh, yeah? If He really *is* with us when we we're born, when we make our first appearance in the world, and later on when we need His help and guidance to make the best and wisest decisions, like when I started college what subject I should major in? I picked history and can't find a job, when all the kids that chose chemistry and computer science are on their way to becoming millionaires? Why didn't He give *me* some good advice, huh, Mildred?"

"Listen, Vivian, anyone with half a brain knows majoring in computer science will give you lots of opportunities. Surely, you don't need to waste God's time on something like *that,* for heaven's sake!"

"You're right, that was silly and childish of me. But I know someone who ruined his early adult life on drugs and booze, and my brother's friend that recently went through a knockdown drag-out divorce, and is taking his hostility out on the two children that resulted from the couple's embattled marriage. Where was God for them? How come He didn't stick around and scoop these *shmucks* out of the soup?"

"He *was* there, but waiting to be *asked* for help. God doesn't just barge in on your privacy. He's respectful and polite. You have to appeal to Him. It's what *prayer* is about!"

"What's Next, If Anything?"

Mystical Jews believe in reincarnation, that a dead person's soul is re-installed in the body of a baby just before it's born. This means death is not the end of human existence. However, other, more modern forms of the Jewish faith system focus mostly on the here-and-now rather than on an afterlife.

As to Orthodox Jews who aren't Kabbalists, believers in the mystical, they even believe that the soul of a righteous person goes to Heaven. Or that it's just on hold until the Messiah comes, and then they'll be made *totally* pure, and resurrected. Regarding the soul of someone who commits evil deeds in his lifetime, Orthodox Jews even believe what Christians do, that he will suffer in a place like Hell. But in the Jewish religion, Hell is a recycle factory, not a place of eternal burning.

Some scholars maintain that belief in an afterlife is a late development to Judaism, so since there's no clear evidence of it in religion's early history it should be rejected, or at best considered a supposition, not an absolute. The reason is that the Torah teaches us our good deeds are rewarded and evil ones are punished while we're alive, not left for when we die.

However, do we not have endless examples to the contrary? That many selfish, greedy people are extremely wealthy, powerful and privileged while hordes of kind, caring, generous people are poor and powerless? So for me it's hard to believe that the good are always God's beneficiaries and that He consistently punishes bad people.

Nevertheless, there *are* some statements in the Torah that clearly comfort even a skeptic like me. One is that after death we unite with people we felt close to in life. The Tanakh has more specificity about that issue.

That resurrection of all the dead will happen when the Messiah arrives is a basic precept in traditional Judaism. It was a belief held by the Pharisees, our more learned and intellectual ancestors. It is also *implied* in various verses, and that too was enough to convince the Pharisees. Ordinary Israelites, the Sadducees, rejected it as an idle guess. Reform Jews do too.

But it may really mean a spiritual afterlife, not a physical one. Oh well, at least when (or *if*) the Messiah really does come, we can expect the world to grow peaceful again, and people whose lives were spent in deprivation to have eternal sufficiency. Part of making the world perfect again is reshaping the righteous dead to a state of blissful love and harmony.

What happens to the evil dead is amorphous. Of course, they will be punished for having disobeyed God, but the severity of the punishment, and whether their punishment is prolonged, and whether in the end they too are is redeemed, all *those* issues are not clarified through erudite sources. In Judaism "life-after-death" is not unveiled with any convincing, absolute firmness.

"Can You Wait? You Better!"

One of our Torah precepts is based on an agricultural restriction. It's that the fruit of a tree must not be picked the first three years. Once the three years have passed we're free to enjoy the fruit. We should, though, express our thanks for the blessing!

The Adam and Eve tale exemplifies our lack of self-control, the foundation of not just emotional, but spiritual growth. The remission of those first human beings, Adam and Eve, was their uncontrollable desire for instant gratification. Although the biblical anecdote is famous, what is not so well known is that the fruit of the forbidden tree was not intended to be endlessly withheld from them. They just had to *delay* their pleasure.

The three years we must wait before eating the fruit of any tree is a reminder of the importance of building restraint, of learning self-control, the ability to rein in our desires of the moment.

The delicacies of the world *were* given to us for enjoyment, but the power to discipline our impulses reminds us that there is more to life than *only* the pleasurable. Creating boundaries around our indulgences helps us become conscious of, and focused on a larger issue. Happiness should be viewed as one segment of an existence filled with other features, a whole series of values, especially the acquisition of a higher purpose. Greed, hedonism are destructive characteristics. They create emptiness, a life that failed to fulfill what God expects of you.

"Why do you want to study Torah while standing on one leg?"

"So I'll Fall For It! Hah, hah."

There's a legend about a Gentile approaching a Sage by the name of Shammai and making the following request: "I'd like you to convert me to Judaism, but it is on condition that you teach me the entire Torah while I stand on one leg."

Shammai frowned in disapproval and chased the man away. The Gentile then approached Hillel with the same request. Hillel responded in the affirmative: Yes, he will do it. After pondering the challenge he encapsulated the Torah into a single sentence. *"What is hateful to you do not do to anyone else."*

The Gentile's request is puzzling, isn't it? What was the man truly seeking? Why did Hillel and Shammai react differently? How was Hillel's responsive precept equivalent to the entire Torah?

To better understand this episode we need to look at Niddah 30b in the Talmud. It is written that while a child is in the womb it is taught the entire Torah, however, at birth an angel strikes the newborn, causing it to completely forget what it had learned.

The reason this happens is that later on when we study Torah we'll be eager to learn it better, more fully, more deeply. And then through years of serious study it will become more meaningful. When Hillel recited that single statement, but very important principle to the Gentile, the man's curiosity was aroused: What was the source of such a demanding requisite in Judaism? Now his interest was sparked to study Torah in its entirety.

Torah study rests on two principles: that God gave us the potential to understand; it is a seed to be nurtured. Because Jewish learning tends to be done with diligence and toil it shaped us into the People of the Book. We need to feel motivated not only to learn, but to learn properly, so that we bring our purpose on this Earth to fruition.

The first principle of Torah study is that God loves those who *want to* study Torah after the head start He gave us and that at least makes it possible. The second is strength, for when we build up our drive to learn more and more, we're building a vast storehouse of knowledge. Hence, we grow in fortitude and knowledge.

"Do not place a stumbling block before the blind."
Leviticus 19:14

The literal meaning of this precept is clear enough: If one suffers a loss of eyesight, either total or substantially diminished, he is hindered from seeing an impediment in his path. The consequence can be a collision with the unseen object, one that results in injury. It may even prove fatal. Any property he might be transporting at the time could also be harmed, destroyed, or lost. He may be prevented from reaching an important destination, or be seriously delayed from doing so. There may be short term, long term or even permanent consequences from the deliberate or thoughtless placement of an obstruction in his way.

If the impediment were put there thoughtlessly the likelihood is that the offender was too self-absorbed to consider it might cause an accident. But if it were done deliberately perhaps it was for one of two reasons: Feelings of resentment, even hostility, a desire for revenge or retribution. Or ambition for personal gain achievable by harming an opponent, disadvantaged by impaired vision.

It's what the words and statements imply and connote that matter. This requires profound scrutiny, and an analysis of their context.

A single word, a phrase, an idea is often studied, interpreted, and written about in a lengthy volume, even in a series of volumes! A truly scholarly person never has the arrogance to say: "I know the Bible."

The connotation of not placing a stumbling block before the blind is that if you know of risks to someone *not* likely to know he's about to encounter a pitfall, you are obliged to warn him, even remove the peril if you can. Here's a few examples:

Ambiguous or obscure language in a contract, a sales pitch, or in advertising may be inadvertent, or inept in expressing oneself. But it could be a deliberate attempt to deceive, mislead, or entrap.

A concealed defect in a product one is selling or promoting may have a complexity that defies understanding by anyone lacking the expertise of specialized training.

Pharmaceuticals frequently contain a myriad of ingredients, many of which are expressed only with confusing chemical names. If there's anything known or even suspected to have any harmful effects and if this isn't disclosed to the trusting consumer, it violates this principle. New, untested products are often urged on buyers who trust the company, and government regulatory power. If the businessperson thinks only of financial gain and puts the consumer at risk by not doing enough testing or when he knows there's a hazard but puts it on the market, he violated the edict.

Scams and schemes play into the slowing down of old people's self-protection power. They're also used to prey on the young and inexperienced, and those who have cultural disadvantages such as language or low levels of education. Enticements that lead the innocent and unsophisticated along a path beset with peril are insidiously evil.

These include businesses, organizations and cults that exploit people desperate for relief from problems by luring them into consuming harmful substances like alcohol and narcotics. They offer these as an escape, a release from their emotional pain. There are predators that capitalize on the fantasies of the innocent, or the loneliness and insecurities of the elderly, or their reduced ability to know someone is committing fraud, enticing the unsuspecting to walk the path of an impediment: a stumbling block before the blind. Scripture warns evildoers: "You shall be held accountable!"

Bakersfield's Three Jewish Congregations:
B'nai Jacob, Temple Beth El, Chabad

In 1988, the Leadership Council of Conservative Judaism issued an official statement of belief, *Emet Ve-Emunah: Statement of Principles of Conservative Judaism*. *Emet Ve-Emunah* affirms belief in God and in the divine inspiration of the Torah; however, it also affirms the legitimacy of *multiple* interpretations of these issues. The commission found that there were seven main beliefs shared by representatives from different segments of the movement:

"In the beginning God ..." Though we differ in our perceptions and experiences of reality, we affirm our faith in God as the Creator and Governor of the universe. His power called the world into being; His wisdom and goodness guide its destiny. Of all the living creatures we know, humanity alone, created in His image and endowed with free will, has been singled out to be the recipient and bearer of God's revelation. The product of this human/Divine encounter is the Torah, the embodiment of God's will revealed pre-eminently to the Jewish people through Moses the Prophets, the Sages, and the righteous and wise of all nations. Hence, by descent and destiny, each Jew stands under the Divine command to obey His will.

Second, we recognize the authority of the *Halakha,* (law) which has never been monolithic or immovable. On the contrary, as modern scholarship has abundantly demonstrated, the *Halakha* has grown and developed through changing times, and diverse circumstances. This life-giving attribute is doubly needed today in a world of dizzying changes.

Third, pluralism has characterized Jewish life and thought through the ages. This is reflected in the variety of views and attitudes of the biblical legislators, priests, prophets, historians, psalmists and wisdom teachers, the hundreds of controversies among the rabbis of the Talmud, and in the codes and responsa of their successors. Any attempt to suppress freedom of inquiry and the right of dissent is basically a foreign import to Jewish life.

Fourth, the rich body of Halakha and of Aggada and the later philosophic and mystical literature, all seeking to come closer to God's presence are a precious resource for deepening the spiritual life of Israel and humankind.

Fifth, all the aspects of Jewish law and practice are designed to underscore the centrality of ethics in Jewish life.

Sixth, Israel is not only the Holy Land where our faith was born; it plays an essential role in our present and our future. Israel is a symbol of the unity of the Jewish people, the homeland for millions of Jews, and a unique arena for Jewish creativity. Together with responsibility to Israel is our obligation to strengthen and enrich Jewish life in the Diaspora.

Seventh, Jewish law and tradition, if properly understood and interpreted, *will* enrich Jewish life and help shape the world closer to prophetic visions of God's Kingdom.

Conservative Judaism affirms monoism, one God. However, its members have varied beliefs about the nature of God, and no one perception is mandated.

Conservative Jews hold a wide array of views on the subject of revelation. Many Conservative Jews reject the traditional Jewish idea that God literally dictated the words of the Torah to Moses. But they hold the traditional Jewish belief that God inspired later prophets to write the rest of the Tanakh.

Many Conservative Jews believe God had inspired Moses, in the manner of later prophets. Conservative Jews who reject the concept of verbal revelation believe that God revealed His Will to Moses and to other prophets in a *non*verbal form; that God's revelation did not include the particular words of the divine texts.

Conservative Judaism is comfortable with the theory that the Torah was redacted from several earlier sources. The movement's rabbinic authorities and official Torah commentary affirm that Jews should use modern critical literary and historical analysis to understand how the Bible developed.

Conservative Judaism rejects the Orthodox position of a direct verbal revelation of the Torah. However, Conservative Judaism also rejects the Reform view: that the Torah was not revealed but was Divinely *inspired.*

Long before this epic council meeting a Conservative Jewish congregation was formed in Bakersfield.

Art Kay & Hy Seiden: *"The Birth of Congregation B'nai Jacob"*

(Edited by Shirley Ann Newman, April, 2012)

The organizational meeting of Congregation B'nai Jacob was held in 1915, but the site of the meeting is not certain. Some say it was in the home of Al Sandler, who accepted chairmanship of the embryo congregation. Others are sure it was in one of Bakersfield's several lodge halls: Taylor's Hall or Eagle's Hall (corner 19th and Chester.)

It *is* known that from 1910 to 1914, *Rosh Hashanah* and *Yom Kippur* services were held in Woodmen of the World's Hall (18th and Eye Sts.) From 1914 to 1916 they were in Taylor's Hall and from 1918 until 1920 in Knights of Pythias Hall.

The first elected president was Morris Rudneck. Other members to hold the office were: Joseph Alpine, A. Becker, Barney Bergensteen, Henry Bergman, Benny Bemson, Abe and Joseph Chain, Jacob Farbstein, J. Garfinckle, Sam Goldman (of Taft), brothers Max, Morris and Willie Himovitz, Charles Hirsh, Samuel Kessler, Joe Landson, Joe Malamud, Israel (Jerry) Miller, Fred Mooney, Teddy Nussbaum, Sam Orloff (of Taft), Abe Riegler, Meyer Rifkin, Samuel Rosenthal, Dave Rottenberg, Isaac Rubin, Oscar Rudnick, Abe and Harry Sandler, Samuel Silverman, Morris Sommers, Joseph Topper, Alphonse Weill, and George White.

B'nai Jacob Sisterhood was organized in 1919. Its first president was Mary Himovitz. Her successor was Mrs. Pincus Katz, renowned for her culinary abilities.

In 1920 the congregation bought the Bakersfield Woman's Club building for $5,500 (16th and H Streets). It was a large sum in those days and took two fundraisers to acquire $3,900. The

154

balance was a loan from Arthur S. Crites, president of the Security Bank, at 5% interest.

On the 2nd day of Rosh Hashana, 1920 the membership voted in favor of buying the building for Bakersfield's first synagogue. Rabbi David Rosenthal was engaged.

Sisterhood's first members were Mollie Bemson, Anna Daniels, Rae Fingerhut, Mary Himovitz, Marie Himovits, Pauline Himovitz, Mrs. Katz, Rose Landson, Eva Rubin, Fannie Shapiro, Hanna Sommers and Goldie Winer.

In 1921 Morris Himovitz was elected president of the Congregation and Goldie Winer Sisterhood president.

Rabbi Cooperson replaced Rabbi Rosenthal in 1925, followed by Rabbi B.J. Riseman, Rabbi Joseph Goodman and in 1929, Rabbi Benjamin Cohen. Profound of thought and eloquent in speech was Rabbi Cohen. A sermon of his was published in the March 21, 1931 edition of *The Bakersfield Californian*.

"The Humble and the Proud:" ...*and the serpent said unto the woman, ye shall not surely die; for God doth know that in the way ye eat thereof then your eyes shall be opened, and ye shall be as God, knowing good and evil. Genesis III 4-5.*

With this speech of the serpent, began man's downfall. He was tempted to pride, to rise above his station, to be even as his Creator. How much pain and sorrow has foolish pride and worthless aspiration caused in this world! How many people forget God when they get a little material wealth! How many people in their hour of need, call on God to save themselves or their dear ones, and how soon after the crisis is God forgotten. Though money can do much that is good, it cannot buy everything. And saddest of all, so many people are led astray either morally or spiritually by the Golden Calf.

There are many that give freely to the poor, and comfort many with their money. Then there are many that forget that they are only a clay-bound spirit like many another clay-bound spirit, and these people sitting on their insecure pedestal of money, think themselves above the "common run" of people.

Yet it is strange that the same troubles, the same sickness, the same death, the same growing old, attack these demi-gods, sufficient unto themselves, and often it attacks them sooner than it does their poorer but less dissolute brethren.

155

Until the darkest hour, when a dear one is sinking fast, or overwhelming troubles are unleashed in all their fury, do these higher-ups remember they are only human, and pray to God that has infinite mercy, infinite compassion, and infinite forgiveness.

When man shall stop trying to "be as God, knowing good and evil" when man, in the last analysis realizes that by the grace of the Almighty, he was placed on an earth with many another human, and entitled to what he really makes for himself, no more. Then shall man have been made as perfect as is possible.

We all know the man that feels himself entitled to a fortune or special privileges because his great-grandfather was distantly related to some famous person. How boring it is to see a cheap picture of bombast and bloated self-confidence parade the honors of his ancestors for which they worked!

He is usually a mixture of cheap cocksureness and loudness. Because some person remote from the conceited descendent has done something that helped his country, this caricature shines in reflected glory, he fondly believes, his ancestor probably groans in his grave.

Man! Humble thyself before the Lord. Be proud of the works that thou hast earned by honest works. Be proud of thy reputation, be proud of thy children, but in thy pride be humble before God, even if thou art an Emperor, for he put the poorest laborer on earth as well as thee.

Do not forget God when great fortunes have been amassed, do not figure it "smart" to deck one's self with tinfoil, and pass it for silver. For some day, someone will brush the tinfoil off the bright shining cloths and one will be but one of a billion mortals standing before God.'

This sermonette is not intended to make one fear having honest pride. But to consider one's self above his fellow, to think that one is of a higher class than one's neighbor, to look at the sky while one walks over a cliff is a sin.

There are some people who are selfish, rationalizing it with: 'If I don't give, there are plenty of others that will.'

Rabbi's concluding words were, in effect: *In that darkest hour, one of crisis, even the agnostic isn't afraid to dirty his knees on the floor, admitting to himself there is a Being higher than humankind.*

Desperate for guidance and help he appeals to the Being he declined to recognize before.

Congregation B'nai Jacob created a series of cemetery plots on a portion of land donated by Charles Cohen, and consecrated the designated area September 1921. In 1927 the synagogue building was expanded to accommodate enough space for a religion school, a meeting hall and the rabbi's office.

Note: for a full listing of Congregation B'nai Jacob's rabbis please refer to: *We Brought Sinai to San Joaquin, story of the Jews of Kern County* by Shirley Ann Newman;

In 1939 B'nai Jacob rabbi Jack Levy received a cherished award. An article about it appeared in the Sept.7, 1939 edition of *The Bakersfield Californian:* Rabbi Jack Levy Returns With A Fine Prize. *Rabbi Jack Levy, spiritual leader of Bakersfield's Congregation B'nai Jacob, has just returned from San Francisco after winning a national prize. He had been honored at a conference of the Oxford Graduate Writers and Speakers Association.*

In the introduction of his address to the attendees he declared with strong conviction that under the concept of government by the people, the state is a creature of the people, not that the people are creatures of the state. He closed with a powerful argument on behalf of faith in God, and in the triumph of His justice and righteousness!

In conclusion he firmly exhorted, "That is what America treasures: its tradition of free men, of the glory and joy of a democratic form of government. That is its shield of safety against the outrageous darts of a dictator's propaganda. That gives me the assurance that America can and will always sustain a government of the people, by the people and for the people. And by preserving a democratic form of government for itself, will preserve it for all humanity!"

The following reveals an *un*pleasant experience in the rabbi's life. Rabbi Jack Levy Seeks Justice: On February 27, 1949 at about 5 p. m. Mr. and Mrs. Reinik entered Bakersfield's El Tejon Hotel; they sat down in the dining room and ordered a meal. Mr. and Mrs.

Hill, together with three other couples, were seated in a booth in the same room, approximately 18 from the Reinik couple.

In Jack Levy's testimony he said he began to hear loud conversation with the consistent use of the word "Jews," and that Mr. Hill had stated, "If they couldn't sell potatoes to the Armenians, they always could to the Goddamn Jews! Mr. Hitler took care of the Jews of Germany and they will take care of the rest of them!"

Mr. Hill's conversation was apparently centered on a potatoes deal, and of acreage in Cuyama where they were going to plant potatoes. However, it wouldn't matter whether or not they were paid; the government would give them $1.45 or up to $2.45 a sack. No Goddamn Jews were going to let a deal like *that* be taken away from them.

The conversation that included profane language went on and on for 10 or 15 minutes. Finally, Mr. Reinik rose up from his seat and told Hill, "I listened long enough, so quit it; there are women present!"

Hill's heated reaction was, *"No son-of-a-bitch is going to make me shut up!"* And he continued his anti-Jewish remarks.

Reinik left the room to contact the hotel manager. Hill did the same, went to see the manager. Then they both returned to the dining room where there was *more* profanity.

Reinik called the police and when they arrived a few moments later, in the presence of the officers he told Hill he was under arrest. The officers took Hill in custody and to jail, where he was held for about an hour.

On April 14, 1949 he filed an official complaint against Hill, charging him with disturbance of the peace. A jury trial resulted in the defendant's acquittal. Hill's testimony of what had taken place in the hotel was that he and his companions were discussing raising 160 acres of potatoes; that someone said the potatoes could be sold to Jews, to Gentiles or to anyone.

With that, Levy stood up and addressed Hill and his party saying, "You fellows are talking loud and boisterously and I don't like it! If you don't shut up, I'll call a cop and have you arrested."

Mr. Hill replied, "If you're going to call a cop, call a whole bunch of them. Calling one would be a waste of your time and mine." Jack Levy left the room and returned with the hotel manager. He demanded that the manager arrest Hill, but he declined to make an arrest. After a conversation between the manager and Levy, police officers came and the arrest was made.

Rabbi Levy had pointed to Hill and said, "I want this man arrested. He is guilty of a breach of the peace by the use of profane language in the presence of women, and by boisterous conduct in a public place." But the trial court apparently based its judgment on the sole ground that the arrest had been illegal because it was made at a time when the plaintiff was not *at the moment* guilty of a breach of the peace.

Approximately a half hour elapsed between the respondent's first breach, and his arrest. A private person making an arrest must act promptly. In this case it was undisputed that the arrest did take place within a very few minutes after the respondent had stopped making remarks. Hill testified that he was placed under arrest "within a matter of a few minutes--pretty soon--roughly 25 minutes after Levy spoke to him."

Rabbi Levy, on the other hand, insisted the objectionable remarks continued after he first spoke to Hill. One witness testified that the officers came possibly 10 minutes or more after Hill left the room and talked to the hotel manager. Another witness testified that not more than 5 or 10 minutes at the most had elapsed after Levy left the room, and until the officers arrived. No one testified that a half hour had passed from the time of the completion of the breach of the peace until the officers arrived and the arrest was made.

Mr. Hill stated it would be a waste of time to call only one officer. Levy attempted to get help from the hotel manager, couldn't, but he promptly sent for the police. Arrest was surely made within a reasonable time frame and the trial court had obviously erred in ruling that it hadn't been lawful.

In the spring of 1957 the City of Bakersfield purchased the synagogue's building at 16th and H Streets for the expansion of city hall facilities. Property for the new synagogue was purchased on 17th Street, opposite S Street, and plans were drawn for a building. Religious services were held for the next year at the Pacific Gas and Electric auditorium, through the company's courtesy.

AUG 1959

A Labor of Love!

Lew Suverkrop, consulting engineer, inventor, amateur painter and wood carver volunteered to carve the Ten Commandments into redwood tablets for the recently completed B'nai Jacob Synagogue, 600 17th St. Not a member of the Jewish faith, nevertheless Mr. Suverkrup devoted six months of his free time researching the details of performing his art project, the carving of Hebrew letters into the wooden plaques. Note: Article was written by Art Kay for the April 18, 1959 edition of the *Bakersfield Californian*. (After the plaques were completed and installed, their unveiling ceremony was May 3rd) Article and photo graciously contributed by Gilbert Gia, member and past president of K C Historical Society)

Rabbi Jack Levy stepped up to the B'nai Jacob bema again in 1960; Cantor Oscar Muster was engaged as his assistant and to teach the classes. Rabbi Levy has thus far been B'nai Jacob's longest serving rabbi. Originally from London he lived in Bakersfield thirty-seven years. In addition to B'nai Jacob's spiritual leader, he had been a Jewish War Veterans chaplain and deputy chaplain of the National JWV. Rabbi Levy was a founder of KC Crippled Children's Society, head of Bakersfield Board of Charity Appeals, active in the Bakersfield Association for Retarded Children, the Interfaith Council Ministerial Union, and Lodge #764 of B'nai Brith, doing service as president.

The earthquake of 1952 damaged B'nai Jacob's structure to the extent that it relocated to 17th St. A new structure, dedicated by Pres. Lou Orloff took 2 years. Rabbi David Darro was first rabbi.

Morris Laba, over 20 years treasurer of B'nai Jacob, always maintained that the congregation's most essential bill to be paid was the mortgage on the building; 2nd to that was their PG &E bill. Of minimal importance was the Rabbi's salary! As a matter of fact, there arose quite a few times the synagogue ran out of money and could *not* pay the Rabbi! However, Morris Laba was a resourceful treasurer and when obliged to "scrounge" for meeting this obligation he would somehow succeed. (Art Kay and Hy

Seiden discreetly avoided disclosing the frequency of this occurrence and the methods Morris Laba used to accomplish the feat!)

The first *bar mitzvah* service in B'nai Jacob synagogue was Stephen Goldwater's. Steve is currently co-owner of Emporium Western. The first *bat mitzvah* celebration was Toby Cohen's. Records indicate that Dorothy Bernard and Frank McKay were the first to be married in B'nai Jacob's 17th Street locale.

While Rabbi Levy was the congregation's spiritual leader Dave Laba, Lou Orloff, and later Howard Silver were its presidents. Jack Levy was B'nai Jacob's rabbi until his death in 1975. Thus far, he has been its longest serving rabbi. Rabbi Pincus Goodblatt accepted the post in 1976 and stayed until his untimely death in 1981.

Rabbi Goodblatt had earned a Ph.D. in UCLA, follow-up of a Master of Hebrew Literature from The Jewish Theological Seminary of America, a Master of Arts degree in Education in John Carroll University, a Bachelor of Science degree in Education at Columbia University, and a Bachelor of Religious Education in The Jewish Theological Seminary of America. His doctoral dissertation was a study of Martin Buber's philosophy.

An article in *The Bakersfield Californian*, Sept. 8, 1977, disclosed that Dr. Rabbi Goodblatt was currently teaching a religion class in CSUB. When the interviewing reporter asked him to describe this introductory course titled, "The Religious Quest of Man," Rabbi said it was a way of introducing young people to the values of religious life. His aim was to impress how religion instills real meaning to human existence. Religious faith offers sympathetic and critical comprehension of man's *innate* search for creation's ultimate purpose.

Rabbi Goodblatt also wrote interesting and enlightening columns for a weekly publication in Cleveland, Ohio. Occasionally he taught a course in that city's Hebrew Teachers, College.

Currently, Congregation B'nai Jacob doesn't have a full-time rabbi. Spiritual leadership is seldom from an outside source; occasionally a yeshiva student is hired to lead major holiday services or to teach Torah classes. Most often a member of the congregation with sufficient background to fulfill the tasks leads services, and teaches the weekly Torah class. A congregant to very often assume these duties is Howard Silver.

Mr. Silver also belongs to several secular organizations that contribute important social services in the community. Howard Silver is in the photograph just below intently watching the scribe engaged in repairing a very ancient Torah scroll.

Restoring Congregation B'nai Jacob's Ancient
Torah Scrolls—May 2011

(Photograph graciously contributed by Alex Horvath: Director of Photography for the local newspaper, *The Bakersfield Californian)*

The hand-inscribed Torah scrolls of Bakersfield's Congregation B'nai Jacob are all of European origin. However, each one is a different age, and the style of the script varies in each. If letters in a scroll become faded or smudged, it is considered "non-kosher," and may not be used for conducting a service, explained Howard Silver, a longtime member and most frequent substitute rabbi when the congregation does not have an officially ordained one, its low membership numbers the reason for this.

Nevertheless, the congregation was highly motivated and profoundly intent on having their scrolls restored for future generations. In a sense, these sacred texts have borne witness to a panoramic history. It is likely European Jews had been reading and praying from the oldest of these three, while America's Founding

163

Fathers were engaged in forming a homeland for people of *all* faiths. It was *especially* important to those who intermittently suffered religious persecution, and the consequences of political bigotry.

Terrified Jewish people try to hide their Torah scrolls, protect them from destruction, to ensure they survive for future generations. Who knows what B'nai Jacob's scrolls may have experienced, witnessed? A pogrom? The Holocaust? Ultimately they found their way to the restful quiet of this dear little congregation in the central valley of California, U.S.A; they *deserve* to be cared for, to be nurtured!

"This is a once-in-a-lifetime moment," B'nai Jacob congregant Aimee Rothkopf declared. "To hold the quill is a great honor."

Note: using quills for writing was unknown in Talmudic times, and in the twelfth century the casuists questioned the legality of writing Torah scrolls with (Löw: "Ha-Mafteah" p. 349; Lewysohn, "Die Zoologie des Talmuds" p. 161.

Rabbi, the Torah scribe, also known as a *sofer,* averred that not the slightest error is permitted in his painstaking endeavor. Restoring the Hebrew lettering must be to perfection. Renowned for his skill he is petitioned worldwide to do this highly specialized function. And yet he is very modest about his skill. "I'm a glorified forger," he jested while smiling coyly.

The oldest of B'nai Jacob's three scrolls is about two hundred forty years. Maintaining the style and integrity of the script is an imperative so due to the faded ink the Board of Directors agreed to have all three scrolls restored. This is a vast undertaking; impaired letters are only repaired with a quill dipped in ink.

"The cost is expected to be between $10,000 and $12,000," Mr. Silver remarked. "Restoration can take nearly a year." But Rabbi Druin said he expects to complete the work of these in about 40 hours. He compared a Torah to a computer. "Take out one tiny chip or one letter in the Torah, and the originality of either ceases to exist."

Mr. Fabian Glazer half-jokingly but noticeably moved by his moment ago experience uttered, "I can die now that I completed my final mitzvah" (obligation). Proud father of two young sons to care for he plans to stay around for years. But his statement illustrates the tradition and significance behind the 613th mitzvah.

Torah contains hundreds of commandments. Belief held by traditional Jews is that at some point in our lives we really must inscribe in a Torah scroll at least one letter of the Hebrew alphabet. With plume in hand, writing a single letter constitutes fulfillment of the mitzvah.

Holding the interest of B'nai Jacob's attending members, the rabbi related several stories, each related to the letter a participant was repairing. Young Spencer Glazer listened attentively as the rabbi recited the principle of repeating lessons after learning them. Imparting your enlightenment has a worthy purpose; it benefits others. Be generous and share the sacred values of Judaism!

Torah scrolls embody not only the history of the Jewish people that started many thousands of years ago, but contain a series of dos and don'ts, principles of behavior. Protectively robed in velvet or other fine fabric a scroll is tenderly enfolded in the arms of a worshipper committed to obeying the laws Moses recited to his people at the foot of Mount Sinai. Their sacredness is locked in the hearts, and in the forefront of the minds of those who cradle the scroll, kiss it, dance with it, all the while safeguarding what they view their treasure of treasures!

As the scribe continued his work, Carol Schaefer pointed to a few old photographs on the synagogue walls, images of middle-aged members of the congregation when they had been young boys. "This is my family away from home," she informed other people in the room. "We've been around a long time; we want to be here many more generations."

Let's hope your heartfelt wish *is* fulfilled, Carol; that *your* future family members too will tenderly enfold in their arms these ancient and again purified Torah scrolls.

Howard Silver was born in Bangor, Maine. It had been a small town and yet with three synagogues and a Jewish Community Center. His home was traditional, including observance of the dietary laws; his mother kindled the candles on the eve of *Shabbes,* and the four member family celebrated Jewish holidays.

Howard's mother Rita Fraiman had come to America in 1928 on a music scholarship. She was a student of the violin at The New England Conservatory of Music, in Boston. When she graduated it automatically concluded her student visa and she was expected to return to her native country. Her parents loved her dearly, and deeply missed her, but they did not *want* to see her back in Latvia where frequent pogroms against the Jewish people made their lives bitter and uncertain. Rita's marriage to an American citizen enabled her to remain in this country. The couple had two sons, Howard and Milton.

When Howard was grown he started working in his father's auto dismantling business. It remained his line of work until retirement. Milton had gone off to live in Boston, Massachusetts where he drifted through a series of different jobs. He died at the age of seventy-one. Howard's mother was blessed with an exceptionally long life; she reached the age of *a hundred four!*

Howard had a very close relationship with his father's east European parents. His paternal ancestry boasts ten generations of rabbis! But Howard never had even a nodding acquaintance with his mother's Latvian relatives. Sadly, they perished in the Holocaust.

As a young boy Howard attended Hebrew School twice a week. On Saturdays the students conducted Sabbath services, a wonderful learning experience. One year he had the joy and benefits of attending a summer camp. A visitor came while he was there, Rabbi Morris Silverman. The man took particular notice of how well the Silver boy led a Sabbath service. He contacted Howard's parents to recommend that they enroll him in a New York City yeshiva, the one in which this rabbi was affiliated. It delighted Howard's mother and dad to hear their twelve year-old son had a keen interest and that he was quite knowledgeable in the Jewish faith system! However, they were opposed to letting him leave home so the idea was scuttled.

In 1963, in pursuit of better business opportunities the family moved westward, and settled in Los Angeles. But then, in 1968 Bakersfield became their hometown, and Howard opened his own business. The Silvers joined Congregation B'nai Jacob; it promptly became a 2nd home, and a support system to Howard. It helped him through some mighty difficult times!

Mr. Silver regards his Jewish heritage and upbringing highly effective in his business dealings. "I employed many socially disadvantaged people, and when they became aware of my sense of fairness, my compassionate nature, and my religious teachings they reacted reciprocally, developing admirable work ethics. They regarded me a father figure, friend, and counselor.

In the course of a lifetime, I can tell you, I faced quite a few discriminatory situations. However, on balance, good times have far outweighed evil ones! Indeed, I've really been fortunate to have had friends and business associates who based their judgment on a person's character, not his religion.

Nevertheless, Jewish values *are* the source of my viewpoint and general philosophy. A precept that particularly motivates my behavior is: *When you help one person, you help the entire world.* That belief is the foundation of my support and activity in both religious and secular community organizations. My Jewish faith impels me to care about the welfare of others, and to follow through by offering my time and energy to a series of service organizations: Golden Empire Transit, American Public Transport Association, K. C. Gov. Technical Transport Committee, K.C. Transportation Foundation, Israel Bonds Committee, Community Concerts Association, Workability III Advisory Committee of B. C, Shriners Hospital Association, and K. C. Arthritis Association.

"My great reward is to see a wheelchair-bound child become mobile, needing only a walker due to warm water therapy, to hear that a disabled adult can work again, to represent a group of people needing someone to speak on their behalf, to provide transportation for those with no alternative, to campaign against our air and water pollution; to secure a ramp at the airport for wheel-chair passengers; to obtain affordable tickets to concerts for impoverished music lovers."

Howard Silver perceives his community service emotionally and spiritually uplifting and gratifying! "Also my service on the board of B'nai Jacob synagogue since the 1970s, and several times as president. Currently, I am treasurer, religion chairman, and lay leader/rabbi. I'm not likely to fulfill the flattering goal Rabbi Silverman saw for me, but I still seek to achieve its level of knowledge, (without rabbinic ordination, of course!)"

The Dawn of Reform Judaism

The French Revolution was also a Jewish Revolution, the start of the Reform movement. Jews came out of the closet, lived in the neighborhoods of non-Jews, dressed, ate, spoke, went to school and to work like every other Frenchman and thus became acceptably French! However, when Napoleon lost his leadership of France, the Jews lost their citizenship rights!

Rabbi Abraham Geiger knew a great deal about Judaism's long history, including the changes in Jewish practice during the many centuries. He concluded that if ritual observance grew less stringent the faith system would likely be more appealing to modern people.

Thoughtful Jews were concerned about that. They realized many of the changes had occurred not because of a dislike of Jewish rituals and practice but to make a French Jew more acceptable, more inclined to receive better treatment. Another Jew of prominence, Rabbi Leopold Zunz, proposed something else: that Jewish people familiarize themselves with their history, their great achievements, and their creditable contributions to society in general. While promoting his ideas and hoping this will build his people's self-esteem a movement was started to conduct religious services that were better understood. It was through the use of music *and the local language*.

Between 1810 and 1820, congregations in Seesen, Hamburg and Berlin instituted profoundly fundamental changes in Jewish practice and beliefs, such as mixed seating, single-day observance of holidays, and the addition of a cantor and choir. Many leaders of the Reform movement went too far in rejecting rituals, even circumcision! Nor did a young boy display his knowledge of the Torah on his thirteenth birthday, the day he became a bar mitzvah. Reform synagogue's called it a "Confirmation."

Zionism was of no interest; the Jews had Germany as their new Zion. Shabbat, if observed at all, was on Sunday! Dietary laws and other forms of family purity weren't just archaic, but considered *repugnant*.

Anglo-Saxon and German Jewish immigrants to America in the mid eighteen hundreds brought with them Reform Judaism. Some of the members of Congregation Beth Elohim in Charleston South Carolina left that house of worship and formed the first Reform congregation in the United States. The movement quickly spread through the country and was soon the predominant way of practicing the Jewish faith.

Rabbi Isaac Mayer Wise had emigrated from Bohemia in 1846 and in the United States became its leader. He also shaped the early form of Reform Judaism. In 1857 Rabbi Wise authored *Minhag American,* the first Reform siddur (prayer book). In 1873 he founded the Union of American Jewish Congregations. Two years later, in Cincinnati he founded the first Hebrew Union College. The Central Conference of American Rabbis was initiated by Rabbi Wise in 1875.

Reform Jews established the Educational Alliance on Manhattan, New York City's lower east side, the Young Men's Hebrew Association, the American Jewish Committee, and the Anti-Defamation League of B'nai Brith. By 1880, more than 90 percent of American synagogues were Reform. The time all this was happening coincided with the arrival of a major segment of Eastern Europe's Jewish immigrants.

Most of these people were from countries of great oppression, such as Russia, Poland, and the Ukraine. They were tightly fastened to their Orthodox upbringing and intolerant of these "New Jews," or better yet, *"Former Jews."* After all, many Reform congregations of this era were hard to distinguish from Protestant churches, with preachers in robes, pews with mixed seating, choirs, organs and hymnals.

In line with their counterparts in Germany, America's Reform rabbis, such as David Einhorn, Samuel Holdheim, Bernard Felsenthal and Kaufmann Kohler, adopted a much too extreme approach to Jewish observance.

Although early American Reform rabbis no longer included in their service and study class many traditional prayers and rituals, even they drew a line in the sand. In 1909, the CCAR formally declared its opposition to intermarriage. And, although decried as "archaic" and "barbarian," the practice of circumcision remained a central rite.

Early Reform Judaism was also anti-Zionist, believing the Diaspora was necessary for Jews to be a "light unto the nations." Nevertheless, a number of Reform rabbis in America *were* promoting Zionism, including Gustav and Richard Gottheil, Rabbi Steven S. Wise (founder of the American Jewish Congress) and Justice Louis Brandeis. Following the issuance of Great Britain's Balfour Declaration, a promise to allow the Jewish people of the world to have a national State in the Middle East, the Reform movement began to support creation of Jewish settlements in Palestine, as well as institutions such as Hadassah Hospital and the Hebrew University.

As the years passed, a demi-metamorphosis resulted. Things became a little more reasonable. The level of extremism had been so great it was bringing on revulsion among many Jews: *"Zu viel ist ungesund,"* (too much is not healthy.) By 1935, the movement started restoring a more moderate approach to religious practice. The objective was to keep it distinctly Jewish but with an American flavor.

Starting with the Columbus Platform in 1937, many discarded practices were reincorporated into the Reform canon. The platform also formally shifted its position on Zionism, affirming "the obligation of all Jewry to aid in building a Jewish homeland."

A 1921 Article in the Bakersfield Californian

Note: Article contributed by Gilbert Gia, local historian, member and former president of KC Historical Society. Edited by Shirley Ann Newman.

Rabbi Laffee, who had many friends here, died of a crushed skull in one of San Francisco's hospitals. He was at a hotel the same time as a man wearing a sailor uniform, and was found unconscious from a battering he had received to his skull on April 4th. Laffee had telephoned the desk clerk asking to be called at 6 a. m. At 4 o'clock a stranger was seen to leave the hotel, lingering In the lobby long enough to roll a cigarette.

Later, the clerk went to the men's room and found the rabbi senseless, and with every evidence of a severe beating, and choking. Marks on his neck indicated that a rope or a twisted sheet might have been used on him. The rabbi was rushed to a hospital emergency room where his consciousness returned long enough for him to identify himself.

The police learned later on that Rabbi Laffee had been robbed of a diamond stickpin, a watch and chain and some money, the amount not determined. A few hours after he was brought to the hospital's emergency room he was transferred to Mt. Zion Hospital, still in critical condition.

According to the police, Rabbi Laffee had signed the hotel register as A. Laine. They said they were at a loss to know why he did that. Relatives presumed he had been given a hard luck tale by the stranger, and had offered to assist the man.

Rabbi Laffee was a well-liked pastor of Temple Israel. He also was popular among his congregants for his unusual gift of eloquence. He had the admiration of everyone who knew him.

Congregation Israel deeply regretted losing him last autumn, when Rabbi Laffee was called to a San Francisco temple.

The young rabbi had been Secretary of The Ministerial Association of Bakersfield, and a member of several fraternal orders and businessmen's clubs here.

Diane Andrews: *"Temple Beth El, A Nifty Fifty!"*

(Edited and updated by Shirley Ann Newman, April 2012)

The history of Bakersfield's Temple Beth El was started in March 1947. Thirty-five families gathered in the old American Legion Hall on 17th Street to launch this endeavor. Currently, the Reform synagogue's membership consists of about 165 families, quite a few of these people actively involved in the county's secular community.

A month later at the Woman's Club (18th & D Sts.) the first officers of Temple Beth El were elected. Represented at this meeting were forty-eight families. In May at First Congregational Church (18th & G Sts.), in the presence of visiting Rabbi Alfred Wolf, Rabbi Leonard Greenberg, Rabbi Joseph Jason and Rabbi

Morton Bauman, Temple Beth El's first Sabbath service was conducted. In August, services were moved to PG&E social hall (18th & Oak Sts.) where on Nov. 8th 1947 Temple Beth El was formally chartered as a non-profit religious institution.

Rabbi Sanford E. Rosen was the congregation's first spiritual leader. A choir, consisting of ten men and women was formed and led by Maebelle Gordon. The next major duty was to open a school for religious instruction. A staff of eight teachers and a student roll of 36 youngsters comprised the school's beginning.

The site chosen for a temple building was in its present locale, 2906 Loma Linda Drive. The plot of land was purchased from the Kern County Land Company.

While the building was under construction, services were held in Moose Hall (Magnolia & Goodman Sts.) When the structure was completed Rabbi Wolf and Rabbi Rosen presided over the dedication ceremonies and consecration service. At the laying of the cornerstone Rabbi Wolf referred to it as not just a material object but a spiritual one that embodies good wishes from all of America's faithful. Rabbi Rosen said: "A work that is truly dedicated to God will last forever."

Dr. Sophie Goldman Rudnick turned the first spade of earth, a symbolic gesture eagerly followed by other members, including children. Consecration of the sanctuary was on June 10, 1951, coinciding with the observance of *Shavuot.*

At the time the building was dedicated Abraham Hasselkom was Temple Beth El's rabbi. He was followed by Rabbi Milton Shulman, then Rabbi Arthur Kolatch. After ten years, Rabbi Kolatch, in whose honor the religious school was named, was granted life tenure. However, he took leave of the congregation three years later to open a school in San Francisco, focused on teaching emotionally challenged teenage boys and girls.

Rabbi Stanley Robin rose to the Temple Beth El bema in 1972, and his departure was followed by the arrival of Rabbi Steven Peskind. Rabbi Cheryl Rosenstein has been the Reform Jewish spiritual leader since July 1993.

While in service to Temple Beth El some of the rabbis also taught about Judaism at Bakersfield College and CSUB. Rabbis provide spiritual comfort in prisons and hospitals and in other community facilities. Temple Beth El's religious services and programs are open to anyone's respectful interest, to anyone's wish to acquire an understanding of Judaism.

Membership is not required for attending services, for Torah study, or for any other activity such as the book club that meets once a month.

The materialism of a beautiful synagogue building, its artistic symbols and other accoutrements are inconsequential. A major requisite in the Jewish faith is that we *care* about one another—Jew and non-Jew. And that we act kindly not only to people, but to animals, to the earth, water and air of this world God created. In heartfelt dedication, we have to serve the needs of our community in general.

Many members of Temple Beth El play an active role in the county's social and philanthropic programs. Members bring non-perishables for the Food Bank, give personal service and make monetary gifts to the shelter for the homeless, the shelter for battered women and children, the Henrietta Weill Child Guidance Clinic and any other programs that concern them.

Members serve on the Human Relations Commission of Kern County. The Commission's note-worthy objective is to totally eradicate the racism and discrimination we know exists in this community. Jews and non-Jews work as a team in their urgent endeavor to overcome injustices, acts of unfairness that *still* put our area to shame. Nevertheless, heartwarming to note is a growing closeness, an attitude of brotherhood between Jews and non-Jews in Kern County.

Emotional heights were reached (Feb. 26 1994) when Temple Beth El, in conjunction with the Christian Life Center co-hosted a performance by Shony Alex Braun. Mr. Braun, a survivor of the Holocaust displayed outstanding talent as a violinist and composer. He not only enthralled his audience with his violin concert that included his own compositions, he aroused deep feelings of sadness and remorse over his experiences in the Nazi era. Mr. Braun did this by playing classical and folk music whose parallel purpose was to promote love and tolerance.

Another event of immense proportions had been *A Night To Honor Israel*. This was held at the Canyon Hills Assembly of God Church, (2001 Auburn St.) Christians and Jews participated in song, dance, prayer and lecture, signifying the unity of God, and to proffer an understanding of Christianity's origin as a Jewish sect.

It was an event that heralded interfaith brotherhood. Voluntary donations helped finance the relocation of besieged people to Eretz Israel, a change that was expected to kindle the warm flame of spirituality to their lives. Temple Beth El's rabbi and congregants, and the pastor of Canyon Hills Church and its members were a principal part of the assemblage. Guest speakers of *Bridges For Peace* in Jerusalem were included in the program. The event attracted people from all over the community.

Project Svoboda (Russian word for freedom) was initiated in 1977 by Shirley Lipco and Evelyn Kay, with the cooperation of other Temple Beth El members, and in conjunction with the Hebrew Immigrant Aid Society (HIAS).

Families fortunate to be granted exit visas from Russia were resettled in Bakersfield. This required financial funding to tide them over until they had become self-sustaining. Their basic needs were an apartment, furnishings, moral support, acquisition of the English language, and of course, a job and friendships. Available to them was encouragement and counseling to help them adapt to a self-governing land of freedom.

First to arrive was the Rudashevsky family. (Feb. 1978.) The Levins came next, (Jan. 1979) and were soon joined by seven family members.

In 1992, led by Evelyn Kay, Temple Beth El had a State of Israel anniversary celebration in Jastro Park. The event was well attended by the community at large. Cultural aspects included ethnic food, music and dance. Books, children's activity items, typical Judaica from the temple's gift shop, and baked goods were on sale at the festival.

The Los Angeles Israeli Consulate had sponsored a ticket drawing for a trip to Israel that attracted a lot of interest. Adding to the lively entertainment was a professional storyteller, and a couple of strolling musicians who played Eastern European Jewish music as part of the event's charm, and a way of making Jewish culture an innovative experience for many people. For the children it promoted an appreciation of their heritage.

Michael Miller: *"You will never stand as tall as when you stoop to help a child."* The words of this title, from my Boy Scout Leader's Handbook, echoed through my mind at today's dedication of our new playground. Pictures were taken of some deservedly proud women with scissors in hand; ready to do a ceremonious ribbon-cutting. These were: Norma Schwartz, Sylvia Neal, Linda Hakimi, Irene Christensen, Linda Morales, Judy Black and Cheri Carolus. (Ann Greenberg in spirit.)

If the initiators of Temple Beth El in 1947 hadn't taught their children the eternal values of our faith, this ceremony wouldn't have occurred today. We often forget how important the next generation is. You can't have "tikkun olum" without them.

By instilling the joys and camaraderie of synagogue life in our children, they are encouraged to practice their Jewish faith. When they reach adulthood, they will hopefully pass it along to *their* children. It was the custom of our sages to put honey on the pages of the Chumash, so the children would associate sweetness with learning. The women behind the ribbon at today's event truly understand the concept.

We're deeply grateful that these women undertook the project of a new playground. They kept finding reasons for its success instead of failure. The old one was in a pretty sad state. Here's to the new one: Mazel Tov!

Women of Temple Beth El was formed in 1948, its female members involving themselves in refreshment service: food and beverages, taking charge of the kitchen next to the social hall. Sisterhood has sponsored many fund-raisers and provided money for the building's maintenance, and cost of improvements.

Looking back a bit: September 1992 to August 1993 Temple Beth El was confronted with the challenge of having no rabbi to conduct services and fulfill the other duties of a spiritual leader. In typical family fashion, and with the verve of esprit de corps, temple life sailed along smoothly, not a single wave tipping it over.

More than fifty temple members donned the cloak of leadership, conducting services, delivering sermons, reading from the *Torah* and following it up with a personal interpretation. Contrary to the apprehension that membership would decrease, actually a few new people joined.

In 1994 Temple Beth El's and Congregation B'nai Jacob's religion schools united. Although it's a very small step toward the two congregations merging, it may help to reconcile differences in Jewish observance between Reform and Conservative Jews.

Regarding our pre-adult members, Bakersfield Organization of Temple Youth (BoTY) occasionally brings together youngsters (grades 9-12) of this area, with Jewish youth groups of other areas. They also host the Purim carnival for our younger children. For several years, they have been in charge of TBE's Relay for Life team. In 2013, they put on a wonderful gala, and served the dinner, provided the entertainment and organized the evening with great skill. The funds raised were dedicated to enabling members to attend the NFTY convention.

The Little Sisters of Temple Beth El is a group of teenage girls that host a charming tea party and fashion show yearly for our adult congregants. Much to their credit, the group is highly involved in fundraising, including a hundred dollar donation they added to this year's 'Relay For Life.' Another $100 contribution that came from The Little Sisters was to our Campership Fund.

Keep it going, little ladies; you're off to a great start! It's bound to lead to the important, functions of the synagogue's women.

Norma Schwartz is truly amazing; her enthusiasm, dedication, and extraordinary vigor enable her to still head a committee that turns out delicious potato pancakes commemorating the miracle of Hanukkah. *"Hail Norma, Our Lady of The Latke!"*

Irene Christensen is certainly a skilled and productive gardener! Her heartfelt nurturing of the little darlings budding into colorful flowers, the preschoolers that attend HaGan is crucial. She helps them build a foundation in Judaism, strengthen sturdy roots of pride in their heritage, and develop *self*-pride in who they are. As graduates from HaGan they're headed for an eager understanding of their Jewish culture and long history. This is so important in helping them feel ready for the rite of passage at age thirteen, when the young boy becomes a bar mitzvah (son of the Covenant) and when a girl becomes a bat mitzvah, (daughter of the Covenant.)

The following is an article Irene wrote for the *Shofar*. It gives us eye-opening insights to HaGan:

176

"The spring holidays have kept us very busy at Ha-Gan! Our Purim party was more than funny; it was *silly*. But the kids had a good time throwing beanbags at the picture of Haman. Eva's mother, Tiffany Meyer, helped them make hamentashen. Thanks to Tiffany and all the other parents for making this year's celebration a memorable one.

"We spent weeks learning about Moses and his life, and preparing for a Seder. Highlights were playing with baby Moses in the river, talking to the burning bush and asking Pharaoh to: *'Let My People Go!'*

"I'm pretty sure the children can tell you that Pharaoh's response was, "No, No, No, I will *not* let them go!" The Seder went well but by the time we were done, we had to choose between matzo ball soup and searching for the afikomen. So we all went to the Temple porch where pieces of matzo had been hidden among the plants. Each child found one, and was rewarded with a piece of chocolate matzo; that's the Ha-Gan version of the afikomen hunt: non-competitive!

"Next came lessons about *Mitzvot* and *Tzedakah*. We all made get-well cards for our dear Susie. We have also been watering the plants in the courtyard for her. We miss her a lot and can hardly wait to have her back with us!

"From there it was a hop, skip and a jump to honoring parents, and paying tribute to Mother's Day. We filled out Mother's Day questionnaires: Adison Gartenlaub said she would like to buy her mother a thousand cups of dark wine. Samantha said her mother has too many chores to play with her, like doing the laundry. We also beautifully decorated picture frames with our pictures in them. The pictures were taken in front of the yellow flowers in the playground.

"But when it was Eva's turn, she insisted we take her picture by the carob tree in the Temple front lawn. She was right on; next year I think everyone's picture will be taken there. Carter's picture stood out from the rest because he insisted on wearing his *Superman* costume. He likes to wear it in Ha-Gan. Once it's on, he asks me to put on his seatbelt. I didn't understand what he meant at first, but then I realized he was referring to the belt on the costume. We'll miss him when he and his family move to New York.

We're learning about Shavuot and the Ten Commandments, emphasizing some more than others, i.e. not lying, not stealing, respecting your parents and keeping the Sabbath.

"It is once again time for graduation and this year we have seven graduates: Adison Gartenlaub, Braden Fore, Eva Mayer, Jessica Kessler, Kiamoni Myers, River Mongold, and Tzipporah Escobedo. We're taking bets on whether Braden, or River, will tumble off the bema! We're having a potluck dinner after the service, and hoping it gives families a chance to *schmooze* for a bit. We hope they'll all be back again for kindergarten class."

Rachel Chavez who had just become a bat mitzvah is reading from the Torah scroll, displaying her dedication to the Jewish faith. To Rachel's right is Rabbi Rosenstein. To her left: Kathleen Arnold, Shirley Ann Newman, Linda Morales.

Note: Slightly visible in the lower right corner of the picture is a Torah stand made to represent Mt. Sinai. It was designed, built, and donated by Mike Miller. On the back of the stand are two plaques, the words on one: Dedicated to the memory of David Cody. The other plaque reads: in honor of Marvin and Shirley Lipco.

Sonia Simrin is currently chairing the Simcha Set, originally meant to be a monthly get-together of our "older" members. However, now the age of fifty-five is middle age! Occasionally the meeting was a potluck in the temple's social hall but has evolved to a meal in one of our local restaurants. The gathering is for a lunch-munch and a jolly chat-fest.

Sonia also runs the temple's Judaica Shop. The entrance to it is in the social hall. Her admirable taste is reflected in the beautiful merchandise, and the shop's decorative displays. For many years Sonia headed the Caring Committee, but at the moment the committee is without a chairperson.

Eleven years ago, after I (Shirley Ann Newman) had been in the Heart Hospital where a pacemaker was installed to keep my heart functioning. I then was sent to a convalescent hospital for a few days. Among my many visitors were Mike and Sharon Miller.

One day a few years later one of my neighbors dropped into my home. Gazing both admiringly and curiously at a drawing on the wall of my bedroom she asked me about it. Mike had designed and sketched an uplifting spiritual symbol that is always placed where I can see it from my bed (and always *will* be!) It portrays an open Torah scroll, a large Hebrew letter filling up the center.

"What's that big thing stuffed in the middle of the scroll?" the woman asked me.

"It's an *ahlef.*"

"Oh, I see, *a stuffed ahlef*" she responded, initiating in both of us a burst of giggles and chuckles.

For those who can only come to the temple in someone else's car Mike Miller kindly arranges their transportation. Mike's active service in the temple has been not only very lengthy and varied, but with deep devotion and efficiency. Ditto for Joe Fram! Both these men also served as presidents of Temple Beth El. At the time of writing this, the congregation's president is Robert Sincoff. Mike is the financial secretary, a seemingly never *bored* board member!

Irvin Pike chairs the Religious Practices Committee; Jill Egland is leader of the Social Action Committee; Nancy McCombs is currently Sisterhood President; Recording Secretary is Marsha Parr; Webmaster is Courtenay Edelhart. Lorrie, our temple secretary, edits the monthly *Shofar.* Sally Nighbert has been the Temple Librarian for several years. With Mark Hugo assisting, she upgraded the catalogue system with the effectiveness and modernity of technology. This has taken Sally's admirable skill and experience, and her motivation to vastly improve access to our learning resources. What a worthy contribution, Sally!

Every year on *Yom Ha Shoa,* Day of Destruction, Temple Beth El in conjunction with B'nai Jacob has a program that perpetuates remembrance of the horrors our people experienced in the Holocaust and memorializes its victims. A speaker is engaged, candles are lit, prayers and poems are recited. We respectfully and grievously pay tribute to the multi-million Jews and others the Nazis regarded as worthless scum that should be destroyed. Incredible suffering and losses had come from the acts of hate and malice conducted in the 1930s and first five years of the forties.

Regarding the holiday of *Sukkot,* Rabbi Gunther Plaut has given us his interpretation of its origin and significance: "It is likely that in early days *Sukkot* marked the beginning of the religious year; later it became a major agricultural festival, celebrating the bringing in of the harvest. Its theme is gratitude for God's bounty, and its name betokens its major ritual: The building of *Sukkot,* frail booths, which are to remind the Jew of the deprivations of their years in the wilderness, as well as of God's providential care. In modern times *Sukkot* served to inspire Canadian and American Thanksgiving...."

For the last several years Irv Pike and Pamela Elisheva have graciously made their large acreage available for constructing a large-group sukkot for celebrating the holiday. Irv and Pamela have actively participated in the annual event. (Feast of Booths as the holiday I known in the Christian faith.)

According to Zechariah, in the Messianic era *Sukkot* will become a universal festival and the people of all nations will make an annual pilgrimage to Jerusalem to hold a celebration there.

Purim is a holiday of dual celebrations: a serious aspect is when we listen to the reading of the Megillah. This is a historic account of a modest Jewish girl named Esther who becomes Queen of the land in which her people are captives and at risk of annihilation. On a subsequent evening we mark Purim with a jolly folly called a Purimspiel.

"Chai, Rabbi Rosenstein!"

by Bill Wolfe (Edited by Shirley Ann Newman Apr. 2012)

Chai (pronounced "hi", while clearing one's throat) is the Hebrew word for life. Because it means "life," the Chai is consequently a symbol that captures an important aspect of Judaism. According to the gematria, a mystical tradition that assigns a numerological value to Hebrew letters the letters *het* and *yud* add up to the number 18. The *het* has a value of eight and the *yud* has a value of 10. As a result, 18 is a popular number. At weddings, bar mitzvahs and other events, Jews often present money gifts in multiples of 18, symbolically wishing the recipient the gift of a lucky life.

Rabbi Cheryl Rosenstein arrived in Bakersfield from Minnesota in 1993, just after her 29th birthday. Recently the temple congregation, friends and colleagues of Rabbi Rosenstein and Mayor Harvey Hall celebrated her 18th, (Chai) anniversary as TBE spiritual leader. It has been an eventful 18 years.

"She celebrated many life cycles with us. She has been on the sidelines, the forefront, as well as in the midst, encouraging us forward," explained Nancy McCombs, president of Women of Temple Beth El and a key planner of the event. "On the opposite end of the spectrum, when life has cast its shadow on our pathways, she has been the strength at the helm, even when we felt we could no longer place one foot in front of the other."

Rabbi tracks her years in Bakersfield by the "Age of Sage." Sage Russinsky, born June 7, 1993, was the first baby Rabbi Rosenstein had the privilege of naming. Sage turned 18 and left for college this year. Rabbi's first Confirmation service was for a group that included the current vice president of Temple Beth El, attorney Elliott Magnus. In her first bar-bat mitzvah class were two students for whose weddings she later officiated.

Rabbi's first sad duty was the burial service November 9, 1993, for Max Newman, Holocaust survivor and war hero. After the funeral Rabbi attended the meal of consolation in the home of Mr. Newman's daughter and son-in-law, Heidi and Bob Allison. Also present, of course, was Shirley Ann Newman, Max's widow.

The Allisons joined Temple Beth El in 1968. They have a warm, family feeling for the congregation. This was clearly exemplified by Heidi's recent memo to the April 2012 edition of *The Shofar*, as she recovered from the difficulties of surgery:

Dear Temple Family,

As many of you know, I was hospitalized for 3 weeks during February/March with an impacted colon. A number of members pitched in. I want to thank all of you for your help and support. I had a lot of visitors at the hospital. Some walked with me during physical therapy, making the arduous process easier and less boring as they distracted me. Others brought goodies to perk up my appetite, some brought me magazines. Others cooked for Bob and my kids while they were in town. I want you to know that each of you contributed in a significant way to my recovery and I appreciate your visits, your smiles, your cheerful cards and all that you did for me. My recovery would have been much more difficult without you. *Heidi Allison*

Heidi had been a mathematics teacher at Washington Middle School. Before adding a fifth year of university study to her bachelor's degree, and thus becoming a credentialed teacher, Heidi Allison had been a public assistance social worker.

Robert Allison's entire career as an educator has been at Bakersfield College. He started teaching chemistry there in 1963, first as an instructor, then a professor. Bob acquired a chairmanship, became vice president of Bakersfield College, and ultimately, though briefly, the presidency. He is currently Director of The Levan Institute of Lifelong Learning, at Bakersfield College.

Shirley Lipco Baker: *"My Legacy Is In Trusted Hands."*

All my children became a bar or bat mitzvah while our family belonged to Temple Beth El. Danny, our oldest child was first, and lucky enough to work with Rabbi Arthur Kolatch.

Danny became a legendary leader in Bakersfield's business community. He began as a young retailer at the Emporium Western store where his hustle and drive led him to become part owner. Eventually he took over Vallitix ticketing and expanded the business from mostly local to state concerts. Later, he took the lead at the Fox Theatre Foundation, and was instrumental in fundraising to pay for Fox Theatre's needed renovation. He then managed the leasing and operation of Fox Theatre concerts.

Danny's business sense, his *menschlichkeit,* manliness, ability to connect with people, to treat everyone respectfully, earned him the highest praise and status in this community. Danny and my other children were generous to Temple Beth El. He facilitated a boulder on the temple's "Tree of Life."

My son was a beloved resident of not only Bakersfield, but of California. As a tribute to his admirable way of conducting his life, more than 600 people attended Daniel Lipco's funeral. His sudden death January 14, 2012 was due to a liver ailment. His blessed spirit, the memory of his exemplary life's work, permeates his family. Even so, losing their daddy is a great loss to his youngsters, three little girls named Olivia, Gabrielle and Alexandra.

My daughter Lisa was particularly drawn to Jewish life. At the age of 10 she became a singer in Temple Beth El's choir, even though the rest of the group was comprised of adults! She acquired her early education of the Jewish faith at Temple Beth El's religious school, and through her regular attendance at Shabbat and Holiday services. Lisa became a bat mitzvah and was confirmed in the presence of Temple Beth El's congregation, her family and friends.

One of the best things Marvin and I ever did for eager young Lisa was to, send her to Camp Swig during the summer. There her love of Jewish music, and her commitment to it evolved. This led to her decision to become a cantor.

Lisa became president of the Temple Beth El youth group, and was active in NIFTY (National Federation of Temple Youth). She also spent one year abroad to study in Israel. She served as a soloist for many congregations in the U.C. Irvine area where she earned an undergraduate degree. Later she studied cantorial arts at New York City's Hebrew Union College, and in 1989 was ordained a cantor.

Rabbi Kolatch was one of Lisa's most important mentors, and until his death in 2010 the two remained close over the many years of Lisa's career. Lisa's original Jewish healing song: *Misheberach*, and other liturgies are sung throughout the world. She travels around the country with a book she wrote called *Yoga Shalom*, published by URJ Press, sharing that and other spiritually inspiring pieces of liturgical music.

Lisa is cantor in Temple Shalom, Chevy Chase, Maryland. Her daughter Emily and son Lois are Jewish through and through! They attend a Jewish camp, travel to Israel and are active in BBYO and Hillel.

From a humble beginning Marvin and I joined Temple Beth El. Now our grandchildren are links in our Jewish legacy, carrying into the future the values we treasure. All my children have supported Temple Beth El over the years and continue to value Bakersfield's amazing Jewish community.

I'm proud to say my children funded the Big Tree Restoration Project as part of Save The Redwoods League. The deck and bench with a tribute plaque is to Marvin and me, a permanent reminder of the good works and values we instilled in our children that will exist in perpetuity.

Note: Shirley Baker's death occurred 12/21/12, a few months after she submitted the above for my book. She was born in Brooklyn, New York in 1926, but at the close of WWII her family moved to Los Angeles, where she met and married war veteran Marvin Lipco. His uncle established him in business in Bakersfield and Shirley worked with her husband in the enterprise. The couple enjoyed traveling, hiking and fishing. For 40 years they spent the summer in Klamath, California with their children; eventually with their grandchildren too. Shirley's avocations included involvement in social service programs. She was part of a Temple Beth El committee that aided families to come from Russia and settle in this area. She also served as a docent in the California Living Museum, lecturing young people about wildlife and conservation. Before Marvin's death the couple had been married 50 years! Currently, Shirley's widowed husband is Irving Herbert Baker.

The two daughters of Rabbi Rosenstein and Richard Shiell were born in Bakersfield and have grown up at Temple Beth El. In 2011, the older daughter, Jessica, was confirmed and the younger girl, Ariana celebrated becoming a bat mitzvah on Nov. 12. The Rabbi's husband, Rick, is an active member of the community as well.

In 1993, it was still very rare to have women in the clergy. One of the selling points for Bakersfield and Temple Beth El was that no one asked any "leading or outrageous questions" just because she was female. Since coming to Bakersfield, Rosenstein has been a convener and leader of the Women's Interfaith Clergy group.

When Rev. Jenell Mahoney, then of the Congregational Church, organized the community prayer event following Sept. 11, Rabbi Rosenstein was one of the first to sign on. She has been involved in many other community events.

In the intervening months that the temple was without a rabbi, Stan Simrin offered to teach the weekly Torah class. Not only did he come well prepared to present the lesson, his manner of teaching was challenging, stimulating, and so *interesting* that the class had mushroom growth! Stan was such a success that even when we became blessed with spiritual leader and admirable role model, Rabbi Cheryl Rosenstein, he said he'd be willing to lighten her load by continuing to be the Torah teacher. Sadly, Stanley Simrin has become Temple Beth El's *deceased* sage, always to be remembered not only for his wisdom and intellectualism, but for his zeal and dedication to an understanding of the foundation of the Jewish faith: the teachings of the Torah that we brought from Sinai to San Joaquin.

"Attempting to fill his shoes each week remains my most daunting assignment," Rabbi Rosenstein reflected. "As I sit and prepare each week, I pray that I am worthy of the task, that my students are not merely learning just to learn but to keep, and to do!"

The invitation to the Chai Celebration was an opportunity for guests to make gifts in her honor, to establish the Rabbi Cheryl Rosenstein Campership. Temple Beth El students from 3rd through 12th grade have the opportunity to attend Camp Newman near Santa Rosa each summer. However, because the kids go for several weeks, it can be expensive. Because the Jewish population in Bakersfield is small, this experience is especially pivotal for Temple Beth El youth.

"I grew up attending camp," the rabbi said. "My parents taught me the value of the Jewish community, and camp was the place where I learned the significance of the Jewish community." She believes that all her students are in some way her children and, thus, she wants each one to share in the experience.

Looking ahead, there are many challenges as well as opportunities. Temple Beth El will officially become a senior citizen with its 65th anniversary in May. There is only one remaining founding member, Florence Makoff, who is 98 and lives out of town. With the deaths of Stanley Simrin and the last founding member, Hulda Magnus, a "changing of the guard was taking place." However, the building of the Torah Learning Center in 2007, led by former presidents Barry Goldner and Joe Fram, made it clear that Temple Beth El is here to stay!

"Welcome, Chabad!"

Orthodox Judaism maintains that on Mount Sinai the Written Law was transmitted along with Oral Law. The words of the Torah were spoken to Moses by God, and included detailed explanations as to how to apply and interpret them. Furthermore, the Oral law includes principles designed to create new rules. Oral law is said to have been transmitted with a high degree of accuracy. Jewish theologians who project Halacha in a more evolutionary manner point to a famous story in the Talmud: Moses is magically transported to Rabbi Akiva's House of Study and finds himself puzzled, unable to follow the ensuing discussion!

Orthodox Jews base their present views of Torah law on a whole series of discussions and debates that are now in classical rabbinic literature, especially the Mishnah and Talmud. Orthodox Jewish belief avers that the Halakha truly fulfills the "will of God" either directly, or as closely as possible. If some of the details of Jewish law were lost over the millennia, they have been reconstructed with well-established consistency.

Orthodoxy avers that, given Jewish law's Divine origin, no principle may be compromised due to changing political, social or economic conditions in our religious *or* secular lives.

Haredi and Modern Orthodox Judaism differ regarding changes. A principle held by many Haredi Jews is that Halakhah is never to be altered or refined. It's inappropriate, and almost certainly heretical. Modern Orthodox Judaism doesn't have a problem with adaptation to recent times.

However, all forms of Orthodoxy embrace Judaism's dietary laws, circumcision of boy babies on their eighth day, a boy's *bar mitzvah* service at the age of thirteen, and *mikvah* immersions.

The Mikvah: Submerging in a pool of water for the purpose not of using the water's physical cleansing properties but expressly to symbolize a change-of-soul is a statement at once deeply spiritual and immensely compelling. No other symbolic act can so totally embrace a person as being submerged in water, which must touch and cover every lesion, every strand of hair, every birthmark. No other religious act is so fraught with meaning as this one. It touches every aspect of life and proclaims a total commitment to a new idea and a new way of life. It eradicates the old and gives birth to the new.

In 2002 Kern County welcomed a Chabad couple, Rabbi Shmuel and Esther Schlanger, and little Leah, their three-month old daughter. They were coming here just in time for the High Holidays. We already had a Jewish community of considerable size, several thousand families! Members of our community had contacted Rabbi Boruch Shlomo Cunin, director of West Coast Chabad, requesting one of their spiritual leaders. The Schlangers were selected by Rabbi Cunin earlier that year. They made several trips to Bakersfield to meet the community, to arrange living accommodations and Chabad's house of worship.

Chabad-Lubavitch is considered the most dynamic force in Jewish life today. The word "Chabad" is a Hebrew acronym for the following three principles: *chochmah* means wisdom, *binah* is comprehension, and *da'at* refers to knowledge. The movement's philosophy is that the deepest dimension of the Torah is to have an understanding, a recognition of the Creator, the role and purpose of creation, and the importance and unique mission that is given to each creature when it comes into the world. This philosophy guides a person to refine and govern his or her every act and feeling through wisdom, comprehension and knowledge.

The word "Lubavitch" was derived from the name of a town in Russia where the movement was based for more than a century. In the Russian language Lubavitch means "city of brotherly love." The term conveys the essence of love and responsibility every Jew must have for every other Jew.

Following its inception 250 years ago, the Chabad-Lubavitch movement, a branch of Hasidism, swept through Russia and spread to surrounding countries. It provided scholars with answers that had eluded them, and simple farmers with a love that had been denied them. Eventually the philosophy of Chabad-Lubavitch and its adherents reached almost every corner of the world, and affected almost every facet of Jewish life.

Chabad is guided by the teachings of seven "Rebbes", beginning with Rabbi Schneur Zalman of Liadi (of righteous memory, 1745–1812). These leaders expounded on the most refined and delicate aspects of Jewish mysticism, creating a corpus of thousands of study books. They personified the age-old Biblical qualities of piety and leadership. They concerned themselves not only with Chabad-Lubavitch, but with the totality of Jewish life, spiritual and physical. No person, no detail is too small or insignificant for their love and dedication.

The origins of the Chabad-Lubavitch organization can be traced to the early 1940s, when the sixth Lubavitcher Rebbe, Rabbi Yosef Yitzchak Schneersohn (of righteous memory, 1880–1950) appointed his son-in-law and later successor, Rabbi Menachem Mendel, to head the newly founded educational and social service arms of the movement. Motivated by his profound love for every

Jew, and spurred by his boundless optimism and self-sacrifice, the Rebbe set into motion a dazzling array of programs, services and institutions to serve every Jew.

Today 4,000 full-time emissary families apply 250-year-old principles and philosophy to direct more than 3,300 institutions (and a workforce that numbers in the tens of thousands) dedicated to the welfare of the Jewish people worldwide.

The Schlangers said they were delighted by the warm reception they received. "Chabad has a proven track record in attracting the youth of the community," said Gail Tenzer, a Bakersfield resident. "We are confident that Rabbi and Mrs. Schlanger will have a powerful, exciting impact on our children, and the community."

Esther Schlanger agreed. "Our first activities after the holidays will focus on youth programming, for the many young families in the Jewish community. We want to establish a firm foundation of Yiddishkeit in the city, says Esther Malka Schlanger. Our future depends on the children, so we need to begin with them. The couple also plan on introducing adult education, holiday awareness activities, and a full range of programs for the entire family.

Born and raised in Lubavitch communities of London, and Brooklyn's Crown Heights, respectively, Rabbi and Mrs. Schlanger are both deeply familiar with the life of Chabad *shluchim.* There's such terrific enthusiasm in Bakersfield, "We can't wait to get started!" said Rabbi Schlanger.

Rabbi and Mrs. Schlanger Are Now the Parents of Five Children!

"With Joy and Gratitude to Hashem we are delighted to announce the birth of our new baby girl, born Elul 26." (Sept.26, 2011).

Shirley Ann Newman: *"What My Rabbi Means to Me"*

Note: The following is an adaptation of an article from *The Bakersfield Californian* written in 1999 by Shirley Ann Newman.

Years ago if the feminine pronoun "she" was used in reference to a rabbi it was met with an air of surprise; sometimes a furrowed brow of perplexity. A woman rabbi? Yes! Why not? It had to do with the human reluctance to surrender a tradition. This one was that women are family homemakers and nurturers. The *men* are in charge of worldly affairs, including the "other world," the abode of God.

In the past few generations, especially during the era of the Second World War when so many men were in the military, the functions of women started to grow increasingly responsible *outside* the home. Also, their interests were becoming far more diverse.

In the late forties women's college attendance started becoming relevant. They were setting their goals on a professional education that would prepare them to become doctors, lawyers, university professors.

Rabbi, Cheryl Rosenstein of Temple Beth El is an example and a valuable role model of spiritual leadership women were assuming. She has a compassionate nature and the knowledge and wisdom of a fine rabbi, truly fulfilling the requisites of the Jewish faith system. It entails not only ministering to our congregants but active involvement in the social issues of the community at large. Her rabbinic duties include conducting synagogue services, teaching classes in Jewish law, history, and the Hebrew language, not only to fellow Jews, but to anyone contemplating conversion to the Jewish faith, or who is merely interested in learning about the predecessor to Christianity.

A rabbi conducts marriage and funeral services, and the religious service that accompanies the circumcising of a Jewish male baby, or the baby-naming ceremony of a girl; rabbi

190

participates in bar and bat mitzvah services that mark the rite of passage of Jewish children when they reach the age of thirteen. A rabbi teaches, counsels and consoles, supports, strengthens and comforts us. A rabbi helps us know the source of our heritage, which leads us to understand ourselves.

Rabbi Rosenstein's personal life is tightly and securely bound up in her role of a loving, caring wife and mother. She is a devoted daughter to her parents. Much of Jewish ritual and ceremony takes place in the home. The "mezuzah," affixed to the doorframe contains a sacred prayer. The dining table represents an altar where the food and wine, God's gifts to our survival and joy, are blessed in gratitude. The table is also graced with candles that are kindled on the eve of the Sabbath and Jewish holidays.

Prayers are recited, hymns and other songs are sung, stories are told or read. The children learn to understand their history, their culture, their faith not only through their attendance in the synagogue but by means of a loving, moral and ethical lifestyle.

Lynne Rosenstein: *"My Cheryl's Pathway to the Rabbinate"*

My daughter, Cheryl Rosenstein, seems to have come into the world destined to be a rabbi! So many of her early experiences set her on the path toward choosing it as her career. For one thing, we were living in Long Beach, California which has a vibrant Jewish community: several synagogues, an active Jewish Community Center, Jewish Federation, Jewish Family and Children's Services, Hadassah, National Council of Jewish Women, B'nai B'rith and other organizations with a connection to Judaism.

Her parents, Neil and I, were involved in Jewish communal life; I served as the first woman president of Temple Israel, a Reform synagogue, and had my own career at the Jewish Community Center. Neil gave substantial support to the Jewish Federation, and took an active part in its annual campaign.

As a youngster Cheryl truly enjoyed going to religious school. Right after her bat mitzvah service, Rabbi Wolli Kaelter expressed his compliments, telling her how impressed he was with her poise, and the beauty of her voice, lovelier than that of anyone else he had prepared for their bar or bat mitzvah service. Years later, Rabbi Kaelter was one of Cheryl's teachers at the L.A. Hebrew Union College.

Jewish camp life played a significant role in our daughter's formative years. She attended Camp Komaroff, the Long Beach Jewish community camp in Lake Arrowhead, and Camp Young Judea, under the sponsorship of Hadassah. At age sixteen Cheryl spent the summer at Young Judea in Israel. Upon her return she became a *madricha* (group leader) of the movement's young children.

Because of her skill in dealing with people, Cheryl was chosen to receive leadership training in Young Judea's international camp, located in the Catskill Mountains just outside New York City.

Weekly voice lessons tutored by our temple's cantorial soloist began when Cheryl was a teenage high school student. It led her into the role of alternative soloist during High Holy Day services. She studied, too, under Cantor Alan Weiner, and later became a member of choir Kol Echad.

Cheryl excelled in Israel folk dancing, and this ability earned her the best job she had in high school, and later in college.

She was a sophomore in UC Santa Barbara, when one of her classmates invited her to become a founding member of *bayit,* a Jewish co-op house. She lived with her *bayit-mates* the remainder of her undergraduate years, and forged a strong friendship with them that continues into the present.

At the UCSB Hillel, Cheryl filled the role of cantorial soloist during High Holy Day services. And in her sophomore, junior and senior years she taught in the religious school of Santa Barbara's Reform Temple. Director of Hillel Sandy Bogin was a female rabbi, and working with her seemed to awaken in Cheryl the idea of becoming a rabbi.

Long Beach Jewish Center's day camp engaged Cheryl to teach Israeli dancing. Despite all this participation in Jewish life and Jewish music--her many accomplishments in things "Jewish," it surprised her to hear peers and campmates refer to her as

'Rabbi.' She was their *go-to* girl, source of reference, when a question arose about liturgy, and regarding Judaism's rituals.

Innumerable experiences in the Jewish faith system are probably what fanned the flames in Cheryl's mind, initiating a soul search while she was a college student: What precisely is expected of a rabbi? What will make *her* a good rabbi? Is the rabbinate really the right career for *her?* She wondered in depth.

Cheryl contacted rabbis she knew personally and peppered them with a heavy sprinkle of significant questions. Their answers must have convinced her to become a rabbi, because at the start of her senior year one evening she called Neil and me, gushing into the phone jubilantly "I decided to be a rabbi!" She was accepted at HUC, and after graduation from UCSB she launched into the five-year program that led to her ordination.

Reflective Commentaries of Three Rabbis

Rabbi Cheryl Rosenstein:

In 1993, when I was chosen as spiritual leader of Temple Beth El's congregation, it was understood (and clearly spelled out in the contract) that my first obligation is always to the congregation. And it *has* been! Most of my waking hours are filled with temple business: teaching children and adults, and preparing the lessons; tutoring bar and bat mitzvah candidates in Hebrew; studying Torah and preparing weekly messages for Shabbat evening services; writing sermons and newsletter articles; visiting shut-ins and patients in a hospital; engaging in prenuptial counseling; preparing students for confirmation; attending and contributing to various meetings (the Board of Trustees, temple committees, the choir); teaching non-Jewish people considering conversion; officiating at funerals, etc., everything one expects to do in a modern congregation.

But it was also made clear at the outset that my services would not be limited to the congregation's needs. "Small town

Bakersfield" requires a high degree of outreach both to unaffiliated Jews and to the non-Jewish community.

At the beginning, I was the only full-time rabbi in Kern County, therefore with the responsibility of officiating on all issues that relate to Judaism and the Jewish people. I was in the line of fire for any and all inquiries by the local media, on everything from Jewish cuisine to Israeli politics. I was called upon to educate hundreds of non-Jews each year about Judaism and Jewish practice ces.

Even now I give lectures to both public and private school elementary and high school students. (Garces High School, next door, regularly sends six or seven classes of students once a year for a tour of our Sanctuary). I have numerous interviews with students from Bakersfield's two local colleges. I field countless questions from Christians seeking information about Christianity's Jewish roots. I address church groups. Occasionally I go to the area prisons to visit Jewish inmates. I deliver invocations at private and public events, including Rotary meetings, political party fundraisers, and not long ago, the groundbreaking for the city's Centennial Plaza project.

While president of the local interfaith ministerial association I had the opportunity to inform my Christian colleagues of many Jewish customs and beliefs, and to invite their participation in appropriate ecumenical temple events. I also became involved in the formation of an interfaith Women Clergy forum.

Once a year I would take my place on the dais of Canyon Hills Assembly of God church, sponsors of a "Night to Honor Israel." The program, devoid of any proselytizing, was an unprecedented, unadulterated expression of love for Israel, and for the Jewish community! (The funds raised at this event were forwarded to Bridges for Peace, a Christian Zionist organization based in Israel and dedicated to resettling Jewish immigrants in their Homeland). I was always respectfully consulted about the content of the program, from its musical lyrics to the script for the drama, to publicity graphics, to Israeli dance.

I helped the choral director of Bakersfield College find a text for a commissioned piece that reflects a Jewish "take" on the Adam and Eve story.

Among my most rewarding labors is an Introduction to Judaism course. I teach it once or twice a year. The class regularly attracts between 10 and 20 students, but with a bit of promotion this student body of mostly unchurched non-Jews, and unaffiliated Jews could be considerably larger. For eighteen weeks we study the fundamentals of Jewish belief and practice, as well as the Hebrew alphabet. Though education is the primary goal of this class, I'm also privileged to sponsor the conversion of many of these students.

My rabbinic functions are never dull, even on the "home front" of congregational life! However, they *are* made much broader and more challenging by the demands of the larger community I serve.

Note: Among Rabbi Rosenstein's inspiring, thought provoking sermons, is one that evoked particularly positive responses from the congregation. It was delivered while she was in mourning for the loss of her grandmother.

For my Grandmother Adosa Rosenstein, from her eldest grandchild. Few grandchildren are privileged to know their grandparents as long as I've known mine. My recollections are many. I share with you just a few. Grandma was always well-coifed and immaculately dressed. Though she usually wore a blond wig, in the mind's eye of my childhood she is a redhead—the better to reflect her spunk and her spirit, the better to set off those intelligent blue eyes—eyes not unlike those that gaze at me from the face of her one and only great-granddaughter.

Her house always smelled of mothballs and cooking. The food was always plentiful at grandma's - even if you only dropped in for a visit. It was an insult if you didn't eat at least a cookie or a piece of fruit. Grandma's cooking was always well-done. That is, she came from the old school: if it was hard, she cooked it until it was soft; if it was soft, she cooked it until it was hard. My father's penchant for burnt toast traces back to his mother's kitchen. Her fruit compote, however, was a reliable staple at all of our family gatherings. When company was at her house, she ran around like a real Jewish mama, making sure everyone had enough to eat. I'm not certain she ever did.

We always had to yell at her to get her to sit down with us and enjoy the meal. My little grandmother always drove a big, plush

American car. It was big to me at the time, anyway. I remember sitting in the passenger seat of one of those Buicks while she asked me question after question: about my studies, the rest of my family, my life, my boyfriends. Always her advice rang in my ears, "Cheryl, find a man who will put you first." I followed that advice. She approved of Rick. Never did I see a woman as happy as she was when she danced at our wedding.

Grandma enjoyed traveling. She and Grandpa went on cruises. We grandchildren collected souvenirs from wherever they went: South America, the Virgin Islands, Alaska. Once or twice, we even got to attend the bon voyage parties on the boats. After Grandpa died, I began calling my grandmother every week to wish her "gut shabbos."

I stopped only when she didn't have a phone of her own anymore, and could not have remembered. Dosa was so loving, and so tough. She loved her grandchildren fiercely, even when she didn't approve of our behavior. We weren't merely hugged. "Give me a squeeze," she used to say. We received checks on our birthdays, checks "just because" she thought we might need a little something extra. She wanted only the best for us.

Grandma was judgmental, even bigoted. Her early life had been hard. But she was part of that generation that was willing to do anything and everything to make sure that the lives of her children and grandchildren were better. She would "bust her buttons" with pride over each one of our accomplishments.

Grandma's memory loss was hard on us—and on her too, for a while. But in this last year, whenever I saw her, she was happy— happy to have visitors whose faces she recognized, even if our names and precise relation to her were beyond recall. Of course, the face that brought the biggest smile was the one she hardly knew at all. 'Delicious,' she would call Jessica over and over again between smooches: 'delicious!'

My little daughter and husband Rick didn't know how much of herself she saw in Jessica's blue eyes. But I will think of her each time I look into my child's face, and I will remember her. 'Our lives are better because of you Grandma. We thank God that you were ours'. The generation of my grandmother—a first-generation, American-born child of her immigrant parents—is fast fading

196

away. And so I mourn not only the person of my grandmother, but also the values she represented.

What are those values? They are values embodied, in part, by the language of and in my grandmother's home. My grandparents were avid readers of the Yiddish newspaper, Die Forverts-The Forward. Even after they moved from L.A. to Long Beach, they continued to send my father and his sister To Der Arbeiter Ring (The Worker's Circle) School in the Boyle Heights neighborhood of Los Angeles—a kind of Socialist cheder. They spoke Yiddish at home, mostly when they didn't want the kinder to understand. (As a consequence, my father and aunt cannot speak Yiddish, but they still understand quite a bit!) Hebrew may be the Holy Tongue, the Loshon Kodesh, of the Jewish people, but for Jews of European background, Yiddish is the mama-loshon—the language of home, family, and daily social intercourse. Some of its vocabulary derives from Hebrew, some of it from German; but is was and is a proper language all its own, with its own rules of grammar and spelling, its own idioms. There are things one can say in Yiddish that one cannot translate into any other language, words that are uniquely expressive, almost onomatopoeic: mensch, chutzpah, schlemiel. Even the ubiquitous "oy veys mir" is possessed of so many nuances of meaning. Yiddish is a language of emotion, singular in its tenderness, a veritable mother-tongue. In English, we say head, hands, feet, nose. In Yiddish, we say them: kepele, hentele, fisele, nazele. In Yiddish, they have the tenderness of the diminutive. In Yiddish, there is character.

My grandmother was a person of character. She was opinionated and biased. But she wasn't afraid to voice her opinions, even when they were wrong-headed. The truth is no one cared about people more. My grandmother cared for her own mother in her home until Bubbie's death. Grandma's kosher kitchen was established in order to accommodate her mother. It remained kosher long after her mother's passing—indeed, until my grandfather died, and she sold the house. By then it was long habit, I suppose, but mostly Grandma continued it out of loyalty to my great-grandmother's memory.

My grandmother played nurse to other infirm family members as well—to her own sister, my great-aunt Ruth, and particularly to her niece, Naomi, both of whom preceded her in death. She fulfilled the Mitzvah of bikur holim, visiting the sick, many times over. She was frugal with her money, rarely spending any on her own needs, so that she could be equally zealous about the Mitzvah of tzedakah.

Adosa Rosenstein knew that *tzedakah* had to do with righteousness, not with love. She set a positive example for her children and grandchildren by giving generously to charitable institutions, even as she taught us the value of saving for our own future needs. She established trusts to help her grandchildren get through college. She gifted us with U.S. Savings Bonds, which instilled in us the values of patience and patriotism. This is the *Torah* I have learned from my grandmother, *aleha shalom* (may she rest in peace): Family loyalty, honoring parents, tradition, tenderness, toughness, *tzedakah, bikur holim,* education, frugality, the courage to own your opinions and express them, flexibility, patience, patriotism, making sound life choices, embracing the promise of the future.

My grandmother's teaching inspires these questions: What *Torah* have you learned from your parents and grandparents? What *Torah* have you transmitted—are you yet transmitting—to your children and grandchildren? I hope that something of my grandmother's teachings inspires you as she inspired me. And I pray that each one of you is as blessed as I have been, to have such a person from whom you may learn in your own lives.

Note: The following is Rabbi Rosenstein's message to the congregation in the June 2012 edition of the Shofar.

An important learning device is through comparisons. After three weeks in the hospital (including a brain "shunt revision," followed by two weeks of rehabilitation therapy), Jessica is back in action. She attends school half time and is completing three classes with home study while her rehab and chemotherapy continue here in town. Your love and blessings have been the best medicine, and we are constantly grateful for your compassion.

At our Seders, we re-learn the lesson that it takes the experience of slavery to truly appreciate freedom. Jessica has a renewed sense of gratitude for the ability to do many things she was unable to do for most of those three weeks, and Rick and I breathe sighs of relief each morning as we awaken to the relative "normalcy" of our family life at home. Gratitude is a wonderful lens through which to view the world, and one too easily forgotten and shunned in the midst of life's hustle and pain. However bitter our lot, however low we might sink, things can always be worse – and the silver lining of the clouds we inhabit is always there, lighting the path ahead with its gleam.

After our departure from Egypt, Mount Sinai is the first stop on our itinerary. Torah teaches us that there can be no freedom without responsibility. The Ten Commandments make it clear: we share responsibility for the well-being of one another and of our community. It is not enough to care only for ourselves and our families; we genuinely need each other to live whole and holy lives. We not only need rules to live by; we need people around us to encourage us to follow the rules – to live rightly and keep each other from succumbing to our lesser, selfish inclinations.

In our Torah study class we are plunging deeper into Leviticus, and we are rediscovering that this challenging book is not merely a collection of antiquated laws regarding ancient and obsolete sacrifices. Long before its vaunted midsection containing the "Holiness Code," Vayikra quickly makes itself apparent as a book about morality. Its opening chapters talk about the measures of sin: when one errs against one's fellow human being, one must first make restitution to the victim and pay a fine. Only then can one offer an offering to "rebalance" the scales and re-enter the community of the holy. When we sin against our fellow, we sin against God – but our atonement is only acceptable on high after we make peace with one another.

We are better human beings, and better Jews, when we live together. Whether we are celebrating Shabbat or festivals or personal milestones, or offering emotional, physical or spiritual support to one another in times of crisis, we help keep each other on the right path, moving forward.

Rabbi Arthur Kolatch:

Note: I had asked Rabbi Arthur Kolatch, formerly of Temple Beth El to kindly add his input to my book. He graciously complied. My next question was, "Did you plan to include cooperative relations with the *non*-Jewish community? And if so, what did it comprise?"

"Yes," Rabbi Kolatch promptly replied. "I thought you would be interested to know what motivated me to have this relationship with the general Jewish and non-Jewish communities. The reasons are two-fold: The first is based on the pronouncement in the Book of Jeremiah (29:7) 'Seek the peace of the city where you abide for in the peace of that city will you find peace.'

The second is based on a phrase in the second paragraph of the *Aleinu* prayer, as it appears in the traditional Hebrew prayer book: It is our responsibility 'to improve the world in accordance with the Divine We alternated providing those who were home-bound with Friday evening Sabbath services over radio station KGEE through the generosity of Dan Speare, the station Program Director. Our relationship was so close that when Rabbi Levy died I was asked by the family to conduct the funeral services.

My involvement with the general community comprised several categories: education, chaplaincy, mental health and community relations.

Besides addressing numerous classes in practically every public high school and Garces High, I also appeared before teachers and parent groups throughout the county. In recognition of my participation in the community educational programs, the Kern County PTA awarded me an honorary life membership. I was appointed instructor of World Religions at Bakersfield Community College and was instrumental in introducing into the curriculum a course in Modern Hebrew, which I then taught. I was also the first instructor at the newly opened California State University in Bakersfield to teach the course: 'Literature of the Old Testament.' I served as president of the Kern County Mental Health Association. Our main function was to provide the public with the need for adequate mental health services in Kern County.

In addition, during my administration, I conducted a survey of those incarcerated in Juvenile Hall and the County Farm. Our concern was that part of the inmates' frustration was their lack of educational skills. As a result of an academic level survey we conducted, we discovered that the average inmate's educational level was at third grade. We presented this information to the Kern County Unified High School District, and it arranged for its Adult Education Division to provide the inmates with teachers and materials on an ongoing basis.

The Guild House was opened to provide much needed financial assistance to the Henrietta Weill Child Guidance Clinic one of my wife's particular interests. Mrs. Kolatch worked closely with this organization. Her concern was not only for the advancement of good mental health, but also for assistance to the visually impaired. She, with several other Temple Sisterhood members, transcribed school textbooks and other reading material into Braille for use in the local public schools.

I served as the first Jewish person in Kern County to sit on the Board of Directors of the Kern County Catholic Social Services. My relationship with Father Ralph Boniface was one of friendship and respect. I was honored to participate in the dedication of the San Felipe Boys Home which serviced young men who were entrusted to its care by Juvenile Hall. I was especially proud to be a speaker at a testimonial dinner given to Father Ralph by the Diocese honoring him for his dedicated and devoted service to the Church and community. Equal rights of all citizens was of great concern among minority groups. I joined the 'Citizens Committee for the Establishment of a Bakersfield Human Relations Committee.' I assumed the presidency of this group. The committee included members of varied races and ethnic backgrounds. After several years of planning, we decided to present the idea of creating a Human Rights Commission to the Bakersfield City Council. The seeds were sown. Ultimately, even though not in my time, this Commission was established.

For my efforts I was presented with a Certificate of Appreciation from the African Methodist Episcopal (AME) Church at a Sunday service. I was also invited by the Mexican community to be the principal speaker at, what I believe was the first, *Cinco de Mayo* Day celebration in Bakersfield. Perhaps the most fulfilling community involvement was during the impassioned grape strike. In an attempt to defuse that critical occasion I wrote a conciliatory article, asking both sides to the dispute to ameliorate their differences. As a result of this article appearing on the front page of the local news section of *The Bakersfield Californian,* I was called by the president of one of the wineries.

He asked me if I could arrange a meeting between himself and a representative of the United Farm Workers. I, together with this representative, spent an entire Sunday in this vintner's home. It was a most amicable day, well spent. In less than a month the vineyard signed a binding agreement with the United Farm Workers.

These were all positive and rewarding experiences spent in representing the Jewish people in the community. At no time do I remember anyone harassing, castigating, vandalizing or using anti-Semitic epithets against me or any member of my family. This was more than adequate reward and an indication of respect and gratitude."

Rabbi Schmuel Schlanger:

Note: Rabbi Schlanger's 6/1/12 *Torah Thought,* edited by Shirley Ann Newman

Defining Unity: The term is not a synonym for singularity. It means that despite our differences we are to have mutual respect, we should care for each other, and attain the same *fundamental* values. We share common, over-all goals, even though we might differ on how to achieve them.

A Torah commandment that Orthodox Jewish men adhere to is donning a 'tefilin' when they pray on weekdays. One function is to fasten a small leather box to their forehead. The other goes on the arm. Tefilin contain four handwritten paragraphs that depict the fundamentals of Jewish belief. In the 'head Tefilin' these paragraphs are inserted into four separate compartments on four **separate** pieces of parchment. However, in the 'hand Tefilin' they are all are written on one scroll. Why the difference?

202

The head symbolizes our power of intellect and cognitive processing. The 'hand Tefilin', placed close to the heart, represents our emotions and feelings. That is why they are different. When it comes to the way we think, we cannot and should not always agree. Multiple opinions breed creativity, fresh ideas and depth of understanding. We can and should have differences of the mind. But we must have one heart. With united feelings of love, respect and shared convictions, our differences can only enrich our togetherness in a more beautiful way. A single instrument generates fine music. But an orchestra with many different instruments, all following one conductor and blending with each other, produces a charming, *harmonious* symphony.

Dear Friends: (July 15, 2012)

We have just completed an awesome summer at Camp Gan Israel Bakersfield. This year we had a record enrollment of forty children and young teens enrolled in camp. The campers had an amazing time! Between interesting and exciting field trips, entertaining workshops and stimulating activities this summer will be one to be remembered. What makes Camp Gan Izzy so unique is that the Judaism is imbued into the children in an exciting and positive manner, leaving them proud and excited about their special heritage. It is our hope that the children of Camp Gan Izzy take this positive Jewish experience with them throughout the entire year. A big "Thank You" to all our generous camp sponsors, parents and community members who volunteered their time, skills and efforts! Camp Gan Israel of Bakersfield would not be the incredible success it is without your partnership. As we enter our tenth year in Bakersfield we look forward to a fabulous year ahead to continue bringing the beauty of Yiddishkeit to our brothers and sisters in the Kern County Area.

Thank you again for all your encouragement and support. Enjoy the rest of your summer!

PART FIVE

Mending, Befriending, Blending

Mending, Befriending, Blending

Blessed Are The Peacemakers!

Indeed, there are countless situations that culminate in litigation, requiring a justice system to sort out who did what to whom and how the injured party is to be compensated by the violator. But a prized member of every family, or within a circle of friends, or a part of the community is that special person known to be the peacemaker. This is someone who has the gift of defusing inflammatory confrontations, of soothing injured feelings, who acts as a sounding board, and who succeeds in convincing the sparring partners of the superiority of perpetuating their relationship rather than breaking up over a conflicted viewpoint.

The peacemaker is adept at pointing out to siblings the benefits of curbing their jealous rivalry, of helping spouses regain compatibility, of promoting loving and respectful parent/child relationships, and the help neighbors should make available to one another.

A miracle worker with the special ability to mend a damaged relationship often accomplishes it by doing little or nothing more than listening quietly and patiently to the anecdotal account of the hurt. Listening to hostile parties who are unburdening their feelings, voicing the firm conviction that they are totally in the right, and how wrong is the "other." Speaking gentle words of understanding and support can quiet resentment, indignation, even rage. It often is the only way to fulfill the practice in Jewish law of shalom beis, peace in the home.

A charming legend comes to mind to exemplify the point of all this. In a small village one Shabbes, a rabbi and his neighbor were out for a sunny afternoon stroll. As they were passing the home of a member of their shul the man came dashing out the door, stopped them in their tracks and began to pour out his troubled emotions on Rabbi Shimmel, concluding it with the words, "I was right, wasn't I, Rabbi?"

"Did you ever once hear me tell you you're wrong, Mendel?"

In happy contentment Mendel practically flew back to his nest.

The rabbi and his companion walked on. A little bit further along, a virtual repetition of the event happened again, this time it was with the other party to the dispute. In astonishment the rabbi's walking companion listened to him reply with the words, "Isaac, go in comfort; you have my assurance you didn't violate the covenant, nothing you did will bring you the wrath of HaShem."

"I was right, wasn't I, Rabbi?"

"My son, you are deserving of Shabbes shalom, His blessed gift to us." Tearfully happy, the man skipped off through the doorway of his house.

As the two men resumed the walk, the rabbi's companion trotting along beside him grasped his arm and uttered sharply: "But Rabbi Shimmel! Those two men just recited opposing views to an issue they had been arguing bitterly over; surely, only one of them can be right, not both!"

"Sure, Nathan, sure," answered the spiritual leader, nodding his kippah-covered head in placid accord, "you're also right."

Rabbi Shimmel lifted his face to the warm sun, and took deep breaths to enjoy the scent of orange blossoms as he loped along in total serenity, in Shabbat shalom.

"Widen Our World!" Wailed Woebegotten Women

In theory, a Jewish wife is treated by her husband with love and respect, with kindness and understanding. On the eve of the Sabbath he honors and praises her admirable attributes as wife and mother. She brings forth as many children as God wishes this man to parent; she conducts a household that is pure and sacred. It leaves the man of the house free to keep rocking forward and back while reading and *davening* (praying) a few times a day.

He feels comfortably assured that his meals are kosher, and that his children are being reared in accordance with the laws

Moses learned directly from God atop Mount Sinai, and that he taught his people, the Israelites.

In theory women are not to be mistreated or in any way demeaned. To exemplify, here is an excerpt from the memoirs of Max Newman, born 1911 in Austria. (*Deflecting My Death, memoirs of a Jewish Resistance Fighter in Nazi-occupied France,* by Shirley Ann Newman) The following is about *Max Newman's* mother:

Shifra, was a tall, slender woman of proud bearing and nervous energy who moved through the house efficiently and confidently. Well trained in the religious expectations and demands of wife and mother, her personality was both firm and gentle, neatly blended in ideal harmony for her prescribed role.

Her husband and children loved and respected her. She disciplined the little ones without inflicting corporal punishment, never reproofing them in a loud voice or quarrelsome manner. A meaningful glance was often enough to redirect a maverick to the right path.

Within the cultural boundaries of early-to-mid-twentieth century Europe, the era in which Shifra lived, and despite the unworldliness of Orthodox Jews, especially females, everyone regarded her as highly knowledgeable, apprised of a wealth of understandings.

This is what the life of a Jewish wife and mother was supposed to be, but it wasn't happening for large numbers of Jewish women. Not until the birth of feminism.

A leader and promoter of enlightenment concerning the mode of life for Jewish women was Judah Leib Gordon (1831-1892). Beginning in the1870s, women in the Jewish Pale of Settlement in Russia, and female students in various cities of Europe considered him one of the few people to display sensitivity and empathy regarding their difficult lives.

He wrote a radical protest poem that began: "Hebrew woman, who knows your life? In darkness you came, and in darkness you shall go. A Jewish woman's life is eternal servitude. You shall be pregnant, give birth, suckle, wean, bake and cook and untimely wither."

It reflected the very poignant cry of woman, at the mercy of hard-hearted rabbis, locked away from enlightenment and worldly pleasures. But then, in one of his last poems, he wrote a stinging satire mocking more sophisticated women who were already prominent in many urban communities of Eastern Europe:

"Oh, the learned woman has harmed me," the poet lamented, having anticipated a better married life than that of his peers, that his wife would be a source of joy, and yet she became a shrew!

"Learning has altered the gender hierarchy beyond recognition, infusing self-confidence in females, allowing them to argue with their husbands, to insist on their own point of view, and to a husband's chagrin, often reject his demands for sexual intimacy!"

Major figures in Europe's enlightenment came to realize the difficulties of this change they had brought about. The most outspoken of them was Jean Jacques Rousseau (1712-1778) known for his revolutionary theory, and Enlightenment's most important feminist work. In it the main character demanded nothing less for women than equality, universalism, humanism, and intellectualism.

None of these values, Mary Wollstonecraft argued, is sex-dependent. No one should set a double, contradictory standard of values. Ethics and reason, she wrote, have no sexual identity. And in any case, who made people of male gender the sole determiner of whether woman shared their gift of intellect? Women gifted with reason and ethical standards must participate equally in intellectual life.

Indeed, this provocative work by Wollstonecraft, whom her opponents called "the philosophizing serpent," not only raised the issue of women in the public sphere, but also established the topic as a touchstone for the entire Enlightenment movement.

What has been the positive impact of this struggle, if any, on women of the Jewish faith? An exhilarating winner's race for Reform Jewish girls and women, a slow, steady advance for those in the Conservative movement, but not much for the Orthodox Jewish female.

Many Jewish feminists have significantly altered the character of Jewish religious, intellectual, cultural, and communal life in the United States. In the stormy late 1960s and early 1970s, when the rising stars of contemporary American feminism were publicly denounced from synagogue pulpits as aberrant and destructive, feminist attitudes and goals seemed revolutionary.

But by now many feminist attitudes and aspirations have been infused into mainstream American Judaism. Female rabbis and cantors are trained and ordained in Reform, Reconstructionist, and

Conservative seminaries. Life-cycle events for females such as bat mitzvah ceremonies are commonplace. A few decades ago even women's organizations were ambivalent about the impact of feminism but now support it.

The Women's Division of the Council of Jewish Federations featured a number of feminist figures at its 1987 General Assembly in Miami. Calling themselves "feminists," officers of the Women's Division gave the platform to Amira Dotan, a female Israeli brigadier general; Alice Shalvi, founder of the Israel Women's Network; Susan Weidman Schneider, editor of Lilith magazine; and others identified as feminists.

In their private lives as well, American Jews display the impact of feminism. Their women have been a highly educated group, and today are even more educated. Moreover, the women are by and large focusing on career goals, rather than open-ended liberal arts and sciences that had typified educated females in the 1950s and 1960s. Partly because of career objectives, American Jewish women marry later and bear children later than they did 25 years ago. They are far more likely than married Jewish women of the past, to continue working outside the home after they marry; even when they become mothers.

The late-forming, dual-career family has become the norm. While feminism has become mainstream many important feminists have pulled back from radicalism. Celebrated Betty Friedan reassessed family and career life as worthy goals for women. Through their personal experiences many feminists have denounced the anti-Judaism in some strands of feminism, Letty Cottin Pogrebrin, editor of Ms. magazine attests. Some of her appealing novels are about strong, intelligent, accomplished women, who nevertheless are very vulnerable. Jewish women have also helped diminish the radicalized form and face of feminism.

The gap between American Jewish tradition and contemporary American feminism seems to have narrowed. A quasi-feminist stance appears to be *de rigeur* in the American Jewish community. However, the extent of influence exerted by general and Jewish feminism on America's secular and religious life, and on the family life of both has yet to be analyzed.

The Innovation of Female Rabbis!

It was a standing-room-only crowd June 3, 2012 at a celebration honoring "Four Firsts." These were the first women in America ordained as rabbis in Reform, Conservative, Reconstructionist, and Open Orthodox denominations.

The momentous event had been co-chaired by Monmouth Reform Temple and the Jewish Heritage Museum of Monmouth County. Paving the way for more than 1,000 female rabbis who followed her was an honor, said Priesand in an interview with *New Jersey Jewish News*. All four honored rabbis have been privileged to open the doors of spiritual leadership to Jewish American women. It reflects our constitutional values of gender equality, and equal opportunity, and it affirms Rabbi Cheryl Rosenstein, religion leader of Bakersfield's Temple Beth El.

Intermarriage and Conversion to Judaism

The substantial increase in intermarriages between Gentiles and Jews in the past half century has permanently changed the texture of Jewish American life. Although the phenomenon is not heavy among Orthodox Jews, intermarriage has had a profound impact on the vast majority of Jewish families.

For years, many Jews kept hoping intermarriages could be substantially reduced. And most population studies indicate that Conservative congregations, through the use of a wide range of initiatives did succeed in lowering the rate. However, in our open society, intermarriages: Jews with non-Jews, is going to continue to significantly flourish.

There are growing numbers of initiatives that welcome intermarried couples into the fold. But our error is in limiting ourselves to the following two approaches: either outright rejection or be welcoming them, but with the hope of influencing them to feel comfortable in our congregations.

The Conservative movement ought to embark on a bold new initiative that reflects the long-ignored wisdom at the end of Hillel's statement: After telling the non-Jew that the essence of the Torah is, "Do not do unto others what is hateful to you," Hillel stated an addendum, *"Zeel g'mor"* – "Now go and *learn* the Torah." His message was a challenge, but it was also an inspiration and encouragement. It was as though he had said, "I know you *can* learn the whole Torah, and I shall be here to support you. I will stand with you and help you."

Rejecting the intermarried family must *not* be our response! Welcoming and being open is a vital first step. Too often, we act as if being warm, welcoming, and supportive is a sufficient goal, that such behavior is enough to meet the challenge. It is not. Although attitudes of welcome and warmth are important, and creating Jewish cultural and social interconnections should be applauded, these can only be vital first steps. These actions will hardly suffice in guaranteeing Jewish survival. To achieve that end we must focus our outreach. Our ultimate objective must be to raise the number Jewish descendants. We must create Jewish families to ensure continuity, and to create the Jewish renaissance of which we dream. But we also must inspire intermarried Jews to choose Judaism out of conviction that Jewish lifestyle enriches family life, especially the children's. Our outreach must reflect our values. We must shape a movement that passionately encourages conversion and the rearing of Jewish children.

In response to increased intermarriage the Jewish community has formulated a spectrum of initiatives called "keruv," a Hebrew word whose root is, "to bring close." As the word implies, keruv initiatives are aimed at bringing people nearer the Jewish culture, to the Jewish community, to Jewish life as a whole. The foundation of keruv initiatives constitutes a change of attitude, of conveying a warm, welcoming openness to *all*, particularly to a blended family.

Studies have demonstrated that in 96 percent of the homes in which there are two Jewish parents the children are raised as Jews, but in only a third of homes with one Jewish parent are children brought up Jewishly. Their intermarriage rate is a staggering 74 percent, while the rate for children of two Jewish parents is 22 percent. Even the latter is disheartening. Thus the challenge for Conservative Judaism is to focus more effort, more energy!

Shirley Ann Newman: *"Mix 'n Match"*

When I was a teen-ager, and then a young woman, (eons ago!) intermarriage was not an issue in my life. I never contemplated it as a possibility; it never entered my mind. As a matter of fact, I never even dated a Gentile boy or man. Thinking about whether or not I should marry someone of a different religion would've been like considering marriage to my dearly loved puppy. In fact, although I had dozens of boyfriends, I don't remember a non-Jewish boy asking me to go out with him.

That was pretty much the way things were in New York during the 1930s. Intermarriage was strongly connected to how your family members, particularly your parents and grandparents, would accept it. Interestingly, among couples that did intermarry, the most harmonious relationships were between a Jew and an Italian.

The reason for this seemed to be because of our effusive, demonstrably affectionate personalities, and various other cultural similarities, such as family closeness. This was a condition that reduced the tendency to stray from the fold. It impelled friendship between these two peoples—Jews and Italians.

After a usual period of boy/girl dating, and the admission of love for each other, there would blossom a happy marriage between a second generation Italian and Jew. Despite their wide difference in religious practice, Jews and Italians felt comfortable with one another. And since their families could easily co-mingle, it increased the chance of happening.

In general, Anglo-Saxons tend to be more reserved than persons of *my* culture, *my* background, which evolved into American from my father's German ancestry and my mother's Hungarian. In dealing with emotional situations, whether it's a very happy event, or a deeply sad one, English, German and Scandinavian people do not display their feelings as freely as those that descended from, or whose predecessors came from a Mediterranean or Middle Eastern country.

This difference in overt emotionalism is true even when the event is highly personal, one that was wrenchingly sad, such as the death of a loved one. Or it could be a glowingly happy one, such as the longed-for birth of a child or grandchild. By nature Nordics more or less hold their feelings in check. Frequently, and sad to say, they show disdain for people that do *not* display the same sedate, reserved mannerisms that they do.

In my husband's Orthodox Jewish family, marriage to a Gentile person, and any offspring that result would have no recognition. It would not be considered a valid marriage. The man and woman were merely engaging in extra-marital sex, disgracing the family, putting it to shame within its circle of ultra Orthodox Jews.

A number of years ago I attended the wedding of two friends. One had been born to a Jewish family; the other had converted to Judaism in Temple Beth El, a Reform synagogue. There had been lengthy instruction in the conversion process, guided and sanctified by a Reform Jewish rabbi, who soon joined the two in marriage.

The couple parented two children, and several years later they started to practice Orthodox Judaism. Well, now the marriage was *not!* It took a whole series of ritualistic procedures incorporated in Jewish Orthodoxy and its legal technicalities for the "Gentile" to be considered Jewish, and for the couple to be *properly* joined in marriage.

From Two Christian Spiritual Leaders

"We Feel Connected With The Jewish Community."

Rev. James Imel:

"What's the favorite hymn of Jewish merchants the day after Christmas?" I professed ignorance of the existence of any Jewish liturgical practice for the 26th of December. Michael Miller responded with the answer: "What a friend we have in Jesus..." We both had a good laugh. This reflects the relationship of camaraderie between me and some of the people of Temple Beth El in Bakersfield. Mike has been President of the Congregation a few terms and will continue to serve the membership. I am an ordained Baptist minister in what is known as a conservative, evangelical denomination. One does not risk making ethnic or religious jokes with someone if there is the slightest unease over the possibility of offending him or her.

I've been the pastor of five inter-denominational churches and administrator of three Christian schools. Between churches, I was a technical writer for nine years in the Silicon Valley area in and around San Jose, California. I started a small publishing company, specializing in religious non-fiction.

My relationship with the Jewish people of Kern County was non-existent until Mrs. Shirley Ann Newman and I joined the non-fiction critique group of the Writers of Kern in Bakersfield. Critiquing each other's written work and that of others engendered mutual academic respect which in turn led to a personal friendship between her, my wife, and me.

Shirley Ann Newman invited me to visit the Thursday night *Torah* studies at Temple Beth El. Stanley Simrin, one of Bakersfield's most outstanding criminal defense attorneys, teaches the class. I was quickly and warmly received, and before long I began to develop friendships among the congregants. They good-naturedly referred to me as the "temple minister" and as their "token Christian." We have had a lot of laughs over this and

216

related things. The book by Mrs. Newman, *Some Wars Never End,* was such an intriguing and well written, human interest story that I published it for her. It is the story of her late husband, Max Newman, a World War II hero.

It became evident to her after several years of marriage that Max was suffering from a traumatic post war syndrome. It was only after several decades that Shirley Ann was able to persuade her husband to unburden his soul of the things so inordinately troubling to him. It was during a ten-year span of time that she faithfully recorded the episodes of his early life, followed by the years that Max spent in Paris, France, working for his mother's cousin, Helena Rubinstein in her institute for the development of cosmetics and other beauty aids.

Max related his service in various anti-Fascist organizations and how he fought on the losing side—the Republicans—during the Spanish Civil War. Then came his experiences in the Second World War, the fall of France and how he spent the next eighteen months in the *Maquis,* the French Resistance to the Nazi invasion of France, his beloved adopted country. He escaped successfully after a year and a half as a resistance fighter but was arrested in Spain as an illegal entrant. After nine months of incarceration in that country he joined General Charles de Gaulle, head of the Free French, stationed in England where he became a tail gunner in the heavy bomber, *The Halifax,* whose macabre nickname was "The Flying Coffin."

Every Friday evening at Temple Beth El, when the Sabbath service commences, Rabbi Cheryl Rosenstein invites members of the congregation to come forward and light a candle if he or she had some event during the week that was noteworthy or particularly joyful and to share the good news with the congregation. Several times I have lighted a candle and related to the attendees something special that happened in my life that I felt they could rejoice with me. They have always been gracious enough to applaud on these occasions.

Sometimes I am asked about the Christian perspective on a *Torah* passage, or some question of Christian theology, or differences between Christian denominational practices. One example was an incident in the national news: A Protestant bishop proclaimed that we should find it in our hearts to forgive a certain convicted murderer that he had visited in prison. He said he had forgiven him and so should we. Class members protested that only the one who was slain could forgive the murderer, and that was impossible since the victim was dead. Also, they thought God would most likely not forgive such a heinous crime. The bishop's attitude was castigated among the members of the *Torah* class, and I was asked my opinion. I explained that the bishop was likely influenced by the teaching of Jesus to forgive those who sin against *us*. We were able to agree that forgiveness was the choice of God and that we might find it in our hearts to forgive a murderer for whatever pain or wrong *we* suffered as individuals as the result of his crime.

My wife Merilyn Imel attended several *Torah* classes with me as well as special Friday night services. When she passed away in March of 1997, thirteen of our friends from the synagogue came to her Sunday afternoon memorial service at Shalimar Baptist Church.

My wife and I became acquainted with Temple Beth El members David and Rochelle Cody at *Torah* studies and at Friday services. When David was diagnosed with cancer, he and Rochelle joined the cancer support group that Merilyn and I belonged to and which we had found to be so very helpful over a period of several years. David passed away in November of 1996, and Merilyn passed away four months later.

That spring Rochelle and I began dating for mutual consolation. We found we had much in common as we sought strength to cope with our grief. We soon discovered we had fallen in love. We married in July of 1997 at the county courthouse with several Jewish and Christian friends as guests. We now attend *Torah* studies and the Friday temple services together and other events important to Rochelle. We attend Wednesday night Bible study and Sunday morning services at my church, where Dick Hunter is pastor. She accompanies me when I am called to go somewhere to preach.

My relationship with Rochelle and Temple Beth El has caused me to analyze more carefully the Christian Scriptures. Christian believers are admonished: "Be ye not unequally yoked with unbelievers" (the Apostle Paul in II Corinthian 6:14). Therefore, some have questioned how could marry a Jewish widow. As I read again Romans Chapter 11, I realized Jewish believers in God are children of God through the same faith in Him as modeled by

Abraham in Genesis 15:6. This is exactly the same kind of faith professed by Gentile believers in God. Since she and I were believers in God through the same faith Abraham had, this did not constitute a hindrance to our union.

I feel tremendously benefited from studying the Bible from the Jewish perspective after having studied the same Scriptures for years from the Christian perspective; I appreciate this as a rounding out of my education. Mr. Simrin reads far and wide among the Jewish scholars to bring a wealth of thought provoking light to bear on the particular verses under discussion.

As I contemplate the wisdom and writings of the Rabbis, I am gaining newfound appreciation for the work of these early devout men of faith and mental acumen. I had been predisposed to disparage the *Talmud* and the *Midrash* as of little value because these were commentaries written about the Bible by mere men. But I was impressed by their insights and sometimes startling applications to real life situations. Then I realized that we Christians have our own "Talmudic" writings and "Midrashes" by scholars of renown, such as Martin Luther, John Calvin, Matthew Henry, and C. Scofield. All these "mere men" have had a hand in shaping modern Judaism and Christianity.

Also, I see that many Christians have been remiss in their treatment of Jewish people, Judaism, and the Hebrew history and language. The Hebrew Bible was the only Bible known by the early Christian believers and writers. They wrote to help all the many new Gentile believers in God to overcome their deficiency of background. Gentile believers were likened to wild olive branches, grafted into the domestic stock. Thus, we have what is called the New Testament of twenty-seven books.

Of course, in regard to major differences, there is the matter of my belief in Jesus as the Jewish Messiah. However, Jews and Christians alike believe the Messiah will come to earth to set up His throne and begin the Messianic Period. We Christians believe He has come once to set up the Church Age in preparation for the coming Messianic rule that we call the Millennia.

Rev. Martin Murdock, Wesley United Methodist Church:

I am deeply honored to be asked to offer my perspectives on Jewish/Christian dialogue and relations in Kern County, based upon my personal experiences as a United Methodist Minister in Bakersfield. Thank you for asking. After my arrival in Bakersfield the summer of 1996 I began to seek organizations or gatherings through which I could become acquainted with other members of the clergy: ministers, priests and rabbis. What a delight it was to find that there was a Bakersfield Interfaith Ministerial Association, which met monthly, and that its president was Rabbi Cheryl Rosenstein of Temple Beth El.

The fact that there was limited Jewish institutional life in Bakersfield, due to the small number of Jewish residents made it especially interesting to note that Rabbi Rosenstein was the current elected leader of B.I.M.A. among so many Christian and Catholic clergymen. An additional pleasure was in finding that her leadership projected warmth, humor, insight and courage, all of which reflected her person and her work. It was good to be in Bakersfield and to be connected to this group of people.

Soon I developed an ongoing, friendly relationship with Cheryl, and continue to be the beneficiary of her insight, vision, and caring. We have been together at a number of significant events, including those of particular relevance to Jews: such as the Yom *Hashoa* program, the annual memorial service for the victims of the Holocaust. She and I have pointed out to the City of Bakersfield that a celebration of the city's centennial which is including its religious heritage must not be limited to the Evangelical Christian perspective.

It has always been important to me to build bridges rather than moats, to seek out connections, to bring everyone closer together by discovering our common values and visions rather than focusing on our differences. Certainly we are aware that this is necessary for couples of "mixed" marriages, and often in politics, as well as in multi-cultural neighborhoods. Somehow we tend to overlook the need for finding common ground among people of differing religious traditions.

My first church assignment was 27 years ago. Shortly after settling in and acquainting myself with the members of my congregation I set out to meet other pastors and priests in a community so small there was no rabbi at all. I expressed the hope that one of the pastors of a nearby village would meet with me from time to time, for coffee and conversation. I was astonished to learn that he had no desire for that kind of relationship with me. He expressed himself this way: "No, I don't have enough in common with you to even consider getting together. For one thing, your church is part of the National Council of Churches!" he said, accusingly.

"Yes, we are. We're proud to work cooperatively with other groups to affirm that God has brought us together and that we can combine our efforts to make a better world!" I retorted arrogantly. Indeed, I was younger and less tactful then, but I even now find it offensive to be excluded from personal relationship simply because of differences in religious association. This attitude is very familiar to people of color, those with various disabilities, as well as to Jews. It is not surprising to them that this happened to me because they, unfortunately, have experienced it to such an extent that they frequently allow themselves to become resigned to such exclusionary tactics.

Fortunately Rabbi Rosenstein shares my continual effort to build bridges between disparate people. Together with others we have been successful in forming strong, trusting friendships that recognize difference, but build on commonalities. To our dismay we have had to learn that difficulties can come into play in the community when these bridges are connected to non-compatible allies:

In the spring of this year, 1998 the Bakersfield Interfaith Ministerial Association was still very open and welcoming not only to Protestant, Catholic and Jew but also to Unitarian, Sufi, Mormon and Bahai. The challenge to our organization arose when a witch from a local coven of the Church of Tyressian Wicca applied for membership. The incident was "leaked" to the press, where it was given prominent coverage. The statement of our mission clearly excludes no one who can be construed to be part of an "interfaith" representation. Most of the church memberships would have been relieved if we had voted against admitting a Wicca into the organization. However, we did have others who were deeply committed to the broadest definition of interfaith representation. For Rabbi it was particularly a dilemma since she is so personally aware of the consequences of restrictive policies, and yet she was aware that it might fragment the organization.

The vote favored permission and the Tyressian Wiccan became an official member. We became publicly known as the "witch group" and no longer had a useful voice for representing the religious community. We decided to terminate the group and make a new beginning. Not surprisingly Rabbi Cheryl Rosenstein and I were both appointed to the steering committee currently working to create a new organization for inter-religious cooperation.

My confidence in how disparate religions can work together derives from the experience I had as pastor of a church in Santa Rosa. We shared the building with a Reform Jewish congregation; from the financial perspective it was of benefit to both groups. Congregation Shomrei Torah was too small to maintain the cost of its own building and Christ Church United Methodist was well able to use the rent it received to help pay our own bills. We rarely got in each other's way! On Friday nights it was a synagogue and on Sunday mornings it was a church. A movable Ark and a portable cross were put into place as required for each of the faiths.

Once a year the rabbi and I held a pulpit exchange; I was the pulpit guest on a Friday night and the rabbi was our guest on Sunday morning. Same pulpit, merely a different time and "props." At Thanksgiving we held a combined service that included elements of both traditions, including in our prayers, thanks for our shared situation. Our mutual concerns for the world—for justice and righteousness, the needs of the poor, and such issues as nuclear disarmament—were all issues we had in common. These precipitated a number of seminars and adult education classes conducted jointly. These activities built bridges of understanding and multiplied our effectiveness within the community.

Interestingly, we as a Christian and Jewish group working together seemed to have more in common on some of these issues than my church had with very conservative Christian churches or that Congregation Shomrei Torah had with other, more conservative synagogues of the city.

For some unfathomable reason a member of the congregation had removed the Torah from the Ark that weekend and put it in the rabbi's office, a part of the building that hadn't been touched by a destructive fire.

For the next few years the two congregations worked together, planning and constructing the replacement of a sanctuary. We made improvements over the old building, designing an octagonal roof that reflected the styles of worship we shared. We improved the kitchen and bathroom facilities, building bathrooms a greater distance from the sanctuary so that the noise of flushing toilets would not be heard during services.

We held fund-raising events together, and did much of the actual construction. We dug trenches, hammered nails painted, and did the clean-ups after each stage. We designed this place of worship for the dual-faiths, to meet the style preference of both groups. A tower was constructed, its stained glass panels designed to include symbols of both traditions.

We saw wonderful increases in our sense of connectedness to each other after all the shared, cooperative work on the building. We resumed the pulpit exchanges, joint seminars and adult education classes. We added new activities: When it came time for a special community-wide remembrance of *Kristallnacht,* the Night of Broken Glass, when synagogues all over Germany had been destroyed by the Nazis, and holy books and scrolls destroyed, we formed a committee to put together a huge remembrance gathering composed of Christians and Jews from all over Sonoma County. It's hard work to build bridges, but the benefits are enormous, well-worth the effort.

Congregation *Shomrei Torah* has grown; it is large enough to have a full-time rabbi and there is discussion on the subject of erecting another building on the present site and ultimately constructing a synagogue building on its own ground.

This saga does not have anything directly to do with Bakersfield but it gives the reader a sense of my experience and why I came so naturally and readily to an organization such as the Bakersfield Interfaith Ministerial Association. I celebrate the opportunity for interfaith dialogue, especially for Jewish/Christian dialogue and cooperation. Again, building bridges is the way to connect people in ways that are life giving and constructive action to improve our community.

I celebrate the vision and courage of Rabbi Cheryl Rosenstein and her work as the spiritual leader of Temple Beth El. Clearly she has answered God's call for her life as a minister to her people. She is a guiding force for teaching and for the spiritual development of all the residents of Bakersfield and of Kern County. I am grateful for the opportunity to work together with her in affirming the common roots of social conscience, righteousness and justice that so clearly emanate from our shared Judeo-Christian heritage. I thank God for the satisfaction and stimulation I derive from working together with her to build the bridges across our differing cultures and religious traditions. Our objective is for a future that is bright, insightful and tolerant, a far better future that any one of us or any single group could create alone. God is good and we offer our gratitude to Him. *Shalom!*

"The Triviality of Symbols."

Which is yours, the cross, the six-point star, the crescent? Symbols are comforting to those they belong to; so are ceremonials and rituals. They have a cohesive factor that binds us together as a distinctive group, the security of fellowship. It helps us believe our way is the right way, and that "we" are better than "they." This is true of political factions, of social groups, *and* of different religious faiths!

Our spirit of patriotism is stirred when we stand with our hand placed across our chest over our heart, a gesture of paying homage to our nation, and to its symbolic flag. We display reverence for our country when we sing the national anthem, or just listen respectfully while it is being played. When uniformed soldiers, sailors or marines, defenders of our land come marching by in a parade, not only they but we too are primed up by the vibrant sounds of martial music.

When will we acquire the sensibility to regard symbolism a triviality? It is a leftover of the past, the *entrails of paganism!*

It's how we regard everyone, treat everyone that is meaningful! Furthermore, Jews are not to limit their acts of beneficence to other Jewish people. It should not have to do with whether a fellow seeking help wears a kippah on his *kepalah,* whether there's a mezuzah on the door frame of his mansion, whether hanging from his wife Fanny's flabby neck is a three inch six-point star with a twinkling sapphire in the middle, or whether she is bundled into a mink coat or shivering in a cheap flannel jacket.

It's the way we treat *everyone*, *all* people, regardless of how they worship God, whether or not they *do* worship God, what the color of their skin is. Yes even if it's flame red from drinking too much alcohol. Even if it's blue as a corpse's from hardly eating in the last few days, because they had spent all their money on lottery tickets. Nevertheless they're people, *people,* so be nice to them!

"Pleasure and Pain In Our Rose Garden."

To quote Reb Pesach: "God didn't give us a rose garden."

Sorry, Rebbe, I disagree. Indeed, a rose garden is exactly what God gave us! Let's examine this difference of opinion between lowly "me," Shirley Ann Newman, and holy "he," Rabbi Pesach.

The rose is truly exquisite; its visual image includes charming colors, its petals have an appearance of the soft and gentle. Its delightful fragrance permeates the atmosphere.

BUT, you had better exercise caution when you reach out to tear the rose from the bush!—God created the stem of the rose with threateningly sharp thorns! They prick your skin, demanding that you surrender a bit of your precious blood. The rose garden *is* symbolic, *highly* symbolic, of the planet Earth upon which God set us.

Our world is a garden that includes the soft, gentle, beautiful rose, but also the sharp, painful sting of thorns. It represents the pleasurable and the undesirable. That which is to be enjoyed exists in the rose garden, but that which is to be avoided, as well. In the rose garden are what enhances life, and what makes life difficult and challenging.

With the right to occupy—not to own but to *occupy*—the Earth, metaphorically a rose garden, God gave us a set of rules for occupying His rose garden. It's important that we know and follow those rules. That means not just reading them, not just casually skimming through God's book of instructions, called The Holy Scriptures, but to thoroughly and analytically study and learn these requisites that teach us how to nurture and perpetuate the rose garden.

God gave us dominion over all forms of life. It means we are the stewards, the protectors, not the *destroyers!* It's time—long past the time--to show we're grateful for the garden, even though its lovely roses are also thorny!

"Dialectical Progression To Perfection."

Thesis: The Holy
Antithesis: The Profane
Synthesis: A blend of the natural and the spiritual are what
    helps defects mend, ultimately resulting in the godly.

 The progress of forward movement toward purity is a painstaking evolutionary process. Its ultimate objective is mankind's harmonious relationship with all of nature. The bible depicts that the final, universal act is a condition of peaceful coexistence: "The lion shall lie down with the lamb," a metaphor we can decode as meaning that when natural law and moral behavior are finally reconciled, the universe will achieve perfection. It will follow that the souls of the dead unite with their bodies, and constitute "the last day." Heaven (at present, an illusion!) will come into being, a haven for the deserving dead.

    Also the intended outcome will finally occur: a man-and-God partnership. A perfect universe will be the blending of The Spiritual (God) with the natural, man and his material creations. The metamorphosis requires man's commitment, dedication and multiplicity of energetic efforts.

    Not only was *man* made in God's image, indeed, so was everything else, resulting from how God pictured it all, how He created everything from the precise images in his mind.

"Let's Make What's Proper More Popular!"

Spiritual leaders even while imparting what makes their religious faith different (and the right one!) can also teach society's secular ethical values. Religious and temporal messages should be aimed at promoting peace and harmony, halting acts of destruction. This does not just mean world conflicts but in our own neighborhood, our own home! This idea of maintaining peaceful relations among all people can be found in everyone's biblical text.

The philosophy of Martin Buber, known as the "I-Thou" concept is specifically about how we relate to one another, deal with one another, how we perceive other human beings. An "I-Thou" attitude demonstrates recognition that we should respect each other, that all mankind has the same inherent value.

The opposite is what Buber calls the "I-it" relationship that we often treat others as commodities to be used solely for our convenience and pleasure. An unsatisfying commodity may be dispassionately disposed of. Oh sure, it's all right to trash your outmoded VCR, troublesome car, imperfectly functioning dishwasher. It's *not* all right to do it to the people in your life you have the power to control.

"I-Thou" is meant to be our attitude toward everyone, it is supposed to be practiced universally, applicable to all persons, despite their ethnicity, race, religion, intellectual or social construct. Not only does everyone's bible teach the precept, it is the platform, the foundation, the political philosophy on which our American Constitution is based, the framework that structures our laws and statutes.

However, for the unkind, the selfish, the greedy, the overly aggressive, the exploitive, the hypocritical, we need emphasis from the pulpit about the evils of that sort of behavior! It can be the most responsible message emanating from every church, synagogue and

228

mosque. Differences in how we worship God do not preclude the basic one: We were all created by God in His image.

In summoning your flock with the words: "And now let us pray," I beseech you, Rabbi, Priest, Pastor or Emir, to make it abundantly, unequivocally clear that your message is not and never will be "Let us *prey!*"

"Helping Humans Become Humane!"

The philosophical and legal foundation of our land is the ideal of equality and justice. At times it has proven to be only an ideal, an abstract concept, one that is unfulfilled.

Kern County has not been without ugly acts of racism, religious intolerance, and demeaned ethnicity. We have also seen age, low educational level, poverty and various life-style prejudices.

Even if it's not targeted at you, it should not be ignored. Acts of violence, destruction, threats that invoke fear, or that merely insult and humiliate, other members of our community deserve to be defended. As Jews we are required to support, champion the cause, come to the aid of the physically, emotionally, politically, economically, socially afflicted, handicapped, thus disadvantaged.

That is one of the reasons for the Kern County Human Relations Commission. We are very proud that one of its past presidents, Dr. Barry Jacobs, had been a member of Temple Beth El.

The situation that led to establishing the Commission, how it functions, and its level of effectiveness were clearly detailed, described, and explained to us by Dr. Jacobs:

"On November 22, 1990 the Kern County Board of Supervisors duly passed and adopted Ordinance # G-5400, thereby establishing the Kern County Human Rights Commission (HR. C.)

The purpose of the H.R.C. is to study, evaluate and recommend to the Board of Supervisors plans and programs for the elimination of prejudice and discrimination, as well as to safeguard and promote the equal rights of, and respect for all Kern County people in such areas as employment, education and housing. Social and economic justice are expected to be the imperatives of our community.

The Commission is the official channel through which the Board of Supervisors and the public at large can investigate, and provide help in resolving these matters. It is the community's responsibility to inculcate mutual respect and understanding among individuals who are diverse in ethnicity, race, and religion. There is, too, the necessity of promoting positive attitudes regarding age, physical and mental disabilities, variations in life-style and sexual orientation.

The H.R.C. conducts studies in these fields of human relationship that assist in effectuating its general purpose. It also inquires into incidents of tension and conflict that concern prejudice and discrimination, and that attempts to ameliorate the problems through conciliation, conferences among disputants, and the use of educational and persuasive techniques.

The H.R.C. comprises eleven persons: two appointed by each of the five Supervisors, and one member appointed by the Board at large. The Commissioners are expected to be broadly representative of the different racial, ethnic, religious and socio-economic strata, as well as differences in age, sex, marital status and possible impairments. However, it was not until January 1996 that a person of Jewish heritage was offered a place on the Commission. It was Barbara Patrick who offered the appointment to me at that time.

I, Barry Jacobs was the designated replacement for an open position. I was gratified to notice that my influence was immediate; I pointed out to the Commission that its annual essay awards banquet sometimes was scheduled to take place on a Friday night and that this caused a conflict to Jews who observe Friday night and Saturday as the weekly Sabbath, and Seventh Day Adventists who also adhere to the Saturday Sabbath.

Furthermore, prayers and music—as Gospel music—that invoke the name of Jesus Christ create a level of discomfort to non-Christians who may be attending the public function.

I enlightened members on the Commission of the fact that the Jewish High Holidays, the days most sacred to the Jewish community generally occur during September or early October, and before functions are scheduled, the Commission should confer with one of the community's rabbis to avoid a date conflict.

In September 1997 I was elected President of the Commission, for a term of two years. It was at a time that I was involved in the formation of an anti-hate-crime network to operate throughout this county It has as its purpose to bring together representatives of all the diverse agencies that fight hate-crimes and hate-violence. Such a network will, I hope, lead to better reporting, greater understanding, and the resolution of these forms of human injustice. It is also my fervent hope that reducing this menace to our community will be my legacy to Kern County. Candidates to public office and the laws that govern us in our Republican form of government are the result of majority or plurality vote. But the majority may not tyrannize those in the minority. Accommodation must be made for the opinions and civil rights of those who differ in their viewpoints from the majority. Minority opinions and minority rights may not be obliterated by criminal acts or even by intimidation. Through the collective association of our high-principled, ethical residents who take responsibility to protect the defenseless and the vulnerable members of our community, along with a system of education that instructs our children in how to value all human beings—similar to them or different from them—we *can* eradicate hate crimes!"

PART SIX

Life's Highway Has Unexpected Turns

Life's Highway Has Unexpected Turns

Note: This segment of the book discloses the deep feelings, the very intimate perspectives of several people in the Jewish community—including the author's. Most are essays are about becoming Jewish. In Mrs. Newman's brief sketch she tells about becoming *aware* of what being Jewish really means, and now that she knows, how she feels about herself.

In 1983 Karen Pike, who was then Karen Pierce, chose to become a Jewess. As she stood poised to enter into the Covenant, to live according to Mosaic law, Karen looked back on the road she had traveled before reaching that significant turning point in her life. She expressed her thoughts and feelings in the form of a letter to herself, herewith revealing its contents to us. Karen studied to become a teacher in our public school system, is the former wife of Irvin Pike, and the mother of their two sons, Ezra and Gabriel.

Karen Pike: *"A Decisive Change, Effected With Deliberation."*

This letter to myself is about why I made the choice to convert to Judaism. Writing this letter is a precious task because in the process I feel myself becoming closer to God and learning more about Karen. There are many things that draw me to Judaism. I feel that if I can identify those things here on paper, and also reflect on the conversion that has taken place in my heart over the past year, then I will more clearly understand how I have arrived at my decision. I will know what it is that now makes me a Jew.

It was less than one year ago when I had my first real exposure to Judaism as a religion and way of life. It happened through a very good friend who eventually became my closest companion and continuing source of inspiration. Irvin invited me to weekly *Shabbat* services at Temple Beth El, and at first I went along to satisfy my curiosity about something entirely new to me. I also accepted Irvin's invitations because I enjoyed sharing time and experiences with him.

Although initially I didn't understand much of the *Shabbat* service, there were parts of it with which I could identify and gain spiritual nourishment from. The Rabbi spoke of several ideas that I recognized as harmonizing with some of the most important values in my life. (I will elaborate on these ideas later). Also, I felt very comfortable reading the prayers from *Gates of Prayer* since they were essentially the same as ones originating in my heart. Basically, I found *Shabbat* services to be a very positive experience because they stimulated both my heart and my mind, and also because the Temple members created such a warm social environment.

As time went on and I continued to attend *Shabbat* services, my initial curiosity about Judaism turned to something much greater. I became very interested in learning more about this perspective on life because I felt that it might offer something of personal spiritual value to me. I decided to look deeper into Judaism through independent study. I checked out six or seven books from the library and began to read. It seems silly now, but in looking back, I felt very shy about revealing my interest in Judaism to others for fear that my motives would be misconstrued. My interest was genuine, and I did not want anyone to think that I was studying Judaism for the sake of my relationship with Irvin.

Most of all, I did not want Irvin to think this. As much as I cared for him, I knew I would never adopt spiritual values that were not already my own. I was too new to Judaism to fully know how I felt about it. I didn't want Irvin or anyone else speculating on my reasons or asking me questions that I wasn't ready to answer. There was also one other reason that I chose to pursue my study of Judaism privately:

From a very early age, I have taken my spiritual development very seriously and have made it a priority in my life. However, like Siddhartha, I felt strongly that I must make my own path. I valued independent thinking and the road of the solitary spiritual quest. I was suspicious that organized religion provided easy answers for people and excused them from the responsibility of seeking Truth for themselves. Now, at this point of my life, I was somewhat surprised to find myself feeling so "at home" with the beliefs I encountered in Judaism. Still regarding myself as an independent thinker, I was not ready to show others that I could learn from a form of organized religion. I guess you might say that I had a spiritual chip on my shoulder. Well, that chip got knocked off the day Irvin found all those books on Judaism crammed behind the seat of my truck where I had hidden them! That's also the day I learned I could trust Irvin, that I didn't need to worry about what other people thought, and that feeling good about Judaism didn't mean I wouldn't think for myself anymore—to the contrary! It was a painful lesson, one I paid for with much embarrassment. It seemed childish to hide the books. However, it was worth living through that lesson because from then on I could be open about my interest in Judaism. Irvin has supported that interest and has contributed to my study by sharing his knowledge and experience. I am thankful to him for this gift.

In November of last year, I enrolled in the Introduction to Judaism course taught by Rabbi Peskind. I have learned much from the Rabbi and the readings he recommended. It has also been a satisfying experience to join with others in exploring Judaism. My previous fears have dissolved and been replaced with a good feeling about myself and this period of my life when so much spiritual growth is occurring. I now ask myself: When did the transformation happen? At what point did I make the decision to convert to Judaism?

When did I know that I wanted to live as a Jew? Well, I don't really think there was one magical moment. With study came knowledge, and with knowledge came the gradual conversion of my heart and mind. I believe that this process has taken place so naturally and easily because Judaism's teachings have served to confirm many basic beliefs about God and life that I already held. What is new is my realization that through continued study of Judaism and striving to live as commanded in *Torah,* I can elevate my life higher and higher to reflect oneness with God. This is my sincere desire and this is the reason that I now choose to make official my conversion to Judaism.

I have now completed one objective that I set before myself in writing this letter. I have recounted my thoughts and the events that led up to my decision to convert. Equally important, I want to include in this letter a brief discussion of some of the ideas and practices that drew me to Judaism and made it my own personal path. It would be an exhausting task to try to discuss all that I value in Judaism, but this is not my goal. Listed below are the aspects of Jewish tradition and belief that currently stand out in my mind.

I have often thought that ideally every moment should be suffused with the awareness of God. When we stay centered in the present, when we are aware that God is recreating the world every minute, every second, and we give thanks for His creation, and then we truly experience our oneness with Him. Judaism, as a way of life, teaches us daily, weekly and seasonally, practices that make it possible to work towards this ideal experience of God. Through daily prayers, celebration of *Shabbat,* and observance of Jewish holidays, I feel I have entered into a greater awareness of God's presence in my life.

Judaism teaches that it is important to set aside one day each week as a day of rest and reflection upon God. This is the *Shabbat,* which commences with the kindling of the candles on Friday night and ends with *Havdalah* on Saturday at sundown. I value *Shabbat* because it has brought to my attention the need for respite from the workweek's "busy-ness." By reserving one day for rest and study, we can re-focus our perspective on God and the larger meaning of life. I admit it is often difficult to let go of work and inappropriate activities, but through consistent effort, I feel that I am moving closer to making it a reality in my life.

I am thankful for *Shabbat.* It is necessary for the nourishment of the soul. Judaism confirms our relationship to God by commemorating certain points in the human life cycle: the birth of a child, the attainment of religious maturity, marriage—important events in the life of a person that are sanctified through special ceremonies. I witnessed a very beautiful baby-naming ceremony at the Temple one *Shabbat* eve. I felt deeply touched by how the parents stood before the congregation and gave thanks to God for the birth of their child. This ceremony was a concrete example to me of how Judaism teaches us to consciously praise God for the many blessings we receive throughout life. Life becomes so rich with meaning when we relate specific life cycles events to our relationship with God. I now invite this practice into my life and wish to pass it on to the children I hope to have in the future.

Judaism validates a major motivational force in my life: that is the desire to serve other people. I believe that mankind is God's most special creation. Therefore, by serving my fellow man—in both great and simple ways—I feel that I am simultaneously serving God. These ideas are in harmony with the teachings of the *Torah*: "Thou shalt love thy neighbor as thyself." In my career, in my daily dealings with people, and in my social/political concerns, I am striving to relate in ways of love.

I have studied hard and learned much about Judaism over the past several months. I still have much to learn. Judaism teaches us that study and the quest for greater knowledge and understanding is a lifelong pursuit. I accept this attitude whole-heartedly. I thank God for my mind and I pray that it continues to serve me well.

Finally, I have this to say about Judaism before ending this letter. I want to know the *Torah*. I believe that all of the answers are there for a world troubled by war, nuclear bombs, environmental pollution, hunger, and man's many injustices to man. I believe that the way to improve the world is to begin by improving myself. To this purpose I now look to the wisdom and laws of the *Torah* as my guide.

I am ending this letter here because it must end somewhere. A letter can never contain all the thoughts and feelings I have about such a special event in my life. That is because I think about being a Jew every day, and I will continue to do so for the rest of my life.

Susan Le Drew: *"My Personal Transformation."*

In tracing the course of my transformation of religious belief from Christianity to Judaism I think a significant turning point might have been the Christmas that my daughter Lindsay was three or four years old. I started to relate to her the story of Christmas, when suddenly I realized it was no longer credible to me! Earlier on, in conversations with an aunt of mine I learned that my grandmother may have been a Jewess. It aroused an interest in Judaism that continued particularly in my college years. I became acquainted there with a highly observant young Jewish woman whose grandparents had perished in the Holocaust. I attended her wedding where I was introduced to many aspects of the culture. They were totally new to me and gave me a new perspective, one to which I had very positive feelings. On another occasion, while at the Vermont home of a best friend of Lindsay I read several texts on Judaism. We were staying with these friends to attend the girl's *bat mitzvah* celebration.

With a waning acceptance of Christianity and a growing affinity to Judaism it is not surprising that I started to read book after book on the subject when we moved to Bakersfield in 1990. I was particularly interested in books I found in the library that analyzed the difference between the two *faiths, and* how they are practiced. I had no doubt about my belief in God but what struck a responsive chord in me was Judaism's focus on deeds rather than heavy reliance on faith. It was a natural stage in my evolution to the Jewish religion.

I tested my feelings about its validity by attending a Friday night synagogue service when in *The Bakersfield Californian* there appeared a notice of one designed specifically for youngsters. It was scheduled for the second Friday of each month. The phrase in the article, "all are welcome" encouraged me. I also regarded this initial visit as a challenge to Temple Beth El itself; would I really be welcomed, and would I really feel I was?

I certainly did feel comfortable there! Soon Lindsay and I enrolled in a course led by Temple Beth El's rabbi, "Introduction to Judaism." I looked forward more eagerly to those classes than I had to anything else I ever studied.

Judaism does not consist of dogma, nor does it attest to being the only valid and true religion. There is no concept of the transmission of "Original Sin." It allows for flexibility and individuality. Most appealing to me is that it does not reject human imperfection. What Judaism does expect is that we strive to improve, to come closer and closer to the fulfillment of God's laws and His expectations of us, that we try to live in accordance with His will.

I find myself at home in Judaism. I feel connected to the Jewish community and that I truly belong to the Jewish people. I am in total accord that life is a process, that even though we do not need to become perfect, as our lives progress we *do* need to try and behave toward one another with steady improvement. The emphasis in Judaism is on human interaction rather than merely on the relationship between man and God.

Judy Black: *"Enlightenment Brought Me Comfort"*

As a child I never really knew much about Judaism. What I did know about religion came from my admittedly sparse attendance to my Southern Baptist Church. I always found it difficult to accept that I—and others—who told lies are so bad that when we die we shall burn in hell! These were the words of my preacher, who I was certain directed them to me, a ten year-old child. My reactions, understandably, were nightmares and the firm conviction of what lay ahead for me when I died. I did tell lies occasionally such as telling my parents I had finished my chores when I had not or that I promised to be home "on time" and didn't do so. Was that really bad enough behavior to condemn me to a sentence of spending eternity burning in hell?

Instead of church attendance and thoughts about God making me feel secure and comfortable I was filled only with dread. I also found it hard to accept that it would not be all right to pray directly to God. Try as I might to believe in everything I heard, a good deal of it somehow lacked credibility to me. As I grew older I learned of other faiths and visited other churches.

I had discussions with friends about the different religions and I read a variety of religious material, including books. I was struggling to find something that would alleviate my continual discomfort. But I couldn't and I merely avoided thinking about it; I put my religious life "on hold."

When I was eighteen years old I met Allan, who after awhile became my husband. It was he who introduced me to Judaism. In numerous long discussions about Judaism based upon his personal understandings in accordance with his Jewish upbringing and education I became acquainted with new ideas. I learned that Jews, in fact, pray directly to God—without an intermediary. Significant to me was the Jewish belief that making a wrong choice in life or behaving badly doesn't mean that we are bad people. How relieved I was! During the next few years I went through the process of acquiring my understanding of Allan's religion.

I attended the Introduction to Judaism classes that were being offered jointly by both Congregation B'nai Jacob and Temple Beth El. I went to *Shabbat* worship services, Passover *Seders,* and High

Holiday services—all of which touched me deeply. Now I realized that Judaism together with its long, profound traditions is right for me, and that it is what I want for my future children. I completed the process of conversion in 1984, and my husband and I are raising our two little daughters Hannah and Lauren to be proud, responsible Jews.

Michael Murphy: *"My Family Adapts To A Turn of Events"*

When I, a life-long Catholic married my wife Marie, very little was known of her heritage. Later on it seemed very curious—but of little concern to us—that our daughter Stephanie, as a very small child would not go to sleep until I sang an eleventh century Jewish lullaby to her called "Dona."

After High School, Stephanie began attending Bakersfield College. To fulfill a requirement in history she felt a strong desire to choose Russian history. Strangely, Stephanie found this course so much easier than classes in her major, forestry. She had selected it because of her special interest in birds of prey. Her grades were also much better in Russian history, achieving them without the struggle she was having in other courses. History then was chosen as her minor while she was still in Bakersfield College.

An interest in events of the past aroused in Stephanie an impulse to research her heritage. When her years at the community college were completed she enrolled in Fresno State University. She decided on a double major: history and political science. Stephanie has aspirations to do foreign service, preferably in Russia or Israel!

I, Stephanie's father, have a very Irish family name, but my ancestry is nebulous; my mother is Dutch and my father's mother is French-Canadian. Without knowing what aroused it, Stephanie somehow developed a feeling that there might be Russian people in her background, perhaps even Russian Jews. This motivated me to write a letter to one of my wife's few living relatives, a cousin of Marie's in Madison, Wisconsin. After long delay his answer did, indeed, confirm that her heritage included Jewish Russians.

Why had this fact remained undisclosed to us until October 1997? Marie's maternal grandmother had reached the decision that the lives of her posterity will be less troubled by the world's anti-Semitism if they merely ignore their Jewish background. My wife's mother died when Marie was only eleven years old and she grew up not knowing—until this very recent revelation—who she really is.

Once Marie's family history came to light we began to collect names, dates, places of residence, whatever we could to try to piece together a genealogy. We learned from an uncle that all documentary evidence had been purposely destroyed after the First World War. It was an attempt to put to rest the pain and trauma of anti-Judaism's impact on the lives of members of that family. All that's left are word-of-mouth reports from those in Marie's family, who still know what happened, who can affirm their Jewish heritage.

As soon as Marie acquired this knowledge we began to attend services at Bakersfield's Temple Beth El. A certain inner unrest that had always existed in my wife and daughter now gave way to a wonderful sense of peace and tranquility! My own heart is always open to God's will; I highly support and favor the pursuit of knowledge about Judaism occurring in our family. We're certain God will lead us on the right path to fulfill His intentions for us.

Maria Chavez: *"We Found Our Way Home"*

Convert: What precisely does the word mean? Webster's dictionary defines it as *transform; change; turn aside.* As such, my family would be considered "converts" by virtue of the fact that my husband Rudie and I, were born into Catholic families. However, *we* don't perceive ourselves converts.

True, our families are members of the Catholic Church and Rudie and I were both well immersed in that religion and in Catholic traditions. The neighborhood I grew up in, a Lubbock, Texas one, consisted of our extended families; our neighbors were also like family members, everyone's life revolving around the neighborhood Catholic Church.

As a youngster I often rebelled against my family's religious expectations of me. I had a lot of unanswered questions and a good deal of guilt about my inability to accept what I was taught. But I refrained from directing questions at my father whose stern looks kept me silent and afraid. It was apparent I was violating a child's obligation to obey the dictates of a parent.

I began to "avoid" church services when I was sent on my own. I'd skip off to the nearby playground keeping careful watch on people's departure from church, so that I arrive home in a timely manner. Whenever my father learned of my negative attitude and my "truancy" he would lecture me in anger and disapproval. I was obliged to confess these remissions to the Priest. For hours and hours I listened to lectures about the human spirit and soul, as my parents tried to "set me on the right path."

They certainly didn't succeed when my mother stated the Jews were evil people; that they were responsible for the agonizing death of Jesus. Ironically, as my mother looked into her child's eyes, trying to instill hatred of the Jewish people, a principle she was spoon fed in her own youth she had no idea she was looking in the eyes of a future practicing, believer in the Jewish faith!

Rudie, his parents' one child grew up in Colorado Springs, Colorado. His mother came from a farming family. It meant that the nearest church was in town, remote from their farm. However, my mother-in-law vividly recalls that even though she didn't regularly attend church services her father conducted weekly bible study. The sessions were at the farm, for his and other families in the vicinity.

When she married and then lived in the city attending Sunday mass became a usual occurrence. And when Rudie started school he was enrolled in a private Catholic school. He also served as an altar boy in their church.

From the very beginning of our relationship Rudie and I would engage in long and serious discussions on every conceivable subject! Although *religion* did not come up in the conversation on our first date we talked with such heart-felt intensity about so many important issues that we knew at once we had both found our "soul mate." We knew that from then on we would be "lifelong partners." We understood one another more profoundly than anyone else did. We united with every fiber of our being and with the mutual desire to search for something that lay deep within each of us.

People don't realize the difficulty of answering their question: *"Why did you convert?"* I *do* know the answer, it's just too hard to express it verbally to those who hadn't experienced in childhood the constant yearning Rudie and I had been plagued with. We sensed something was absent from our lives; we could only "grope and hope," until we finally *did* find it! It was an innermost need and drive that led us to Judaism.

Although by the time Christopher, our first child was born Rudie and I had drifted from the Catholic faith, we did have our baby baptized in the Catholic Church. We continually talked of our belief in God and our commitment to His commandments and we very much wanted God in our child's life. We brought him to the only Church we knew. After that we never returned because of our feeling that we just didn't belong there.

When a child is born to you, suddenly you view the world in a new light: The leaves of the trees have a new beauty; and as you point out the sky to your baby you yourself now see it differently. I believe that is what happened concerning the issue of faith. We wanted *so much more* for our child than *we* had had. It motivated us to try even harder to find our true faith!

Rudie and I had no specific plans about changing our religious connection; it flowed along in a surprisingly natural manner. All at once we felt the inclination to visit a synagogue and attend a service. Christopher was eleven months old when we went to Congregation B'nai Jacob whose spiritual leader was Rabbi Goodblatt. In retrospect we must have looked rather strange to the congregants. But no one questioned the reason for our presence. Everyone was friendly and hospitable; we felt natural and comfortable.

We didn't know any of the words to Judaism's prayers and hymns but our souls recognized them and we joined in. Rabbi Goodblatt spoke to us in the social hall after the service, and introduced us to several congregants. No questions were posed and we felt we "belong" here. It was the start of a new life for us!

We began to study Judaism on our own. Rudie, who loves reading, would read aloud to me about the Jewish people, their faith and their religious practices. The more we learned the greater our eagerness to learn more and more. It was so exciting, like discovering a treasure! We no longer ate pork or other non-kosher foods. We bought a printed copy of *The Torah* and had our son's name inscribed on the cover. Although we had not yet joined a synagogue our lifestyle was Jewish. To everyone we stated that we are Jews. We observed the Jewish holidays in our home.

Our parents and other family members were keenly disapproving and disappointed in us, and they told us so. They were even more upset when David, our second son was born; we did not have him baptized. Our children were not ever going to heaven, was my father's dire warning. "Only by believing in Jesus can you be a good person."

As for Rudie's mother—at first she assumed our new religion was probably just a "passing fancy." We would soon come to our senses and return to our Catholic faith. But as time went by and we became more committed to Judaism, she grew worried. When she had Christopher to herself in secret she would take him to church. After we discovered her deceptive practice we no longer left him in her care.

Some of my sisters and brothers left the Catholic Church in favor of other Christian religions. That was acceptable to my parents. Their struggle to accept Rudie, the children and me as Jews was lengthy and difficult. Nevertheless we perpetuated our convictions, and managed to maintain an ongoing relationship with our extended families.

With the births of our third and fourth children, Jacob and DeeDee, our faith continued to expand. The most difficult part was shielding our children from the hostility and resentment of others. Our children realized our religion was uncommon and that this made our lives different. They accepted it probably because they hadn't known any other. We have sufficient evidence from the way they express their thoughts that they feel neither anger nor emotional pain despite awareness that their grandparents will never be present at our important religious events such as DeeDee's *bat mitzvah.*

Many years have passed and despite our differences we have earned the family's acceptance. We are even respected for the sincerity and fervor of our commitment to the Jewish faith. Our children came through the experience unscathed. Our fifth child,

Rachel, does not have to cope with the initial anger the family displayed. By now all our children have a loving relationship with grandparents, aunts, uncles, and cousins. I keep embracing Rachel and thinking as I write this how thankful I am to have realized our dream. I know we couldn't have given our children a more beautiful gift than their Jewish faith. We had engaged in a long search that finally led us to understanding the reason for such an empty aching in the depths of our souls. There had been an unexplainable need to find *something,* but never knowing quite what that *something* was.

We're now members of Temple Beth El, a wonderful Reform Jewish congregation. The start of our family's relations with Rabbi Cheryl Rosenstein, its spiritual leader was during a period when our lives were overcome with distress and sorrow. The rabbi's support, comfort, and compassion further confirmed our existent firm faith in God and Judaism.

Clearly I can still remember my sentiments the night we were welcomed to Temple Beth El. It felt like a homecoming, as if we had been on a long, exhaustive journey and were now reunited with our badly missed family. The congregation is a family we belonged to all our lives but were separated from until now reuniting. So, you see, we didn't *change,* we haven't been *transformed;* we're not *different.* We simply joined, became connected with *our own* people!

Addendum, July 2012: By now Rudie and I have two married children! David is married to Renée, and DeeDee to Chris Chambers (beloved son of Kathleen Arnold, our close friend and fellow member of Temple Beth El.) David and Renée have launched our family into its next generation. They have a baby daughter named Elena.

The Happily Expanding Chavez Family

Shirley Ann Newman: *"Waking My Jewish Genes"*

The bible of my childhood, my *own* upbringing, the written source of my "proper" behavior, the ethics of my everyday life, the way I'm supposed to treat other people, came from Aesop's Fables. Not until I was in my late thirties, the mother of a teenage daughter, and had just started my 2nd marriage, that my new husband gently awakened me to what "I'm Jewish" means.

My initial attitude toward the faith system was happy and comfortable when we joined a Reform synagogue, regularly attended Friday night and major holiday services, and *especially* when I started going to Torah study. But about a decade before, in the late 'forties when the curtain had ascended on the Holocaust, its views and voices depicting what the Jews of Europe had experienced, they impacted too harshly on my personality's hypersensitivity.

I acquired my own fears, and they were mounting, growing more intense because I had brought forth to a world of such evils a child I adored. Night after night I was afflicted with an emotionally shattering nightmare. Yes, a repetition of the very same hideous dream. Gestapo agents were breaking into a darkened room in which my young child and I were clutching each other in agonized terror. We were alone, crouched in the farthest corner of the room, unprotected, defenseless, helpless, metaphorically enclosed in a box of voracious vipers!

Overcoming this damaging segment of my life was a hard struggle. It took a manifold effort, an extraordinary degree of willpower and determination. Nevertheless, when my marriage to Max Newman started, so did a close connection to synagogue life, to my heritage, to my Jewish identity.

After learning of the good and bad things that happened to the Jewish people in the course of thousands of years of *plight* and *flight*, now that I know our code of ethics and morals emanates from the Torah, the Five Books of Moses, I'm glad to say, *I like who I am!*

EPILOGUE

"I Leave You With This--"

"I LEAVE YOU WITH THIS--"

"A Jew by the very condition of his Jewishness pays the continuing price of Sinai. If Jewishness remains his fate, Judaism remains the framework of his native spiritual existence and God his partner. And therefore as long as The People as a continuing organism in history keep alive the consciousness of Sinai each Jew can find his roots."

Rabbi W. Gunther Plaut

This book contains descriptive and heartfelt accounts of many Jewish families and individuals from foreign lands who settled here, entered into marriage, had children, and used their skills, ingenuity, and experience to support themselves and their families. Some knew how to utilize the potential of especially this pioneer area in the mid 19th Century to become very wealthy. The Jewish people made substantial contributions to the development of Bakersfield and its satellite communities.

Early and later Jewish settlers in California's Central Valley were not all foreign born, but descendants of European Jews. The book also includes born Americans living in the east who were attracted to this locale for various reasons. Biographical accounts of local families typify all or most Kern County Jews who gravitated and settled here at some point in time between the 1850s and now.

The book is not strictly a history; it's a sociological study of what Jewish life *was* and *is* for Kern County residents. It is a mirror image that allows us to view ourselves, and to give some insights to our Gentile friends, neighbors, associates. Even to non-Jewish strangers.

Long Journey With Heavy Luggage--Mt. Sinai to San Joaquin Valley portrays the lives of Jewish families who were part of the mass of pioneers that opened up and initiated America's southwest. We have seen where some of them came from and the circumstances that impelled the move, their social and religious affiliations, and the adjustments they had to make in view of their minority status, including relationships with non-Jews.

From its very inception America has been a haven, a place of refuge for the demeaned, the underclass of all nations. For many European Jews this land has been a sanctuary, an escape to safety from the tyrannies, terrors, despair, and futility of their home country. For the most part it has lived up to its promise. Opportunities existed all over eastern America, but for a great many that came to this part of the country it turned out to be "the right place at the right time."

It's A Lot Cheaper, A Lot Better!"

A significant problem senior citizens are having, well articulated themselves is the high cost of their medications. If they can't sleep or can't keep awake, if they can't remember or would rather forget, if they're too fidgety or too lethargic, those descendants of snake-oil peddlers have something to sell that can help.

A long time ago I found an extraordinarily inexpensive cure-all Not a round or oval pill, not a gel-cap, not a liquid to be taken before meals, after meals, with food, with water. It contains no questionable additives: fillers, colors, flavors. And it does not have a limited shelf life. It is a very old remedy known as *Torah;* it works for me, and it is in no way straining my budget. I can take doses of *Torah* in any amount, at any time of day or night. I never run short of my supply of this beneficial product. The fact that it has no expiration date means I will *never* discard it!

When I feel tense I don't need a tranquilizer. I can clear the crowded channels of my mind, I can slip into relaxed slumber, I can arise to face the day eagerly, enthusiastically, in a positive uplifted attitude, and I can "go-with-the-flow" rather than do battle against the tides. No, I don't reach for a bottle, I reach for a book. It is not the only book I read—far from it. But *Torah* is forever timely, forever interesting and challenging—partly because of its innumerable cryptic messages. It offers remarkable and reliable source material that keeps me mentally, emotionally, spiritually, even physically well. As testimony to how much it helps my memory: I can clearly recall those days—thousands of years ago— received the precious gift of *TORAH!*

Question: Why is Queen Esther a heroine? Why was Jacob angry and unhappy the morning after his wedding night? Why do we use an eight-branched candelabrum for the Hanukkah lights? What was one specific and important reason for me to write this book?

No, this is not a game of "Trivial Pursuit" it is about *profound pursuits.* To my fellow Jews I say, seek to know our Jewish history, our past experiences, some of which go back over three thousand years. If you know where you're coming from it will give

A significant problem for senior citizens, well-articulated by themselves and their advocates—but also the problem of many young people who are hard-working, in stable jobs—is the high cost of prescription and over-the-counter pharmaceuticals. If you can't sleep or can't keep awake, if you can't remember or would feel better if you could forget, if you are too fidgety or too lethargic—those descendants of snake-oil salesmen have something to sell you that can help! Ah, but here's the rub: you may have to spend half your monthly income on those magical aids.

For me there has proven to be an extraordinarily inexpensive, effective, pure-cure. Not a round or oval pill, not a gel-cap, not a liquid to be taken before meals, after meals, with food, with water... It contains no questionable additives: fillers, colors, flavors. And it does not have a limited shelf life. It is a very old remedy, known as *Torah;* it works for me, and it is in no way straining my budget. I can take doses of *Torah* in any amount, at any time of day or night. I never run short of a supply of its benefits. And it has no expiration date, warning me when to discard it.

When I am tense I don't go to the medicine cabinet for a tranquilizer to clear the crowded channels of my mind so I can drift into relaxed slumber, so I can arise to face the day with an eager, enthusiastic, positive attitude, so I can gallantly "go-with-the-flow."

No, I don't reach for a bottle, I reach for a book! It is not the only book I read—far from it. But *Torah* is forever timely, forever interesting and challenging, partly because of its often cryptic messages. It offers remarkable and reliable source material that keeps me mentally, emotionally, spiritually, and physically well. As testimony to how much it helps my memory: I can even recall those days thousands of years ago, when I was encamped at the foot of Mount Sinai. It was and there I received the precious gift of *TORAH!*

Question: Why is Queen Esther a heroine? Why was Jacob angry and unhappy the morning after his wedding night? Why do we use an eight-branched candelabrum for the Hanukkah lights? Why did I write this book?

No, this is not a game of "Trivial Pursuit" it is about *profound pursuits*. To my fellow Jews I say, seek to know our Jewish history, our past experiences, some of which go back over five thousand years. If you know where you're coming from it will give you a better perspective on where you are going. Or at least what your goals should be. You will be better able to shape a constructive purpose to your life, a worthy, ethical one. Rise up in the morning, have a good breakfast, and GET INTO YOUR GENES!

Wishing you good health in body, mind, and spirit,

Shirley Ann Newman

Index

Made in the USA
Charleston, SC
11 May 2013